COUNTERPOINT APPLIED

In the Invention, Fugue, Canon
and other Polyphonic Forms

An Exhaustive Treatise on the Structural and Formal Details of the
Polyphonic or Contrapuntal Forms of Music

FOR THE USE OF

𝕲𝖊𝖓𝖊𝖗𝖆𝖑 𝖆𝖓𝖉 𝕾𝖕𝖊𝖈𝖎𝖆𝖑 𝕾𝖙𝖚𝖉𝖊𝖓𝖙𝖘 𝖔𝖋 𝕸𝖚𝖘𝖎𝖈

BY

PERCY GOETSCHIUS, Mus. Doc.

(Royal Württemberg Professor)

AUTHOR OF

*"The Material Used in Musical Composition," "The Theory
and Practice of Tone-Relations," "The Homophonic
Forms of Musical Composition," "Models of
the Principal Musical Forms," "Exercises in Melody-Writing," etc.*

Price, $3.50

G. SCHIRMER
INCORPORATED
NEW YORK

Printed in the U. S. A.

PREFACE.

THIS book is a sequel to the *Homophonic Forms*, and the system pursued in its preparation corresponds in every detail to that of the latter.

Experience in practical teaching has confirmed the author's belief that no further preparation for the exercise of contrapuntal writing is necessary than the course of harmony given in the *Material used in Musical Composition* (or any equally exhaustive treatise), together with the course of study prescribed in the *Homophonic Forms*. But these courses, especially that in harmony, must be exceedingly thorough; two years of diligent application to *Material* is by no means too much, possibly not enough, for the acquirement of the only basis upon which practical contrapuntal facility can rest, naturally and securely.

Nevertheless, the first Division of the present book is devoted to the specific details of contrapuntal discipline, partly because of their inseparable bearing upon polyphonic form, and partly as a concession, — for the benefit of students not familiar with the method of harmonic discipline peculiar to the *Material*.

The other Divisions owe their design to the author's conviction that the quickest and surest means of acquiring contrapuntal skill consists in the **practical application** of the contrapuntal method to the composition of polyphonic forms. Hence the title of the book.

Therefore, this volume, like the preceding, "undertakes no more than the systematic enumeration and exhaustive explanation of all the formal designs and methods of structural treatment in the polyphonic domain of music composition, as revealed in classic or standard writings."

Further, "the student must regard the conscientious analysis of all the carefully collected references, as a very significant and **distinctly essential** part of his study." On the other hand, it will probably not be necessary for every student to do all of each Exercise. The tasks have been made extremely comprehensive, not because they are indispensable, but rather in order to meet the wants of every class of students.

The following works, to which constant and vital reference is made, should be owned by the student:

Of **Bach,** the Well-tempered Clavichord, Vols. I and II; the 2- and 3-voice Inventions; the English Suites; the Organ Compositions (Peters compl. ed.), Vols. II, III, IV, V, and VI.

Of **Mendelssohn,** Pfte. Works, op. 35 and op. 7; Organ Compositions, op. 37 and op. 65.

Besides these, frequent reference is made to —

Bach, The Art of Fugue, French Suites, Partitas, and other clavichord works;

Händel, Clavichord Suites;

Klengel, 48 Canons and Fugues;

And Oratorios and similar choral works of **Händel, Mendelssohn, Bach, Beethoven, Brahms,** etc. These and all other cited compositions may be obtained, for inspection at least, at any large music store.

Like its predecessor, this book is designed not only for the practical composer, but also for the general music-student. The latter, while studying and analyzing with the same thoroughness as the special student, will simply omit the prescribed Exercises.

PERCY GOETSCHIUS.

Boston, Mass., *September,* 1902.

TABLE OF CONTENTS.

(The figures in parentheses refer to paragraphs.)

DIVISION ONE.

FUNDAMENTAL PRINCIPLES OF 2-VOICE POLYPHONY.

DIVISION TWO.

THE INVENTION-FORMS.

DIVISION FIVE.

THE CANON.

APPLIED COUNTERPOINT.

INTRODUCTION.

THE most concise definition that may be given of good and correct Polyphony is, that it consists in the HARMONIOUS ASSOCIATION of INDIVIDUALLY PERFECT and COÖRDINATE, BUT INDEPENDENT, MELODIES. Correct polyphonic writing is, therefore, subject to the following three conditions: —

> Condition 1: PERFECT MELODY;
> Condition 2: HARMONIOUS UNION;
> Condition 3: INDEPENDENCE OF PARTS;

each of which will be successively treated in the chapters of Division One.

DIVISION ONE.

THE FUNDAMENTAL PRINCIPLES OF THE SIMPLE (TWO–VOICE) POLYPHONIC STYLE.

CHAPTER I.

CONDITION 1: "PERFECT MELODY." THE CONDUCT OF THE SINGLE PART OR VOICE.*

CONJUNCT MOVEMENT.

1. THE first and most comprehensive rule of polyphonic melody is, to lead each single part as smoothly and evenly as possible. CONJUNCT MOVEMENT (that is, stepwise ascending or descending progression along the line of the prevailing scale) is therefore preferable to disjunct movement (that is, by leap or skip), as a general rule. Disjunct movement is, however, by no means undesirable, but should be used in moderate proportion to the stepwise movement.

---

* An exhaustive exposition of the fundamental laws of melodic progression may be found in the author's " *Exercises in Melody-Writing.*" Thorough understanding of Chapters I–V of that book will facilitate (possibly supersede) the study of the above chapter.

BACH.

Ex.
1.

See par. 6.   Disj.   Conj. . . . . Disj. . . . . . Conj. . . . .

2. Diatonic conjunct movement is preferable to chromatic.

a. Chromatic successions are least objectionable in *slow* movement (with tones whose time-values represent whole beats, or at least half-beats); and are generally better in ascending than in descending direction, especially when moderately rapid.

Ex.
2.

See also Ex. 82–1 ; 26–5.

b. A chromatic succession should, if possible, be approached in the corresponding direction; and requires, almost certainly, to *continue* in the same direction. For illustration :

Ex.
3.

Upward.   Downward.   ? ?   ? ? ?   (See par. 5.)

c. It is generally unmelodious to separate a chromatic succession by inserting an intermediate neighboring-tone, in quick movement :

Ex.
4.

?   ? ?

DISJUNCT MOVEMENT.

3. Disjunct progressions are qualified as *narrow* leaps (major or minor 3rds), and *wide* leaps (all skips beyond the intervals of the 3rd).

PERMISSIBLE SKIPS.

a. Narrow leaps are generally permissible.

Wide leaps, or leaps in general, are always permissible *when both tones are common to the momentary chord, i.e., if they occur during* CHORD-REPETITION. For instance :

See also Ex. 52–2.

b. A skip of any reasonable extent (rarely beyond an octave) may be made *downward* to any tone whose natural tendency is *upward;* or upward to any tone whose tendency is to descend; — that is, the skip may be made in the direction *opposite* to that of the natural tendency. (These tendencies are defined in par. 6, which see.) Thus:

These skips are, however, objectionable in the other direction (i.e., that *corresponding* to the natural tendency); — unless in obvious and perfect accord with par. 3*a* (during chord-repetition). For example:

c. Almost any leap, no matter how unusual or awkward in itself, may be justified by *sequence*-progression, i.e., by the reproduction of a melodic figure upon other, higher or lower, scale-steps. Thus:

To be feasible, such a line of sequences should start from a figure that is fault-less. The rectitude of the *initial figure* is the justification of all reasonable sequence-shifts (or reproductions) of it.

d. Unusual, and otherwise doubtful, skips sometimes occur at (im-mediately after) an *accented* tone. For example:

BACH.

Ex. 8.

N.B.   N.B.

This particular passage represents, simply, a continuous scale-passage, with two shifts to the next higher octave-register, — a device which is very common and effective in contrapuntal melodies, and possible in either direction. The rule at *d*, however, applies to other cases also (Ex. 16).

OBJECTIONABLE SKIPS, AND EXCEPTIONS.

4. On the other hand, skips are distinctly faulty

a. After any tone which is obviously *inharmonic* or dissonant, i.e., foreign to the prevailing chord.

To this rule there are two important exceptions:

(1) It is always possible to leap *a 3rd*, from a neighboring-note to the opposite neighboring-note (of the same essential tone); usually, the essential tone follows and concludes the group, — as it also begins it:

Ex. 9a.

That is to say, the figures ═ and ═ are always correct, in any reasonable movement (fast or slow), at any point in the measure, and whether the harmony remains the same, or is changed, during the group. The figure contains a "Double appoggiatura," and results from inserting the upper and lower neighboring-tones successively between the principal tone and its recurrence.

Not infrequently, especially in 3-tone groups, the recurrence of the principal tone is dispensed with. The license then consists in *leaping down a 3rd* from the *upper* neighboring-note; it is rarely applied in the opposite direction (leaping *upward* a 3rd from the lower neighbor).

This is called the "unresolved upper neighboring-note." For example:

(2) It is possible to make an indirect or "ornamental" resolution of a Suspension, and of similar dissonant tones. Thus:

The interposed tones (marked x x), inserted between the Suspension and its resolving-tone, usually belong to the resolving-chord, as seen in the above illustrations; but *brief* diatonic passing-notes may be added. Thus:

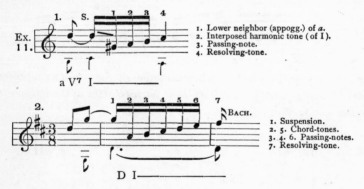

1. Lower neighbor (appogg.) of *a*.
2. Interposed harmonic tone (of I).
3. Passing-note.
4. Resolving-tone.

1. Suspension.
2. 5. Chord-tones.
3. 4. 6. Passing-notes.
7. Resolving-tone.

b. A skip, narrow or wide, *to* any inharmonic or dissonant tone (whereby the latter is deprived of its legitimate "preparation"), is, as a very general rule, objectionable. But it is by no means unpermissible, especially in the lighter (freer) styles of polyphony. See the *g♯* in the preceding illustration; and the following:

c. The leap of an *augmented 4th* is usually, for one reason or another, very objectionable ; and the progression by an *augmented 2nd,* diminished 3rd, major 7th, augmented 5th or 6th, or other awkward intervals, should be avoided.   They are best justified (1) by chord-repetition (par. 3*a*) :

or (2) by sequence-formation (par. 3*c*) :

or (3) when occasioned by such distribution of the tones as represents *the alternate appearance of two adjacent parts* (correct in their respective movements) :

Compare Ex. 7.

or (4), as shown in par. 3*d*, by occurring at (after) an accented tone,— especially when the latter is the *Tonic :*

5. After a *wide* leap (beyond a 3rd) the part should *turn, and progress in the opposite direction.* See Exs. 6*a*, 7, 8, 12, 13. To this very important and general rule there are a few exceptions, as follows:

a. The part may continue in the same direction after a skip, if it passes on *into a tone which belongs to the same chord,* whether the harmony changes meanwhile, or not. Thus:

The following successive skips are all very doubtful, because their aggregate effect is not harmonious:

Compare par. 3*a*.

b. It is almost always correct to pass on *diatonically* in the same direction, after a wide leap, if the direction of the part is *then* changed; i.e., it is usually sufficient to change the direction at the *second* tone after the leap. For example:

In this example the whole structure suggests a distribution of the tones of two adjacent parts (noted in Ex. 15), equivalent to:

Besides, the formation is *sequential* (par. 3*c*).

c. The part need not turn, after a wide leap, if it remains, even briefly, upon the same tone; — whether the latter be *reiterated,*

or simply *held,* for a pulse equivalent to repetition,

or *embellished* by either neighboring-tone:

ACTIVE TONES.

6. The natural or inherent tendencies of certain scale-steps (called Active steps because of their strong natural inclination to move) are as follows:

That of the *7th* scale-step (Leading-tone) is to *ascend diatonically;* that of the *6th* scale-step to *descend diatonically;* and that of the *4th* scale-step to *descend diatonically.*

Besides these, there are a number of acquired tendencies, as follows (all *diatonic*):

That of all *chord-sevenths, chord-ninths,* and *diminished* 5ths and 7ths to *descend;* that of all *raised* (altered) scale-steps to *ascend;* that of all *lowered* scale-steps to *descend;* and that of Suspensions to pass into their respective resolving-tones.

RULE. — *These natural and acquired tendencies should be respected,* as far as is consistent with reasonable freedom of melodic movement.

For illustration of the *natural* tendencies (these being the most significant in the conduct of single melodic parts):

See also Ex. 1; Ex. 6a, Nos. 1 and 3.

As indicated, the *regular* resolution of all active tones is effected diatonically (i.e., stepwise). To the above rule there may be, both as concerns direction and distance, the following

EXCEPTIONS.

a. An active tone may *leap* to any tone that belongs (or might belong) to the *same chord;* compare par. *3a.* The leap may be made either upward or downward, though always best in the *proper* direction (that corresponding to the resolution). Thus:

Such disjunct movements from the active tones constitute, often, examples of the *indirect* (or " deferred ") resolution, referred to in par. 4*a,* (2). That is, the unexpected tone or tones are simply interposed between the active tone and its resolution. Thus:

As a rule, if only *one* tone of the same chord intervenes, the obligation remains, and the resolving-tone should follow; though this depends largely upon whether the interposed tone lies in the direction of the resolution or not, — if the active tone progresses in the *proper* direction, its obligation is at least partly cancelled. For illustration:

If *two* tones of the same chord follow the active tone, its resolution may be evaded; or if the active tone passes *to another active tone,* the resolution of the latter is sufficient. Thus:

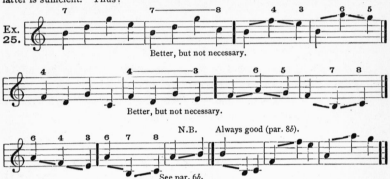

b. The natural tendency of these active scale-steps may be counter-acted by approaching them *stepwise* in the corresponding direction (i.e., that in opposition to their tendency); in which case they may continue in the (false) direction, *along the scale.*

N.B. — This is merely an obvious corroboration of par. 1, in its broadest application.

c. An active scale-step, when approached thus in the "opposite" direction, has the option either of passing onward (as in Ex. 26), or of *turning and fulfilling its natural obligation.* But, if approached in the direction corresponding to its tendency, it is very difficult indeed for the active tone to turn and progress *incorrectly*. The most natural exception (possibly the only defensible one) is when mere melodic embellishment, or deferred resolution, is involved, — i.e., when one of the tones is a neighboring-note, or obviously an interposed tone. For example :

*1) The 4th scale-step is here evidently an auxiliary (embellishing) tone; and f$\natural$ is taken, in preference to f$\sharp$, because of the prevailing C-major key. — *2) Same as note *1). — *3) An embellishment of the Leading-tone *a*, as in Ex. 9*a*, neatly conducted into a sequence of the preceding figure. — *4) A deferred resolution of both the 6th and 4th steps. — *5) Like note *1); *bb* is taken, instead of b$\natural$, to prevent the impression of C major.

7. Care must be taken to avoid any awkward conditions at the transition from one beat into the next. In approaching an accented fraction of the (following) beat, with a *fairly rapid figure*, the latter must be so calculated as to reach the desired point at precisely the right moment, — not too soon (so that awkward anticipation results), nor too late (so that an equally awkward leap is necessary). Supposing *c* to be the tone to be reached, in a rhythm of four tones to the (preceding) beat :

In measure 1 the run is faulty because it reaches the *c* too soon; in measure 2 it is calculated to reach *c* too late; measure 3 is correct.

As a rule, after moving *stepwise* toward the desired tone (at the beginning of the next beat), it is necessary to continue and *enter the new beat stepwise*,—not with a leap. If a leap be necessary, it should be made earlier in the figure, according to the prevailing harmonic conditions:

In the last measure, the awkward leap into *b* is avoided by inserting an *accented* passing-note; this is a very common and excellent device.

While it is usually better to continue thus, and enter the next beat diatonically in the same direction, there is no objection to turning at the transitional point:

8. The reiteration of a tone should be avoided in *rapid* rhythmic succession. It is, however, entirely permissible in *slow* movement; i.e., after a tone of full-beat value or more,—more rarely after one of half-beat value; *always good after a tie.*

a. Rapid reiterations are justified when occurring **several times** in succession, especially in sequences:

b. The most natural remedy, in case of objectionable reiterations, is to *leap up or down an octave*, — always an effective and permissible progression :

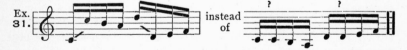

9. The TIE is one of the most effective devices for obtaining the desirable rhythmic independence of the several parts ; it serves to procure time-values of an extent — and at locations — not provided for by the ordinary characters of notation. The tie extends the duration of a tone from one beat into the next, or, with still more striking effect, from the last beat or beats of one metric group into the first beat of the following group (i.e., at, or over into, the *accented* pulses).

a. A *long* tie — from a long or heavy note, of at least a whole (or possibly half) beat value — is everywhere possible.

b. On the contrary, a *short* tie — as a rule, from any value less than a half-beat of the prevailing meter, in moderate tempo, — should be avoided.

Both of these rules coincide, in *rhythmic principle*, with par. 8.

c. As a general rule, the second tone (the one *into* which the tie extends) should not be of longer duration than that of the first (preceding) tone.

d. A *brief* tie, from a tone of less than half-beat duration (see *b*), is best justified when it gives rise to a Suspension :

$$C \quad V_7 \quad I$$

or when several such (brief) ties occur in succession, as syncopated form of an entire passage :

e. After a tie of fairly long duration, the part may progress either quickly or deliberately ; if the tie is brief, however, the part should progress with corresponding promptness, as indicated at *c.*

f. A tie may be followed :

(1) by the *same* tone (reiteration, par. 8) ;

(2) by the *next higher* or *next lower* tone (which progression provides for any " resolution " that may be necessary, — for example, in case of a Suspension) ;

(3) by the tone a *3rd above or below*, either as harmonic skip, involving no further obligation, or as opposite neighboring-note of the resolving-tone, in case such be necessary. See par. 4*a* (1) ;

(4) or by any still more remote tone, belonging to the momentary chord, — again either as harmonic skip, or as interposed tone before resolution. See par. 4*a* (2).

The *choice* of these possible, and equally good, progressions depends principally (often solely) *upon the location of the essential tone required or desired at the beginning of the next beat,* and is governed in any case by the rules of par. 7, which see.

Given the tied note *c*, followed in the next beat by *c:*

10. Brief rests (♩) may be inserted at the *beginning* (generally only at the beginning) of almost any beat, but especially any accented beat. The rest should *not* occur, as a rule, after any inharmonic tone (on account of the resolution); nor after any very short tone,—occupying the last unaccented fraction of the preceding beat; nor in the course of a beat, in such a manner as to impair the rhythm:

Ex. 35.

Longer rests (♩, 𝄾, etc.) are good almost anywhere, but under precisely the same limitations:

See also Ex. 37, No. 2.

11. The influence of *harmonic laws* upon the conduct of each single part (even when isolated, — temporarily unattended by other parts), is obvious from many passages in the foregoing rules; especially par. 3*a*, 4, 5*a*, 6*a*, 9*f.* The next chapter will demonstrate in detail the manifest necessity of basing the polyphonic complex upon a *harmonic* fundament, and of regarding the polyphonic style simply as an advanced stage in the manipulation of *the self-same original factors of Harmony*, — characterized by that superior freedom and independence which advanced growth brings. But, aside from the controlling influence exerted by harmonic law upon the co-operation of two or more simultaneous parts, the same influence is present even in the conception and movements of the single, unaccompanied part; for example, the direct derivation of a melody from a harmonic source, or its dictation by a harmonic purpose, is plainly shown in such motives as the following (all from BACH):

See also Exs. 5, 7, 14, 15, 22, Ex. 30–1, etc.

Such evidences of harmonic design are most palpable in melodies in *disjunct* movement (i.e., with many skips); but are more vague in melodies in preponderantly *conjunct* movement. Hence it is that, according to the rule of par. 1, conjunct or stepwise progression is a characteristic distinction of the *polyphonic* style of composition, in which the parts are more emancipated from the governing power of harmonic bodies; the *homophonic* style, in which this power constantly prevails, being distinguished, on the contrary, by greater frequency of skips, and disjunct movement generally.

12*a.* The above rules apply, with no essential modifications, to the *minor* as well as the major mode. The only noteworthy addition is, that in the *ascending* scale-progression in minor the *6th step* (as defined by the signature) *is generally raised;* and in the *descending* scale-progression, the *7th step is generally lowered.* See par. 20.

b. Further, all of the given rules are most binding in *prominent* parts, namely, the uppermost and lowermost of the polyphonic complex; but are subject to a certain degree of license in the *inner* part or parts.

c. All reasonable violations of the rules are palliated (and even completely justified) by "thematic authority," — that is, when called forth by deference to, or confirmation of, *any perfectly apparent and recognizable thematic design,* involved by the Imitation of a motive or figure (par. 24), by the Sequence (par. 3*c*), or any other sufficiently obvious and plausible melodic purpose.

Summary.

13*a.* Conjunct movement is almost invariably good.

Principal exception, Ex. 27, measures 1–3.

b. Skips are good between *chord-tones*, and justifiable by correct harmonic conditions.

Principal exceptions, Ex. 6*b*, par. 4*a*, 4*c*.

c. Any essential (harmonic) tone may be preceded by its two (upper and lower) neighbors. Par. 4*a*, (1).

d. After a *wide* skip, the part turns, either immediately or at the second next tone.

Principal exception, par. 5*a*.

e. Any progressions are possible which represent the successive (or alternate) distribution, in *one* part, of tones which would constitute two (or possibly more) strictly regular adjacent parts.

Ex. 15, Ex. 19.

f. The tendency of active tones should be respected, and all "resolutions" properly effected.

Principal exceptions, par. 6*a* and *b.*

g. The direction of comparatively rapid figures must be governed by the essential tone (or first tone) of the following beat. Par. 7.

h. The movements of a melodic part must corroborate some rational harmonic purpose; especially applicable to disjunct movement. Par. 11.

i. Cause for almost any irregularity is afforded by the Sequence, or any other entirely obvious and defensible *thematic* purpose. Par. 3*c*, Ex. 14, Ex. 30; Par. 12*c.*

EXERCISE I.

A. Analyze, thoroughly and minutely, the progressions of the solo part at the beginning of every Fugue in the Well-tempered Clavichord of J. S. Bach, for about 5 or 6 measures (even after another part may have joined the first). Every movement, from tone to tone, and the collective relations from measure to measure, are to be tested and demonstrated with reference to the above rules.

B. Write a large number of original melodic sentences (40 or 50), of from one to three or four measures in length, illustrating each rule and exception given in Chapter I., successively. Terminate each sentence upon the first unit of the final measure; employ every variety of measure (from $\frac{2}{4}$ to $\frac{12}{8}$), and all the keys, major and minor alternately. Imitate the rhythm and style of the Bach models.

CHAPTER II.

CONDITION 2: "HARMONIOUS UNION." THE ASSOCIATION OF TWO PARTS (VOICES).

14. The simultaneous conduct of two parts must, naturally, yield a harmonious result; not necessarily wholly, but *preponderantly* so. The consonant intervals must, therefore, dominate all **Essential** tones, while the equally desirable and necessary dissonant intermixtures must be limited to the Unessential tones.

The fundamental distinction [between Essential and Unessential tones is partly a question of harmony, but more largely (at least in the present connection) one of *rhythm*, or, rhythmic prominence. Hence, the Essential tones are those which represent and obviously govern an entire metric unit of moderate duration, that is, the full beats in somewhat rapid tempo, and the half-beats in ordinary or deliberate tempo, — possibly the quarter-beats in decidedly slow tempo. The essential tones, in order thus to govern their beats or half-beats, will usually appear at the beginning, or upon an accented fraction, of the same ; but not necessarily, as the harmonic quality of the tones (their relation to the momentary *chord*) is decisive in all doubtful cases.

The Unessential tones are those whose relation to the chord, or the beat, render them manifestly secondary to the essential tones.

· RULES FOR EXCLUSIVELY ESSENTIAL TONES.

15. The **consonant,** or at least harmonious, intervals which are to govern the association of Essential tones, are of three grades : Primary consonances, secondary consonances, and mild dissonances.

a. The primary consonances are:

>The 3rds, major and minor; and
>the 6ths, major and minor.

The *quality* (major or minor) depends upon the momentary *key;* and the *choice* between 3rd and 6th is dictated by the *harmonic* demands or preference. They are not affected by the enlargement (through an octave of double-octave separation) to 10th, 13th, etc.

These intervals are invariably permissible, at any point, during notes of any reasonable time-value, in practically any order and connection.

An unbroken succession of 3rds (or of 6ths), while inevitably harmonious, and therefore desirable in moderation, nevertheless militates against the necessary independence of the two parts, and should, for that reason, not be protracted beyond 3 or 4 (5) at a time, as a rule.

For illustration (adapted from **Bach,** with omission of the unessential tones contained in the original):

The complete form of these illustrations is given in Ex. 44, Nos. 1, 2, 3.

b. The secondary consonances are:

>The perfect 8ve, or unison; and those
>perfect 5ths which represent strong triads (those of the
>Tonic and Dominant).

The octave is useful, and quite common; it may represent the duplication of any scale-step excepting the Leading-tone (step 7), but is best as Tonic, Dominant, or Subdominant; if it occurs at the weaker steps (2nd, 3rd or 6th) its effect must be carefully tested. The perfect 5th is rare, and always requires to be tested.

Neither of these intervals can occur in succession (8–8, or 5–5), nor should they be interchanged (8–5, or 5–8), as a rule, when the tones are Essential.

Neither of them should be approached in parallel direction, when the *upper* part makes a wide leap, — always excepting during chord-repetition. A wide leap in either direction, in connection with the perfect 5th, is objectionable, especially in the upper part.

For illustration :

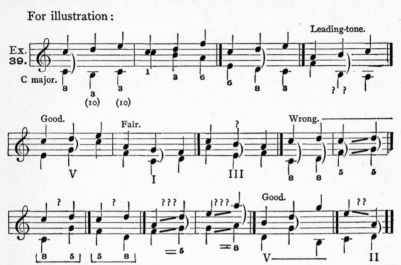

See also Ex. 40, *B;* Ex. 44, Nos. 4, 5.

c. The mildly dissonant intervals, permitted to dominate occasional Essential tones, are :

The diminished 5th; }
the augmented 4th ; } in V⁷ —

The diminished 7th ; }
the augmented 2nd ; } in V⁹ Incomplete (Dim. 7th chord) —

and those **minor 7ths** and **major 2nds** which represent good chords of the seventh.

The diminished and augmented intervals are by no means infrequent; but the major 7ths are very rare.

None of these intervals can be used in succession, nor, as a rule, interchanged; i. e., they should occur only in connection with the primary consonances (3 or 6), or, more cautiously, with secondary ones (par. 15*b*).

They must not be introduced abruptly; the *wide* leap, in either part, toward any of them should be avoided, — excepting during chord-repetition. If a chord-7th or 9th is involved, it must be properly resolved.

For illustration :

See also Ex. 44, No. 2, and Nos. 6–9.

d. Additional general rules :

It is mainly important that each part, **alone by itself, should constitute a perfect, well-designed melody ;** therefore the rules of melodic conduct, given in Chap. I., must be strictly regarded.

And the use of the Sequence, or any other factor which imparts design and purpose to the melody, is of great importance. See par. 17*c;* and par. 21*b*.

Further, a good harmonic result must also be achieved, and for that reason the fundamental principles of chord-succession (detailed in par. 18, to which reference should be made) must be respected. Wide leaps, particularly, are to be tested chiefly with reference to these principles.

It is very difficult to justify a wide leap in *both parts* at the same time, excepting during chord-repetitions.

The two parts should be led, generally, in *opposite directions*, though by no means necessarily. One part may, at almost any time, remain upon the same tone (reiteration, par. 8) while the other part progresses. See par. 17*f.*

EXERCISE 2.

To each of the following given melodies a second part is to be added, according to the rules of par. 15. The two parts are to be essentially similar in rhythm, i.e., a tone in the added part for each tone of the given part; with an occasional exception, as indicated. Every tone, throughout, is to be regarded as essential.

No modulations are to be made.

Each melody is to be manipulated twice; first as upper part, where it is written, and then, transferred to a lower octave, as lower part. The respective added parts must differ from each other.

One staff, or two staves, may be used; if two, the customary G-clef and F-clef. (Should the student chance to be familiar with any of the C-clefs, he may use them also; if not, their use should be deferred. It is unwise to add to the already sufficiently formidable difficulties of the polyphonic style, the difficulty of learning these unfamiliar clefs. *After* the former have been fully mastered, the student can quickly learn as much about the C-clefs as their comparatively limited uses in modern composition — Instrumentation — call for.)

*1) The two parts need not begin together; if the given melody begins on the accent, the added part may rest one beat; and *vice versa*, as indicated in most of the melodies.

*2) Longer tones in the given part may be accompanied by *two* tones (even beats) in the added part; and, *occasionally*, two tones of the given part by one in the added part.

*3) Close upon the Tonic-octave, or unison.

*4) Do not neglect par. 15c.

UNESSENTIAL TONES.

16. The unessential tones may constitute *any* interval, harmonious or dissonant. But every exceptional interval (not enumerated in the preceding paragraph) must appear as *obvious modification of an unobjectionable one*, — as transient (passing) note, neighboring-note, or suspension; and must be employed in such a manner as to confirm the distinction between unessential and essential tones. That is, the objectionable interval must be *followed immediately, or very soon*, by one or another of the perfectly good intervals; thus, 4–3, or 4–6, or 4–5–6; possibly 4–2–6, or 4–2–3; but not 4–2–5–7, or any similar succession. For example :

Ex. 41.

Concisely stated: some good interval (par. 15) must "govern" the ordinary beat, or half-beat, of moderate duration (par. 14, last clauses). If, for any reason, an exceptional interval *governs the beat*, the effect will be poor. No reasonable interval-association is impossible, but all exceptional intervals must be palpably *unessential*, and less prominent than the good ones. The operation of this principle may be tested in the examples which follow, — or in any models of good counterpoint in standard literature.

Further, of the two tones which form an objectionable interval, that one which is obviously non-harmonic (foreign to the chord) should generally enter without leap, though this is not *strictly* necessary (Exs. 12, 32); but it must *progress conjunctly* (stepwise); excepting the two leaps of a 3rd shown in Ex. 9*a* ("double-appoggiatura") and Ex. 9*b* (unresolved upper neighboring-note); and the "ornamental resolutions" of the suspension, Exs. 10, 11.

But an unessential tone that might be regarded as harmonic, as a part of the momentary chord, may *leap* along that chord-line without objection; or may make any reasonable leap even during a change of chord.

Review par. 3*a*, and par. 4*a* and *b*.

For general illustration (unessential tones in parenthesis):

17a. The interval most to be shunned, between two essential (or even semi-essential) tones, is the *perfect 4th.* It is tolerated, as a rule, only between strictly unessential, and brief, tones.

*1) These 4ths, though occupying the accented fractions, are all distinctly unessential.

*2) Here the perfect 4th appears, each time, to govern the beat; but relief (apparently sufficient) is afforded by the consonant interval which accompanies it.

3.

*3) The perfect 4th is best justified by constituting a brief *tonic*–6–4 chord (I_2). This is obviously the case here, and at the first 4th in No. 2.

b. **Each part must progress in a strictly correct melodious manner** (see par. 15*d*). In perfectly good 2-part polyphony it must be **entirely feasible to dissociate the parts and obtain a perfectly good and intelligible melodic result in each alone.** So important is this principle, that it sometimes overpowers the otherwise rigorous rules of part-association (detailed in par. 15, 16, etc.). That is to say, if each one of two associated parts pursues a *definite and obviously justifiable* melodic purpose, they may be conducted with a *certain degree* of indifference to their contrapuntal details. In the conscious fulfilment of a broader melodic aim, the mind of the hearer may waive the demands of euphony to a certain (*limited*) extent. (Compare par. 13*i*.) For example:

The lower of these two parts has the original Motive (par. 38*a*); the upper one has, simultaneously, the same Motive in "contrary motion" (par. 29*a*); — each, therefore, moves according to manifest "thematic authority."

c. For this very reason, it is eminently desirable that each part (but especially the more rapid part, in protracted *uniform rhythm*) should exhibit well-defined and regular formation, i.e., should be compounded of more or less lengthy and regularly recurring *symmetrical figures*, that impart recognizable design to the tone-succession, and prevent it from being a shapeless, rambling, unintelligible, and apparently aimless, melodic line.

This emphasizes the importance of the Sequence, without which truly good and intelligible polyphony can scarcely be imagined. But it refers also to all other means by which the evidence of clear form and broader melodic design may be established, and which are quite as necessary as the sequence, — especially at those places where the sequence itself threatens to become tiresome from overuse. The beginner should never employ, at a time, more than three (four?) sequences of a figure (unless the figure be a very brief one). For example:

The succession of figures in the lower part forms a thoroughly intelligible and coherent melodic line; but the groups differ from exact Sequence just sufficiently to avoid monotony. See also Exs. 88, 92.

d. As stated in par. 15*b* and *c*, it is a part of the limitation of the secondary intervals, that they can only appear singly, — not in succession. Thus, perfect octaves cannot appear in immediate succession under any circumstances; and even when separated by one tone, they are quite as objectionable as immediate octaves, *if the intermediate tone is distinctly unessential:*

But an "oblique" succession of perfect octaves is generally permissible, if one of the tones of the octave itself is obviously unessential; or better, if it is evident that the two parts *maintain their respective melodic independence :*

A succession of perfect 5ths is not permitted between *essential* tones, unless one semi-essential tone, or at least two unessential tones, intervene. When *each* 5th embraces an unessential tone, or when one of the tones of the *second* 5th alone is plainly unessential, the succession is not objectionable. Thus :

A wide leap to or from a tone that is obviously the *Fifth of the momentary chord*, must be made with caution. It is generally bad when the chord-fifth forms the interval of a perfect 5th with the lower part (and is taken by wide leap, — especially parallel with the other part). But is harmless :

(1) During chord-repetition ; and

(2) When the chord is so *inverted* that the interval of a perfect 5th disappears :

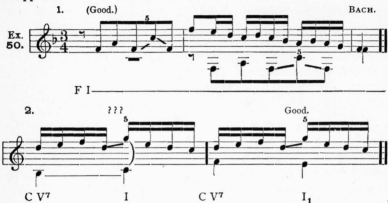

e. The direct succession of any other secondary intervals (i.e., parallel 7ths, 2nds, 4ths, etc.) is permissible only when at least one of the tones involved is *distinctly unessential,* and very brief.   Thus :

* Par. 4*a*, (1).

f. Partly because of the risk of such disagreeable successions as those involved by *parallel* movement of the two parts ; and partly because such parallel conduct deprives both parts of a certain degree of their respective melodic individuality ; it appears desirable to lead the parts in **contrary directions**, as a very general, though by no means binding, rule. Illustrations of wholly or largely opposite motion (at the points where both parts move) are found in Ex. 42–1 ; Ex. 44–2 ; 44–4 ; 44–6 ; Ex. 46 ; — of almost totally parallel motion, in Ex. 44–3 ; — of largely parallel motion, in Ex. 38–2 ; 44–7.

For illustrations of unusually protracted parallel motion, see **Bach,** 2-voice Invention, No. 8, meas. 5, 6 ; 2-voice Invention, No. 14, meas. 14–16. See, also, 2-voice Invention, No. 9, meas. 1, 2, 4 (contrary), meas. 3 (parallel).

HARMONIC INFLUENCE.

18. Strict observance of the above detailed rules must lead to a thoroughly acceptable musical result; but inasmuch as these details themselves are very largely dictated by the principles of harmony and correct chord-progression (without which no style of music can be faultlessly constructed), it follows that constant regard of *fundamental harmonic laws* must facilitate the application of the detailed contrapuntal rules. As already stated (par. 11), the influence of the original harmonic principles is chiefly exhibited wherever *disjunct* movement is employed; but it is never absent, and is the remote power which directs even conjunct movements. The laws of harmonic (chord) succession may be summarized as follows :

I. DIATONIC (within one key).

a. Tonic chords (I or VI) can progress into any other chord of the same key, or of a different key (usually related by adjacent signature).

b. Dominant chords ($V–V^7–V^9-_0V^7-_0V^9$, the $_0$ indicating incomplete forms *) pass, legitimately, into Tonic chords. Other progressions are, however, possible, through the agency of Inversion (i.e., *into* inverted forms of the otherwise inaccessible chords).

c. Second-dominant, or sub-dominant chords (the $II–IV–II^7–IV^7$ **) pass, naturally, into Dominant chords. But their progression into Tonic chords is entirely permissible; best, however, into *inverted* forms of the latter.

d. Subordinate Triads (II, VI, III,) cannot progress into their respective principal Triads (IV–I–V) except by inverting the latter.

e. The III passes legitimately into the IV or VI; into other chords rarely, and only upon inversion, as above.

---

* Triad and 7th-chord on the Leading-tone. See the Author's " Mat. of Mus. Comp.," par. 187, par. 198.

** Idem, par. 206, 207.

f. Any chord may be repeated within the same rhythmic group, but, as a rule, not into a unit which is more accented than that upon which the chord began. This rule, however, is also moderated *somewhat* by inversion, i.e., change of *bass tone* at the accent.

II. Chromatic.

g. If the chromatic inflection is employed, *any* reasonable chordsuccession is feasible, subject to par. 2*a*, and *b*.

The most vital of these rules are *a*, *b*, and *c*, — particularly *b*. For illustration :

*1) See par. 4a, (1). — *2.) See par. 10. —

*3) The effect of this semi-essential perfect 4th is moderated by the embellishing tone *e* (par. 17a).

*4) The ear places the simplest and best construction upon every harmonic effect; therefore this is more likely to *sound like* (and to *be*) a Dominant chord, than the subordinate II.

*5) Comp. note *4). In this whole example the harmonic formations are very clear. See also par. 3a.

*6) The majority of these 8th-notes are essential.

*7) *8) There are here two striking illustrations of the rule given in par. 17b. The progression of the upper part, at note *7), is not interrupted, though it collides quite harshly with the lower part at the accent. Compare par. 7. The still harsher collision at note *8) is justified by the sequential formation of the lower part. Comp. par. 13*i.*

*9) The skip of an augmented 2nd is justified by chord-repetition and straight-forward part-progression (par. 4*c*). — *10) Comp. note *7).
See also Ex. 51–3 (harmonic analysis).

h. In the conduct of the *lowermost* part, the treatment of the chord 5th (as *obvious* 6-4 chord) should be guarded. The established rules apply here also:

1. Avoid leaping either to or from a bass tone that is *obviously* the 5th of the momentary chord, always excepting during chord-repetition. (Comp. Ex. 50, B.)

2. Avoid a *succession* of 6-4 chords. These are always betrayed by *parallel fourths* between the upper and lowermost parts, when the 4ths are *both* essential. (Comp. par. 17*e*.)

3. Further, it is unwise to place any 6-4 chord in a very conspicuous position; hence, it should not appear as very first, or as last, chord of a sentence.

See also par. 62, where these rules are more exhaustively illustrated.

EXERCISE 3.

To each of the following melodies a second part is to be added, according to paragraphs 16, 17, and 18, and the following directions:
The rhythm of the added part is to be more active than that of the given part, so that two, or three, or four tones accompany each beat of the latter, *uniformly.*

Each melody to be manipulated twice, as in the preceding Exercise, adding upper and lower part; and each melody is to be counterpointed throughout in a *uniform* rhythm of two, three, or four notes to each beat, in the following order:

(1)	Adding	lower part,	2	notes	to	each	beat;
(2)	"	upper	"	3	"	"	"	"
(3)	"	lower	"	4	"	"	"	"
(4)	"	upper	"	2	"	"	"	"
(5)	"	lower	"	3	"	"	"	"
(6)	"	upper	"	4	"	"	"	"

It will be well to use two staves (G and F clefs). The added part need not be limited in compass, but it should not diverge an unreasonable distance from the given one; and, as a rule, the parts should not cross.

No modulations (*changes of key*) *are to be made in this exercise.*

Rests may be used, *sparingly;* as a rule, only at the beginning of an occasional *accented* beat. The added part always begins with a rest, as indicated.

Review the directions given in Exercise 2; and refer constantly to the rules of pars. 16, 17, 18, especially the note following Ex. 41; par. **17 b**; **17 c**; 17*f;* 18*b;* 18*f, g.* See also Ex. 8; **Exs. 9 A and B**; Exs. 5 and 17; Exs. 24 and 25; **par. 7**; par. 8; **par. 8 b.** And review the "Summary," par. 13; **par. 21 b.**

Models: (Melody No. 1.)   Seq.

Ex. 9A.

Par. 10.   Ex. 31.   Ex. 5.

Given Melodies.

1.

2.

3.   (Either.)

4.

Par. 12*a*.   *1)

5.   *3)   6.

*1) When the added part has three notes, this figure becomes   or   (see Exercise 6, note *3).

*2) The added melody may end simultaneously with the given part, but it is far better to carry it along, as here, up to the next beat. The final tone must be the Tonic.

*3) When used as lower part, this first tone will be the Root of the Dominant chord.

EXERCISE 4.

To each of the given melodies of Exercise 3 a second part is to be added, as before, in uniform rhythms of two, three, or four notes to each beat, — but introducing a **tie,** from the last note of one group (beat) to the first note of the next, as shown in the subjoined illustrations.

Review, very thoroughly, par. 9, especially *f ;* and observe the following *specific rules* for the treatment of the tie:

Rule A. The tie may be applied to any of the preceding (uniform) species of counterpoint with one, two, or three notes to a beat, and results in a faultless *syncopation* of the same, representing, in each case, the next higher grade of rhythmic motion; i.e., the original formation of one note to each beat becomes one of two notes, two notes become three, and three become four. No further serious condition is involved than that the original formation be uniform rhythm, and *faultless.* Thus :

Model A.
1. (One tone to a beat.)   (Rhythm of 2.)

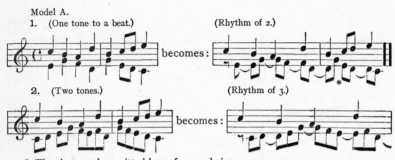

* The tie must be omitted here, for an obvious reason.

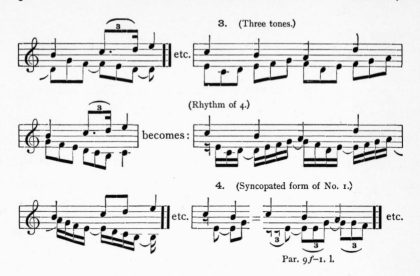

Par. 9*f*–1. 1.

Rule B. A far more comprehensive and fruitful application of the tie is governed by the following directions, to which, for that reason, preference should be given:

(1) The last note of each group (that from which the tie is made) should, as a general rule, constitute one of the *good intervals*, defined in par. 15 as valid for the essential tones, — especially par. 15, *a* and *b*.

(2) The first note of the next group (that which is tied over from the preceding group) may be any interval, *but should be, if possible, a dissonant one, representing a good suspension.* If this is the case, it is not so necessary that the preceding interval be a faultless one (par. 15).

(3) If the first note of the group be, thus, a dissonant interval, its movement is governed by the rules of par. 9*f*; the best progression is the stepwise resolution, upward or downward (most frequently the latter) into one of the " good " intervals; a repetition of the tone, however, before this resolution, is very common and invariably permissible. For example:

(4) It is generally very undesirable to reverse the rule of clauses 1 and 2 above; namely, to tie a poor interval over into a good one:

NOTE. — In some of the solutions in $\frac{3}{4}$ measure the tie may be omitted at the second and third beats, and used at the *bar* only; in $\frac{4}{4}$ measure, it may be omitted at the unaccented (2nd and 4th) beats, or, occasionally, be used at the bar only. Such omissions should, however, be made uniformly throughout.

The tie must be omitted, further, at longer tones in the given melody, — for instance, in melodies Nos. 6 and 8, at the second beat of each half-note.

Each melody may be manipulated in the six different ways specified in **Exercise 3.**

MODULATION.

19. The rules of harmonic progression, given above, also govern the movements of the parts in modulation, i.e., in passing from one key into another.

a. It is always safe, generally necessary, to close each key upon some form of its *Tonic* harmony (I or VI); to pass from this into some *Dominant* or *Second-dominant* chord of the desired key, and from this into its Tonic harmony. Comp. par. 18*a*, and 18*b* and *c*. This modulatory formula is the most common and reliable, whether effected exclusively by diatonic successions, or involving a chromatic inflection (see par. 19*b*). It is least binding for modulation into the *Relative* key (i.e., the key with the same signature); and, of course, it is subject to numerous modifications, especially upon the grounds of par. 17*b*, — unconstrained melodious conduct of the individual parts. For example:

*1) From a Tonic chord of the first key into a Dominant chord of the desired (next-related) one.

*2) From a Tonic chord of old key, into a Second-dominant, and then Dominant chord of new key.

D I   G V————— I——VI bII V——I VI V

c I   f V   I   c IV   V———————I

*3) From the VI (subordinate Tonic chord), into Second-dominant and Dominant chord.

*4) Chromatic inflection in Bass.

*5) The *f*♯ is a raised fourth scale-step only,— not the index of a Modulation; it is evident that no other key than *c*-minor is present.

b. The principal exception to this fundamental rule of modulation is occasioned by the *chromatic inflection;* this melodic device, as stated in par. 18*g*, if properly applied (par. 2*a, b*), renders *every* rational harmonious succession possible and acceptable.

For illustration :

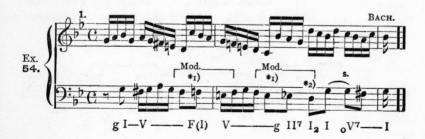

g I—V ———— F(I)   V———— g II[7] I₂ I   ₀V[7]—— I

*1) In both of these cases the first key is abandoned at one of its *Dominant* chords, but *chromatically.* — *2) This illustrates the establishment of the new key through its accented Tonic-$\frac{6}{4}$-chord, which stands for a *Dominant* harmony. — *3) Change of mode, from one Tonic harmony into the other. — *4) Compare note *1). The bracketed analysis is extremely doubtful. See, further, Ex. 44, No. 6.

c. Another somewhat exceptional, though highly effective, modulatory device consists in *introducing an unexpected accidental* in the course of a part-progression, whereby the essential tone involved receives an unpremeditated chromatic inflection (not affecting the *letter*); or, in other words, a foreign tone is *substituted* for the expected one, so as to divert the melody and lead abruptly, but perfectly smoothly, into a new (usually closely related) key. Such a " Substitution " may take place at almost any point; but, of course, only where *either tone* (with or without the accidental) constitutes an equally correct and natural melodic progression from the preceding ones. It is usually safest at accented beats, or accented fractions of beats, and after a Tonic impression of the former key has been imparted — no matter how brief. The parts must be conducted, after the substitution, in a manner calculated naturally to confirm the new key. For illustration :

2.

C II———I———d VI———V———G V⁷———

3.

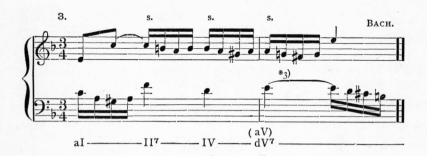

aI———II⁷———IV———dV⁷———

4.

C I———g ₀V⁹———

5.

g V———I———II———c II⁷———V⁷———

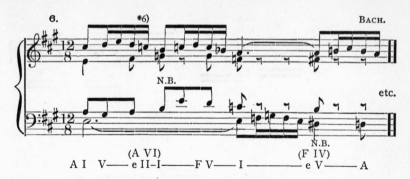

6.   *6)   BACH.

N.B.

etc.

N.B.
(A VI)   (F IV)
A I V——— e II–I———F V—— I ——————— e V——— A

*1) By inserting the sharp, the expected *c* (as part of the expected I of *C* major) becomes *c♯*, and the modulatory current is deftly turned from *C* into *d* minor. In the following measure the expected V of *d* minor is averted by changing the accidental before *c* from ♯ to ♮. — *2) B-*flat* is substituted for the expected b-*natural*. In the next measure a *sharp* is substituted for the natural before *f.* In each case, the expected chord, which would have confirmed the natural harmonic succession, is indicated in brackets. — *3) G♮ is substituted for *g♯*— *4) *Eb* is substituted for *e♮.* — *5) The ♮, substituted for the expected ♯ before this prominent *f,* is an almost unwelcome surprise. — *6) This unexpected *c-natural* leads to the unique mod. into F major. See, further, Ex. 32, third beat; *e♮* instead of the expected *e♭.* — Ex. 57, note *6).

How peculiarly prolific and potent this seductive little device may prove to be when skilfully employed, and how perfectly natural and justifiable its operations may be when prudently conducted, is shown by the following test, in which, it is true, the best possible conditions are provided by the sequential formations (comp. par. 13*i*):

Original form without Modulation:

Ex.   1.
56.   etc.

C I   II   V   VI   IV   V   (III)   VI   II
                                          I

Modified by Substitutions (accidentals):

2.   (♯)
                                                   or:

C   (♯)   F ——————————— d ——— (gV)
    (G)   dI

C   a——————————e —————————— DV——————I

or, if the most extreme treatment be justified or demanded:

and:

*1) The accidentals suggested in the brackets above are doubtless too "extreme"; though they might, perhaps, be justly adopted in slower movement. — *2) The comparison of these two widely different terminations of one and the same series of letters, with the same starting-point, proves that *any* modulatory design may be speedily realized by judicious application of this principle of "substitution." Still, as with all other somewhat irregular factors of musical texture, its best results are emphasized with peculiar effectiveness by *moderation*. A very striking, almost startling, example of substitution occurs in BACH, Well-tempered Clavichord, Vol. I, Fugue 20 (*a* minor), measure 14, beat 3, g♯ in tenor, which abruptly follows g♮ in the soprano. This change is due to the modulatory design as a whole.

d. Finally, any reasonable irregularity with regard to the method of modulation, or the *choice of key*, is justified at a Cadence, or at any obvious point of separation between members of the structural design (i.e., between Sections, Phrases, Motives or Figures; the latter, especially, when sequential in arrangement; compare par. 13*i*). For illustration:

Ex. 57.

a   V——————I   g   II—————— V

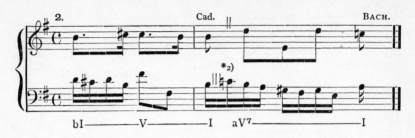

$$c \text{———} V \quad VI \quad B\flat V^7 \text{——————} I \text{——} c V^7 \text{—————} I$$

*1) The irregularity here consists in passing immediately from *a* minor into *g* minor (non-related keys), at — i.e., after — the cadence. — *2) Similar, — from *b* minor into *a* minor. In each of these cases, however, the chords employed accord with the rule (par. 19*a*). — *3) Here the keys are related, but the modulatory process is irregular — from I into I. — *4) Similar (from V of the old key into I of the new). — *5) This extraordinary series of modulations is justified by the sequential formation of the lower part. The unessential intervals are in brackets. The *c♯* in Soprano is the minor 9th (lowered 6th scale-step) of *E*. — *6) The *a♯* in Bass is substituted for the expected *a♮* (par. 19*c*). — *7) Here the chromatic successions are made in an irregular manner, involving the Cross-relation. They are rectified by the Sequences.

20. The notation of the minor scale depends chiefly upon the *harmony*, and is subject to the following rules :

a. The harmonic form (lowered 6th step and legitimate leading-tone) is rarely used, though possible during the *Dominant* harmony. — See Ex. 52, Note *9).—

b. The melodic forms, with raised 6th scale-step in ascending and lowered 7th step in descending, are used during *Tonic* harmonies. Thus :

Ex. 58.

$$c \, I \text{————————————————} IV^7$$

(An illustration in three-part counterpoint is given, because of the superior distinctness of the harmony.)

c. The "ascending" form (with raised 6th step) is used in preference to the harmonic form, in *descending also,* when the harmony is
Dominant; this is because of the proper leading-tone (7th scale-step),
which is characteristic of the Dominant harmony, and not to be altered.
Thus:

*1) The $a\natural$ is used, instead of $a\flat$, because of the $b\natural$ which is indispensable in the
Dominant harmony.

*2) Here $d\natural$ is used in Bass, in descending, although it clashes very harshly
with the $d\flat$ in the Soprano. —***3)** The $a\flat$ in Bass illustrates the force of the rule in
par. 17*b.* It is even doubtful that this $a\flat$ is an essential tone, though it indicates
the Tonic chord (*expected* at this accent) quite forcibly, and thus imparts the appearance of suspension-harmony to the upper tones. At all events, whether essential or
not, the $a\flat$ is "picked up" again at the next accented unit (4th beat) and disposed
of in conjunct movement; and, further, the whole 16th-note passage is sequential.

d. Inversely, the " descending " form (with lowered 7th scale-step) may be used in *ascending also,* when the harmony is *Sub-* (or *Second-*) *Dominant;* or when it is Tonic, immediately *followed* by Subdominant. This, however, is far rarer than the foregoing.

For illustration :

Ex. 60.

c V^9————I————VI————IV————V^7

a I————V^7————————I————————IV————

*1) In both of these cases the notation is influenced by the *coming* Subdominant harmony. See par. *20e.*

e. These exceptional regulations will be seen to corroborate the general rule that *the notation of all passing-notes usually conforms to the scale represented by the chord upon the momentary beat, — or by the chord upon the next-following beat* (if near enough to be affected by the latter rather than by its own beat).

Illustrations are very numerous, in classic writings, of this rational principle of defining the notation of all passing-notes which fall within the limits of a certain chord, as if that chord were, for the time being, a " Tonic " chord. Apparently, it is most commonly the *coming chord* that exercises this dominating power. Exceptions are found, where the influence of the *momentary* chord is weighty enough to overpower that of the coming one ; and, further, at cadences and other points of separation (alluded to in par. 19*d*), where abrupt effects are desired.

General illustrations :

*1) There is scarcely sufficient proof that a genuine, decisive modulation from *F* into *B♭* is here being made; the distinctive tones (*e♭* and *e♮*) are so unessential in effect, that they do not appear to cancel the prevalent *F*-major impression. The *c♭*, and *c♮*, near the end of each measure, are chosen to blend with the *scale*-quality of the coming chord. The *e♭* on the second beat of the measure conforms to the momentary chord.

*2) This whole measure is, more than likely, the Tonic harmony of *F;* the letters *b* and *c* are so inflected as to blend with the coming *d*-minor chord; but *b♭* and *c♮* would sound quite as well, as far as that measure alone is concerned, or if the key remained unchanged.

*3) A modulation takes place at this point, from *d* minor into *F* major, through the altered IV of the latter (with *d♭*, the lowered 6th scale-step); this chord representing the Tonic harmony of *b♭* minor, the passing-notes follow the line of that scale, in descending succession. The analysis of *actual* key-conditions is noted below the brace; that of the scale-conditions governing each group of passing-notes, is given between the staves.

f. The same rule applies also to the *upper* one of the two neighboring-notes which attend each chord-interval. The notation of the *lower* neighbor may either correspond, likewise, to the momentary scale, or it may be a *half-step* (minor second) below its principal tone; the former notation is generally chosen in stately, more serious polyphony; the latter in lighter, more lively, music. For example:

*1) The chord upon this beat is manifestly a II (of *D* major), but, representing *e* minor, the upper neighbor within its radius is written *c♮*. — *2) All of these lower neighbors (marked o) confirm the scale *(D* major). — *3) The lower neighbor is here persistently the *half*-step, despite the key, and the *a♭* above. — *4) This lower neighbor confirms the scale, — as is the case with nearly all the neighboring-notes in the entire composition (W.-t. Cl., Vol. II, Prelude 2 — which see). — *5) Lower neighbor the half-step, but evidently influenced by the coming chord (key).

*6) The lower neighbor of the *Leading-tone* (7th step) is almost always a *whole-step*.

SUMMARY.

21a. In two-part Polyphony, the intervals of the 3rd and 6th prevail, and govern the majority of simultaneous essential tones.

The perfect 8th and 5th, — diminished 5th and 7th, — augmented 4th and 2nd, — govern occasional essential tones, when they represent rational harmonies.

All positively objectionable intervals must be the *obvious modification of some permissible interval* (defined by the harmony).

b. Each part must be so conducted as to constitute, *by itself*, a perfect, interesting, and well-formulated melody, independent of its fellow-part. In order to verify this, **the student must play or sing his added part alone,** after each melodic task is completed.

Further, the parts are conducted, *generally*, in opposite directions.

c. The concerted operations of the two parts must be in manifest keeping with the laws of harmonic (chord-) progression, and modulation.

Principal exception : par. 18*g.*

d. Smooth and effective modulatory inflections (transient or definite) may be made by the substitution of an inflected tone (by an unexpected accidental) for the expected scale-tone, at the appropriate time and place.

e. The notation of passing-notes, within a certain narrow harmonic range, is defined upon the assumption that the chord which *governs* that range is temporarily the representative of the corresponding key (usually as Tonic chord), irrespective of its actual name in the prevailing tonality.

f. Sequential (or generally symmetrical) formations justify any not unreasonable dissonance, irregularity of melody, harmonic succession, or modulation.

EXERCISE 5.

A. Analyze the harmony and the notation of BACH, Well-tempered Cl., Vol. I, Prelude 10 (*e* minor).

B. Fill out the Bass part of the following phrase, in scale-runs of 32nd-notes, as on the first (given) beat; observing the rules of Notation given in par. 20 (particularly 20*e*); refer to par. 21*e*.

C. Manipulate the following phrase according to the principle of Substitution expounded in par. 19c (particularly Ex. 56). Any signature may be chosen for the beginning; and the introduction or substitution of modulating accidentals, in the course, is to be freely practised. The Cadence is to be completed, each time, upon the 3rd beat of the last measure, with the Tonic harmony of the appropriate key:

(May be done at the pfte.)

D. Add a second part to each of the following melodies, with reference to pars. 19 and 20, and in the manner described in Exercise 3, namely: each melody to be used alternately as upper and lower part, and the added part to be in a uniform rhythm of either 2, 3 or 4 notes to each beat, successively. A few experiments may be made with ties (syncopation), as shown in Exercise 4. Refer to par. 21, *b, c, d, f.*

Model.
(Mel. No. 1.)

*1) Scan the melody first as a whole, and determine, at least approximately, where and what changes of key are likely to be necessary.

*2) For 3 notes (♩ ³ ♩ or ♩ · ³ ♩).

*3) For 3 notes (♩ ³ ♩ or ♩ · ³ ♩).

CHAPTER III.

CONDITION 3: "INDIVIDUALITY OF PARTS.'

THE RHYTHMIC RELATION OF ONE PART TO ANOTHER.

22. The fundamental rule is, *diversity* and *contrast* between the rhythms of the separate parts. But the *collective* effect of the rhythm of two associated contrapuntal parts is generally that of uniform movement.

a. A certain grade of tone-values is adopted as the uniform basis of motion (most commonly the 8th- or 16th-note, sometimes as triplet), and this fundamental rate is sustained with predominating regularity. It is rarely pursued in *either part alone,* or in *both parts at once,* for many successive beats; but alternates more or less regularly between the parts, — the part not conducting the fundamental rhythm relaxing, meanwhile, to tone-values of any reasonable length.

Distinction in rhythmic formation must be regarded as the most powerful means of realizing the necessary *independence* and *individuality* of the several parts of a polyphonic complex. Hence, the fundamental law of *Contrasting* Rhythm, and *Alternation.* Similar rhythm in both parts at once (as in Ex. 46), or persistent uniform rhythm in either part (as in the examples made in Exercise 3, etc.), militates against this vital principle of rhythmic *individuality*, and must be used sparingly, as an exception to the rule. For example (correct rhythm):

See, further, Ex. 44–2 (16th-triplets at first in lower, and then in upper part). Ex. 52–1, — the rhythm of 16th-notes in alternating parts during two measures; then maintained for a time in upper part alone. — Ex. 52–2, similar. — Ex. 55–3.

In Ex. 46 the fundamental rhythm is maintained in both parts at once; in Ex. 53–2, it is uniform in each part for some time; both cases are somewhat exceptional, as already stated. In Ex. 54–1, the upper part is uniform, but the lower one diversified.

b. Modifications of the fundamental rate of motion, for the sake of variety, in either or both of the parts, conform *usually* to the laws of regular rhythm; i.e., comparatively heavy (long) tones should occupy the heavier beats, and lighter (short) tones the light beats. In other words, relaxation to longer tone-values should generally occur at accented pulses, and acceleration to shorter tone-values at unaccented pulses.

See Ex. 44, No. 1 (lower part, 16th-notes on beats 2–3, 5–6; the 8th-notes on accented beats 1 and 4). Ex. 44, No. 2, the change of rhythm from 16ths to 8ths takes place at the accented unit (lower part). Ex. 45, No. 1, heaviest note at beginning of measure. Ex. 45-2, fundamental rhythm of 8th-notes, accelerated to 16ths on unaccented fractions of 2nd and 4th beats. Ex. 57-3, fundamental rhythms of 16th-notes, accelerated to 32nds on unaccented fractions.

c. Still, as long as either one of the two parts is conducted in *uniform* rhythm, it appears easy to justify irregularities of rhythm in the other part.

See Ex. 44, No. 6; the upper part is practically uniform (8ths), while the lower, near the end, is distinctly irregular. Ex. 47, lower part uniform 16ths, upper part irregular. Ex. 52-3, lower part uniform, upper part irregular. Ex. 52-5 similar. Ex. 54-1, and 3. Ex. 57-5, end of measure 1. Ex. 40, B.

d. The importance of the **tie** must here again be emphasized. By no other means can an equally effective and legitimate result be obtained, as tending toward the *mutual independence of the parts*. All forms of syncopation are simply the consequence of ties (*actual*, or — according to their location in the measure — *implied*), and therefore serve the same important end. The treatment of the tie is defined in par. 9, which review.

An especially felicitous illustration of the tie is given in Ex. 44, No. 11. See also Ex. 45-2. Ex. 50-1 (syncopation). In each of these cases the general rhythmic effect is *regular*, and preponderantly uniform, because of the correct alternation of the parts, as shown in par. 22a. Ex. 64-3 (syncopation).

The *absence* of ties will be observed most frequently in *two-part* counterpoint of a somewhat lively character and movement, where but little opportunity is afforded for the check which ties naturally occasion (comp. par. 9b). See Ex. 47; Ex. 52-1, 2, 4.

Of barely less importance is the occasional **rest,** which, in the proper place, and in judicious proportion, *is quite as valuable as any tone, often far more so.* See par. 10. Its use is exemplified in Ex. 63; Ex. 64, No. 2; Ex. 91.

e. Distinctly irregular rhythmic formations are justified by sequences, or any other form of *symmetrical successive recurrence;* comp. par. 21f. For example:

Ex.
64.

*1) The rhythmic irregularities here are: the division of the *first* (accented) beat into 16ths, while the 2nd and 3rd beats remain undivided; and the division of the entire second group of 8ths, while the (less weighty) *third* group remains undivided. The self-same irregularities, however, are repeated, and thereby balanced, in the following measure. *2) The irregularities of the first measure are reproduced in the next. *3) The syncopation of the upper part is continued, symmetrically, for three measures. See also Ex. 6A–3, measures 2 and 3, uniformly irregular; Ex. 54–3 (the irregular division of the first beat is sufficiently, if not totally, balanced by similar treatment of the next accent, — 3rd beat). See also BACH, W.-t. Cl., Vol. I, Prelude 13, measures 2–4; Vol. II, Prelude 13, measures 1, 2.

EXERCISE 6.

A. Analyze **Bach**, Two-voice Invention, No. 7, chiefly with reference to the rhythmic treatment of the two parts. Also, Two-voice Invention, No. 1. Also, Well-tempered Clav., Vol. II, Prelude 8, measures 1–5; Prelude 10, measures 23–48.

B. Add a second part (above and below, as before) to each of the following melodic motives or sentences. Refer, constantly, to pars. 7; 9 (particularly *a*, *b*, *f*, Ex. 34); 10; 17*b* and *f;* the summaries, pars. 13, 21; and par. 22.

N. B. Perhaps the most helpful and important rule is, **to look constantly forward, mentally defining the tone necessary or desirable at the next accent,** and guiding the added part accordingly.

1. *Moderato.*

*1) The added part may begin, in each case, exactly with the given one; but it is better that it do so a little after, or before, the latter. Further, the student should make *several* different versions of each task.

*2) *After having concluded his own experiments* with these last melodic extracts from 2-voice polyphonic passages of **Bach**, the student may compare them with the respective original versions; No. 9 occurs in the 2nd French Suite, " Air," measures 1–4; No. 10, in the Art of Fugue, Fugue 9, measures 8–17; No. 11, in the same, Fugue 13, measures 5–9; No. 12, in the 9th Two-voice Invention, measures 17–29; No. 13, clavichord-fugue on " *B-a-c-h*," measures 5–8.

*3) In earlier methods of notation, this figure ♩♪ represented the modern ♩ ₃ ♪ *whenever employed in connection with triplets* (as here).

CHAPTER IV.

THE DEVELOPMENT OF THEMATIC RESOURCES. THE VARIOUS MODES OF IMITATION.

23. The necessary co-ordination of two associated contrapuntal melodies is due largely, it is true, to *contrasting rhythmic formation,* whereby mutual independence of melodic effect is achieved. See par. 22*a,* second clause.

But, besides this independence or individuality, another condition, that of thematic (or melodic) *equality,* is vitally essential to a proper co-ordination of the parts; and this condition of thematic equality is obtained by the device known as **Imitation,** — a device peculiarly characteristic of true polyphonic style.

24. Imitation is the highest of the three progressive species of melodic *recurrence.*

The first grade, (1) simple "Repetition," is the recurrence of a melodic figure in the *same voice,* and upon the *same scale-steps.* This has its natural types in the echo, bird-calls, and other preponderantly physical manifestations.

The second grade, (2) the "Sequence," is the recurrence of a melodic figure in the *same voice,* but upon *other scale-steps.* This, unless purely accidental, implies the exercise of a certain degree of mental power, and therefore enters actively and significantly into the processes of artistic music.

The third grade, (3) "Imitation" proper, is the recurrence of a melodic figure **in some other voice,** either literally or with modifications. This involves the unanimous co-operation of *different individuals,* and therefore calls forth still more comprehensive faculties, enters more deeply into the artistic methods of composition, and becomes the most vital factor of Polyphony. For illustration:

Imitation.

25. The Imitation of a given melodic figure or motive may occur either *above* or *below* the latter; and *at any time*, — though, as a rule, the temporal relation is regular, i.e., the Imitation appears at the same part of the (next) metric group, so that the arrangement of accented or unaccented units is not disturbed (see Exs. 66, 67, etc.).

Further, the Imitation may be effected in a great variety of ways, affecting both the temporal and interval relations. These various modes of Imitation, which constitute an important part of so-called thematic resources, are explained in detail below.

The principal general distinction is that made between **Strict** (or Rigid) Imitation, and **Free** Imitation.

STRICT IMITATION.

26. An Imitation is strict when it adheres exactly to the successive interval-progressions of the initial figure (or motive). This is certain to be the case when it is made upon the same steps of the same scale, i.e., with the selfsame tones, either in the same register (in which case it is called an Imitation in **Unison**) or, as is far more common, in the next higher or next lower register (called an Imitation in the **Octave**); possibly in a more distant register, for which, however, no special designation is necessary.

a. The 8ve-Imitation, because of its perfect agreement with, and confirmation of, the motive (par. 38*a*), is the most natural, simple and frequent, especially for the beginning of a polyphonic section. For illustration :

*1) The "Motive," or leading figure.

*2) The "Imitation" of the motive, in the *upper octave* (or, in the upper part, in the octave).

*3) What takes place here in the leading part during the Imitation, has nothing to do with the latter, and will be considered later (par. 34).

*4) Imitation of the motive in the *lower octave.*

*5) Imitation in *unison* (in lower part).

b. It is also possible to imitate a motive upon other, higher or lower, steps of the scale, without altering any of the given intervals (i.e., strictly):

*1) Imitation of the motive *in the 5th*, above; i.e., each tone of the Imitation is the perfect 5th of the corresponding tone of the motive. It is a "strict" Imitation because the successive progressions coincide exactly, in quantity and quality, with those of the motive. This is quickly verified by observing that the Imitation represents the same scale-steps in *B* major that the motive does in *E* major. Consequently, the melodic and harmonic conditions have remained unchanged (though a change of *key* is implied), — and this is the result peculiar to all Strict Imitations.

*2) Imitation of the motive in the 5th, below, — not in the " 5th reckoned downward," but in a " lower part " in the 5th. It must be borne in mind that interval-relations are always determined by counting **upward**, along the line of the scale, — precisely as the scale-steps are numbered, irrespective of their accidental location above or below a given Tonic. The Imitation in the 5th, of a figure beginning upon *d*, will always begin upon *a*, whether placed in a higher or lower part.

*3) The Imitation is strict ; but an inflection of the scale, resulting in a modulation from *d* into *a* minor, is necessary, to prevent alteration of the original series of interval-progressions.

c. But, as seen already in the second of the above illustrations, the Strict Imitation in any other interval than the octave, is quite likely to call for inflections of the original scale, equivalent to more or less pronounced modulations. Thus :

*1) Imitation above, in the perfect 4th (strict, each tone in the perfect 4th — the key changing from *G* to *C*).

*2) Imitation below, in the 4th (strict, — modulation from *C* to *F*).

*3) Imitation above, in the minor 7th (strict, — the same scale-steps in *f* minor as before in *g* minor).

*4) Imitation above, in the major 2nd (strict, — modulation from *C* to *D*).

*5) Imitation below, in the 2nd (strict, — *e* minor to *f* ♯ minor).

*6) Imitation above, in the minor 3rd (strict).

*7) Imitation below, in the major 6th (strict, — modulation from *C* to *d* minor).

Free Imitation.

27. The precision of interval-succession observed in all the above examples of Strict Imitation, is, however, too whimsical and irksome to be insisted upon ; and, therefore, such desirable licences, or intentional modifications, as come under head of **Free** Imitation, are not only sanctioned but required, as conducing to greater freedom of manipulation, and to more complete development of the possibilities latent in the adopted thematic material (Motive).

These licences may affect either the *melodic* or *rhythmic* form of the motive to be imitated ; they may be either *essential* or *unessential* in nature (according to the extent and quality of the changes) ; or they may even assume complex forms by associating different varieties of modification. The extent to which the licences of Imitation may be carried, is subject to but one limitation, namely, the *ready recognizability* of the original motive; that is, all the essential, or striking, characteristics of the motive should be preserved. Upon this unquestionable recognizability of the leading figure (motive), the argument of par. 23 depends.

Unessential Melodic Changes.

28. In Free Imitation with Unessential melodic changes, the modifications may affect

a. The *quality* of one or more of the original interval-successions.

That is, a perfect interval may be altered to its augmented or diminished form; or a major one to its minor form, or vice versa; etc.

These qualitative changes are illustrated in the following:

***1)** In order to be a " strict " Imitation in the perfect 5th, *each and every tone* of the motive should be answered in that interval, so that the tones of the Imitation would agree with the *F♯* major scale, as those of the motive do with *B* major.   But this is not the case here: the first and second tones (*b, c♯*) are answered in the perfect 5th (by *f♯, g♯*); but the next tone, *d♯*, is answered by *a ♮*, the *diminished* 5th, hence altered in quality of interval-succession.   The same is true of the following *g* (answered by *d♮*).

*2) This "later" version does not follow the motive as immediate Imitation of the latter.   But "Imitation" in the broader sense means not only Reproduction with special reference to the preceding tones of some other part, but the general *Recurrence* or reappearance of the motive at different times and in different parts, in the design of the whole.

*3) In order to be a strict Imitation in the major 6th, these tones should conform to the scale of *E* major (beginning with *g♯*); or, if an Imitation in the minor 6th, they should represent the *E♭* major scale.   Instead of either of these, the tones are so chosen as to *confirm the original scale* (*G* major).   This illustrates the prime advantage, and even necessity, of occasional qualitative changes; while infringing somewhat upon the original melodic and harmonic conditions of the motive (comp. Ex. 67, note *1), they tend toward a far more desirable *modulatory* unity.

*4) The motive is simply transferred to the next lower (or 7th higher) step of the same scale (*g* minor); this involves such changes in the quality of the interval-successions as the concession to the prevailing scale demands.

*5) Imitation upon the next higher step of the original scale.

b. Further, the unessential melodic changes may affect the *quantity* of one or more of the original interval-successions.

. That is, the interval of a 3rd may be enlarged to a 4th or 5th, or contracted to a 2nd, etc.

For illustration :

*1) See Ex. 69, note *2).— Compare this version with the motive, and observe what enlargements of the corresponding original interval-successions occur, at the brackets ;—the first tone (*b♭*) is answered in the 6th (*g*); the next four tones are answered in the 5th; the next in the 7th; and the last four again in the 6th.   From this it is evident that the " interval of Imitation " cannot, in such cases, be exactly specified, because of the changes in quantity.   It is customary to define the Imitation according to the interval most frequently used, — generally, though not always, that indicated by the very first tone.

*2) Here a contraction from 8ve to 7th occurs.   This reveals another of the favorable features of the change in interval-quantity, namely, that it *alters the harmonic aspect* of the motive.   In this case the original motive, which represents a "triad " form, is modified to a " chord of the seventh."

At *3) the triad-form of the motive is changed, both by enlargement and con- traction, to the form of a " chord of the sixth."

At *4) it is changed to a chord of the seventh.

c. As important as these alterations of the melodic and harmonic form of the original motive may appear to be, in themselves, the par- ticular object of the unessential melodic changes will be found to consist, chiefly, in *facilitating the adjustment* of the motive (upon its periodic recurrences) to the prevailing modulatory conditions, or to any immediate or general requirement of the total design.

When the motive is imitated in any other interval than the 8*ve*,— that is, when it is shifted to other steps of the scale than those which it originally occupied, — the melodic conditions are changed, of course, and possibly seriously disturbed.   To counteract this, two things may be done :

(1) A *modulation* may be made (into any *next-related* key), changing the scale in such a way that the new location of the motive shall repre- sent correct step-progressions.   Or,

(2) The above quantitative melodic changes may be undertaken *in the Imitation itself*, so that the otherwise faulty successions are removed.

For example, the following motive, in C major:

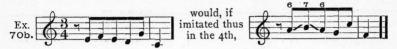

would, if
imitated thus
in the 4th,

assume an awkward and defective form, if retained in C major without change of interval-quantity; but it may be redeemed, either by changing the key:

(to *F* major.)   (to *G* major or *e* minor.)

or by altering the size of the first interval:

or by resorting to both devices; if transferred to *a* minor or *d* minor, without further change, the result would again be faulty:

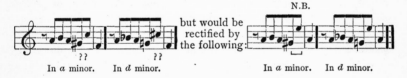

but would be
rectified by
the following:

In *a* minor.   In *d* minor.   In *a* minor.   In *d* minor.

ESSENTIAL MELODIC CHANGES.

29. In free Imitation with Essential melodic changes, the following distinctions of species are made:

a. Imitation in **contrary motion.** Here, the *direction* of each tone-succession of the Motive is reversed in the Imitation; i.e., all ascending progressions are changed to descending ones, and vice versa. As these changes, though radical in their nature, affect each and every tone alike, the result is a legitimate uniform modification; though turned "upside down," it is the same melodic line, and invariably recognizable as such.

The term "inverted motive" is permissible; but it is judicious to restrict the word "inversion" rigidly to the local relation of *two or more parts to each other*, as involved in so-called double-counterpoint (see par. 55).

For illustration :

The size of the interval-progressions may be in " strict " accordance with those of the Motive, but this is by no means necessary, or even desirable. The "interval of Imitation" cannot be defined as in par. 26, obviously, because the melodic lines are not parallel, but contrary ; but they appear to revolve, in opposite directions, about a certain *mutual axis*, or corresponding tone, and the choice of this tone is significant in determining the degree of coincidence, both harmonic and melodic, between the Motive and its Imitation.

If, for instance, every *Mediant* (3rd Scale-step) in the Motive is answered by a *Mediant* in the Imitation, the several tones of the Tonic chord and also of the Incomplete Dominant 9th chord (the most important fundamental harmonies) will reappear, in reverse order. Thus :

The harmonic similarity is therefore complete.

This coincidence may also be defined as *tonic* note responding to *dominant* note, for that is the natural consequence of Mediant responding to Mediant.

The same is true of the corresponding *minor* (*c* minor).   And it applies to these tones *either in their simple harmonic form, or embellished,—as basis of an ornate melodic motive.*

If, further, each *Mediant* in the Motive be answered by a *Tonic* note, the result will be:

which constitutes very nearly the same degree of harmonic coincidence as above.   Consequently, these two varieties of melodic relation,—*Mediant responding to Mediant* (= *Tonic to Dominant*) and *Mediant responding to Tonic,* — are the best for the Imitation in Contrary motion. These, and other conditions, are illustrated in the following:

*1) The Mediant (*f*) in the motive becomes each time again *f* in the Imitation: i.e., Mediant responds to Mediant; or Tonic (*d*) responds to Dominant (*a*), and vice versa.

*2) Mediant responds to Mediant (or Tonic to Dominant) up to the 2nd beat of the fourth measure, when one of the quantitative changes shown in Ex. 70A takes place.

*3) Here, Mediant responds to Tonic. The same is true of Ex. 71, No. 2.

*4) Tonic responds to Tonic. See also Ex. 71, No. 1.

*5) Might just as well have been *d♮*, but for the desirable modulation.

While such melodic coincidences may, and perhaps should, be adopted as a means of obtaining the *first* (and best) version of the Imitation in Contrary motion, it must be understood that when the melodic line or figure of the "Contrary motion" has been once thus fixed, it may be shifted about to any steps in its own, or some other, scale — possibly with such *unessential changes* as are indicated in par. 28. Comp. Ex. 69, Note *2).

b. **Retrograde** Imitation (*cancrizans*), in which the motive is reproduced *backward.* This alteration so seriously endangers the recognizability of the motive, that it may scarcely be regarded as a legitimate or permissible mode of Imitation; and, in truth, its adoption in modern Polyphony is extremely rare. See par. 27, last clause.

An extraordinary example of Retrograde Imitation may be found in **Beethoven's** Pfte. Sonata, op. 106, in B♭ major, last movement. The long and unique Subject at the beginning of the *Allegro risoluto* reappears in reversed order (i.e., backward) at

very nearly its full length, in the first nine measures of the section with the 2♯ signature, — in the lower part; the same form follows immediately in the upper part,
and then in the lowermost part.   It is characteristic of **Bach's** conception of pure
Polyphony, that this device does not appear at all in his "Art of Fugue," a work
replete with all the *legitimate* devices of contrapuntal texture.

Unessential Rhythmic Changes.

30. In Free Imitation with Unessential rhythmic changes, the
following licences occur :

a. The value of the *final* tone of the motive may be either increased
or reduced.   This utterly harmless modification is illustrated in Ex. 67,
No. 1 ; Ex. 68, No. 2 ; Ex. 69, No. 1 ; Ex. 70A, No. 3 ; and Ex. 74,
No. 3, — which see.

b. The value of the *first* tone of the motive, also, may be increased
or decreased (by beginning the Imitation correspondingly earlier or
later).   Neither of these modifications is purely arbitrary, but will, in
the majority of cases, be dictated by the necessity of adjusting the
thematic figure, at either of its extremities, to the general design, —
especially as concerns the harmony and modulation.   For illustration :

*1) The first tone is lengthened, from ♩♩ to ♩.♩ —.

*2) The first tone is reduced, from ♩♩ to ♩ —.

*3) Both the first and second tones are lengthened, from ♩ to ♩ —.

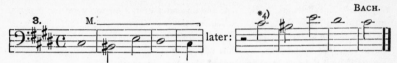

*4) The first tone is reduced, and the value of the last tone is also changed. The reasons for these and similar changes are amply apparent in the context of the original.

c. More rarely, the value of certain tones in the *course* of the motive may be modified, — generally in such a manner that what is added to one beat is subtracted from the neighboring beat, so that the rhythm of the remaining tones, and the effect as a whole, is not disturbed. These changes are largely arbitrary, and are made more for the sake of variety and heightened effect, than from necessity of adjustment. For illustration:

*1) The rhythm of the 2nd beat is altered from ♪ ♪ to ♪·♪; the first and last tones are also modified.

*2) The value of the 7th and 9th tones is decreased, and, as no equalization takes place, the second half of the motive appears dwarfed. The first tone is lengthened.

Essential Rhythmic Changes.

31. Free Imitation with Essential rhythmic changes involves the following modifications:

a. Imitation in **Augmentation.** Here the time-value of *each tone and rest* is multiplied in uniform ratio. Thus, the length of the motive is usually exactly *doubled*, although three-fold and even four-fold augmentation sometimes occurs. This applies naturally to motives in duple rhythm; whereas in triple time it is often necessary to resort to uneven proportions of augmentation, in order to preserve the original arrangement of accented and unaccented tones. This change, though essential, does not jeopardize the recognizability of the motive, for it has usually simply the effect of decreasing the *tempo* without affecting any of the melodic or rhythmic proportions of the original tones. For illustration:

*1) The principle of Augmentation operates from the *accented* units, and there-fore affects, in this case, the initial *rest* also. — *2) The ♩-rest contracts the value of the first (augmented) tone from 𝅝 to 𝅗𝅥· It is a four-fold enlargement, — sometimes called *double* Augmentation. — *3) This example of Augmentation also involves a shift of rhythm, — explained in par. 31c. — At *4) the proportions of Augmentation are uneven (three- and four-fold). — *5) Here the proportions of Augmentation are *necessarily* uneven; otherwise, the triple measure would be transformed into duple. — The version at *6) conforms a little more closely to the prosodic effect of the origi-nal motive.

b. Imitation in **Diminution.** This is exactly the reverse of the above, and has the effect of increasing the *tempo* without changing the design of the motive. It is hardly feasible in any other than duple measure. For example:

*1) The rhythm of these four notes is equalized by cancelling the dots. — *2) A reduction to *one-third* of the original values. The prosodic effect of the motive is totally changed. — *3) A fragment, only, of the motive, in still more extreme Dimi-nution.

c. Imitation in **Shifted rhythm ;** that is, the reproduction of the motive at a *different part of the measure,* so that the original arrange-ment of accented and unaccented tones is more or less completely changed.

In 4-4 measure, a shift of *two* beats simply produces an exchange of accents, without appreciable change of prosodic effect. This is illustrated in Ex. 66, No. 1 (the motive begins in the 3rd beat, the Imitation in the 1st); Ex. 68, Nos. 2, 3, 4, and 7; Ex. 69, No. 4; Ex. 71, Nos. 1 and 2.

In 4-4, or any other variety of duple measure, an entirely new arrangement is obtained by shifting the motive *one beat, forward or backward;* or, as is more rarely the case, by shifting it a fraction of one or more beats, so that the original full beats fall between the pulses, and the Motive assumes a *syncopated* form. For example:

*1) The Motive, as Imitation, is shifted *forward* one beat. Observe the change in the location of the accented tones; play each version several times, with very marked accentuations. — *2) In slow tempo, this will appear to be the simple exchange of primary and secondary accents; but the difference in effect is, nevertheless, sufficiently noticeable. — *3) Shifted *backward* one beat. — *4) Shifted forward one-half beat (syncopated Imitation).

In 3-4, or any other variety of triple measure, the prosodic transformations are still more numerous, because the accented tones may be

shifted to *either* of the two unaccented units, with totally different results. Besides this, syncopated Imitation is also possible, as above.
For illustration :

*1) This phrase is borrowed from the pianoforte-quartet in *A* (3rd movement),
merely to illustrate, in a peculiarly effective manner, the two-fold transformation
possible in triple measure. At *2) the motive is shifted forward, and at *3) backward, one beat.

32. Complex forms of Imitation, such as Contrary motion, and, at
the same time, unessential melodic or rhythmic changes ; or simultaneous Contrary motion and Augmentation, Diminution, or Shifted
rhythm, and so on, — are possible and not uncommon. But it must be
remembered that the more these licences are multiplied, the more
likely they are to endanger, or destroy, that *recognizability of the original
motive* designated in par. 27 as the inexorable limit, beyond which it
would be inconsistent to pass. For example :

Cont. Motion and Augm.

*1) Imitation in Contrary motion and Diminution; the value of the first tone abbreviated. — A few other cases of slight complication are shown in Ex. 74, No. 2: Ex. 78, No. 3; and Ex. 79, No. 2.

33. Finally, more exceptional forms of modified Imitation are occasionally encountered in the polyphony of **Bach** and others, consisting, (1) in the addition of intermediate embellishing tones; (2) in the contrary motion of some *single* interval; (3) the transposition of a portion of the motive to a higher or lower octave; and (4) the *partial* application of certain essential modifications (i.e., to certain figures, only, of the motive). Such miscellaneous changes are most justifiable when made for the sake of adjusting the Imitation to some *legitimate and obvious thematic purpose;* or to facilitate obstinate and awkward, but *manifestly necessary,* contrapuntal movements. (Comp. par 12*c*.) And, as usual, they should not infringe upon the recognizability of the original motive. For illustration :

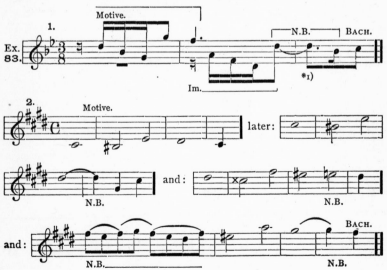

*1) Comp. par, 4*a*, 1 (Ex. 9*A*).

*2) These last tones are transferred to the lower octave, evidently to avoid carrying the part too high.

*3) A curious example of *partial* augmentation.

*4) The motive is shifted one beat forward, and embellished, during three measures.

*5) This final fragment is transferred to another part.

*6) The motive is shifted backward one beat, and the 6th tone is altered, from the expected $g\sharp$ to $d\sharp$. Compare No. 5, of this Example.

*7) This well-nigh unrecognizable Imitation is complicated by change of register at single tones.

The Contrapuntal Associate.

34. After the leading part has terminated its Motive, and the Imitation of the latter is annunciated in the other part, the leading part does not discontinue its movement, or even pause briefly, but carries its melodic line along, apparently independent of the Imitation. This projection of the motive-melody must, however, constitute a harmonious contrapuntal associate of the Imitation, and therefore its conduct must be defined according to the rules of two-part polyphony, detailed in Chapter II. It is usually called the " Counter-motive," or, briefly, the " Counterpoint."

35. To the general details.of contrapuntal association given in the second chapter, the following special rules must be added :

a. The " Counterpoint " must be a *perfectly natural continuation of the Motive-melody* which precedes it, — as if the imitatory appearance of the other part were rather accidental than intentional, and did not concern the progressive movement of the leading part.

This rule is of the utmost moment in genuine polyphonic texture. For illustration :

*1) The leading part runs on, apparently regardless of the Imitation (observe the collision at N. B.), in sequential projection of its final member. The importance of the Sequence is here again vindicated; *by no other means can melodic evolution be more easily and naturally effected than by the Sequence.* See par. 17c. As to the points marked N. B., see par. 17b and 13i.

*2) Here also, the " Counterpoint " is a nearly sequential continuation of the motive itself.

*3) The Counterpoint is all derived, somewhat disguised, from the motive.

*4) See Ex. 45, No. 2.

See also, **Bach**, Well-tempered Clav., Vol. I, Fugue 5, meas. 1–3; Fugue 9, meas. 1–3; 16, meas. 1–4; Vol. II, Fugue 5, meas. 1–4; 11, meas. 1–8; 12, meas. 1–8.

b. *The beginning of the Imitation must be properly adjusted* (as regards harmony and modulation) *to the termination of the motive.* This will influence the choice of the interval of Imitation (par. 26a, b, c); may induce the employment of the unessential rhythmic changes noted in par. 30b; and will possibly necessitate the unessential melodic changes given in par. 28a and b, at the beginning of the Imitation.

For example:

*1)*1) The adjustment of the beginning of the Imitation to the termination of the motive is perfect, both as concerns interval and chord, in each of these cases. This is to be expected, when either the Imitation in the 8ve or 5th is chosen; i.e., these intervals are " safe."—*2) Imitation in the 3rd. It is adjusted well at the very beginning, but leads to a somewhat hasty and undesirable modulation. —*3) Imitation in the 7th. This is good, because the chord-connection (harmonic adjustment) is complete. —*4) Imitation in the 2nd. Like the preceding case. —*5) The size of the first interval is in one case extended, in the other contracted. — *6) The objectionable interval at the outset is softened by shortening the first tone. — *7) Improved by lengthening first tone. See also Ex. 76, No. 1; Ex. 77, No. 3.

c. It suffices, as a rule, to provide thus for harmonic agreement at and during *the first beat or two of the Imitation.* The subsequent beats may easily be so manipulated, — either by unessential modification of the *Imitation itself* (par. 28*a*, *b*), or by consistent and careful conduct of the " *Counterpoint*," — as to achieve good harmonic conditions.

The Imitation once correctly launched, the succeeding movements of the contrapuntal associate are determined, as already stated, by the principles of two-part polyphony, but with more particular regard of the primary rule given at *a* above (par. 35).

Examine the methods of adjusting the beginning of the Imitation to the termination of the motive, in Exs. 66, 67, 68, 69, 70*A*, 71 ; 74, No. 3 ; 83, No. 1.

THE STRETTO.

36. The Imitation is said to be in "stretto" when it *overlaps* a portion of the motive ; i.e., when the Imitation sets in before the motive is finished.

The section of the motive thus covered by a section of the Imitation is, consequently, at the same time the contrapuntal associate of the latter ; and, therefore, the practicability of the Stretto is conditional upon reasonable contrapuntal agreement between these sections. This depends

(1) upon the choice of Strict or Free Imitation (pars. 26, 27) ; if Strict, —if no concessions are to be made, — then but few Stretti will be found feasible, though the rules of par. 12*c* and par. 17*b* (which see) provide an excuse, at least, for *some* harshness of effect ; if Free, then the judicious application of the unessential licences of par. 28 *a*, *b*, will make almost any Stretto possible. It depends, further,

(2) upon the length of the overlapping section.

The earlier the Imitation appears, the longer will the overlapping section be, and, consequently, the more protracted the risk of disagreement. Hence, fewer Stretti will be practicable after only one or two beats (i.e., from the beginning of the motive) than after a longer period, nearer the end of the motive. But, here again, slight alterations in interval-quantity will facilitate even such extreme Stretto-Imitations.

Specimens of *incipient* forms of the Stretto are seen in Ex. 66, No. 3, and Ex. 67, No. 1, where the Imitation begins *simultaneously with the final unit* of the motive ; this brief interlinking of the two parts (not strictly " overlapping ") involves no more than the rule of par. 35*b*. See also Ex. 68, Nos. 1, 5, 6 ; Ex. 69, Nos. 1, 3, 5.

Illustrations of the genuine Stretto : —

*1) In defining a Stretto-Imitation, both the melodic and rhythmic intervals are specified: At (*a*) it is a Stretto "in the 5th, after six beats;" at (*b*) in the 4th, after one measure; at (*c*) in the octave, after one measure; at (*d*) in the 5th, after three beats; at (*e*) in the 5th, after two beats; and at (*f*) in the 6th, after one beat. This motive is peculiarly adapted for the Stretto, as it yields all of these grades without a single alteration in interval-quantity. — *2) After two beats, in the 5th. The collision at N. B. is justified by the principle of par. 12*c*. — *3) After two beats, in the 4th, Strict. — *4) After one beat, in the octave, Strict. — *5) The quantity of the first interval-progression is changed, to facilitate the Stretto. — *6) The same Stretto as in the preceding measure, but with inverted parts. — *7) The Stretto begins in the 4th, after *one-half* beat ; at this point the tone *g* is inserted, and the Stretto then continues, at the distance of a *whole* beat.   In the next measure, a change in interval-quantity is made, for an evident reason. — *8) Comp. Ex. 10 and context.   This is a Stretto " in Contrary motion." — *9) *10) An extraordinary example of the Stretto : first in the 7th, *after one beat;* and then in Contrary motion, *after one beat,* — without changing a single interval, during almost the entire length of the unusually long motive.   The student's experiments with his own motives will contribute most convincingly to his admiration of such contrapuntal feats as this. — *11) Stretto in Augmentation. — See also Ex. 85, No. 3. — See further, **Bach,** Well-temp. Clav., Vol. I, Fugue 1, meas. 7–8, 17–18 (Tenor and Bass) ; 6, meas. 21–25 ; 20, meas. 27–31 (Soprano and Tenor), meas. 64–68 (Bass and Tenor).   Vol. II, Fugue 2, meas. 14–15 (in Augmentation) ; 3, meas. 1–3 (cont. motion) ; 6, meas. 14–15.

EXERCISE 7.

A. Each of the following given Motives is to be extended by an Imitation (in the specified interval) and a Contrapuntal associate, as shown in the subjoined model.

As a rule, two staves are to be used, and care should be taken to prevent the two parts from diverging too widely from each other, — very rarely more than two octaves apart, usually much less.

Each Motive is to occupy first the upper part, followed by its Imitation in the lower ; then the lower part, with Imitation in the upper ; and each time a *different Counterpoint* must be devised.

Review the summaries, par. 13 and par. 21 ; also par. 22*a;* par. 35 *a, b, c.*

This exercise is to be limited to par. 26*a,* — **Strict Imitation in the Octave.**

The student is expected to manipulate this (No. 1) again, in his own way. Then Exercise 6B (page 58), Nos. 3, 4, 5, 2, 6, 7, 8. Then the following:—

*1) Final tone optional, both as regards choice and *duration.* — *2) The tempo-indications must not be overlooked; they may affect the rhythm of the Counter-point. — *3) Duration optional; and the same in every succeeding case. — *4) The Motive ceases with this tone, whose value, and the continuation of the part, up to the entrance of the Imitation, are optional. — *5) The tie is optional.

B. A number of these motives (as specified below) to be manipulated according to par. 26*b*,—**Strict Imitation in the 5th.**

Each motive, as before, imitated both above and below. Especial attention to par. 35*b* (*c*) will be necessary.

Motives adapted to this exercise:

    Exercise 6*B*, Nos. 2, 3, 4, 6, 7, 8;

    Exercise 7*A*, Nos. 1, 5, 6, 7, 8, 9, 11, 13, 14, 15, 18, 20, 21, 23, 25.

EXERCISE 8.

A. Manipulate the motives specified below, in various **other intervals** of Imitation (in the 3rd, 4th, 6th, possibly 2nd or 7th); all in **Free** Imitation, according to par. 28*a* and *b*.

The practicable intervals of Imitation will be determined in keeping with par. 35*b*; and it must be understood that the unessential melodic changes there referred to are not arbitrary, but should be resorted to only as an *expedient*, when the Strict Imitation baffles harmonious adjustment, — or in order to secure better modulation. Review Ex. 69, Note *3), and Ex. 70*A*, Note *2).   And observe particularly par. 28*c*.

For this purpose, employ the following Motives:

    Exercise 6*B*, Nos. 2, 5;

    Exercise 7*A*, Nos. 2, 4, 6, 8, 10, 16, 18, 20, 21, 25.

B. Manipulate a few motives (Exercise 7*A*, Nos. 1, 7, 9, 11, 26) with the licences of par. 30*b*, and, occasionally, *c*, — Imitation with unessential rhythmic changes. Any interval of Imitation may be used (especially 8ve, 5th or 3rd).

EXERCISE 9.

A. Manipulate the following motives according to par. 29*a* **(Contrary motion)**, in various methods of response (Exs. 72, 73 ; Ex. 74, Note *4) :

  Exercise 6*B*, Nos. 3, 4, 5, 6, 7, 8;

  Exercise 7*A*, Nos. 3, 6, 10, 13, 14, 15, 16, 17, 19, 22, 23, 26.

B. Manipulate the motives specified below, according to par. 31*a* **(Augmentation)**. Any interval of Imitation may be used, preferably the 8ve, 5th or 3rd.

*1) It is necessary, in the contrapuntal associate of an Augmentation (because of its length and persistently heavy rhythm), to check the rhythmic current from time to time, — especially at the outset, and at any heavy accent.

For this purpose, employ Exercise 6*B*, Nos. 2, 3, 6;

  Exercise 7*A*, Nos. 2, 12, 16, 4, 5, 11, 17.

C. Manipulate the following, according to par. 31*b* **(Diminution)** :

  Exercise 6*B*, Nos. 3, 7 ;

  Exercise 7*A*, Nos. 4, 19, 26 (10).

D. Manipulate the motives specified below according to par. 31*c* **(Shifted rhythm)** :

*1) The Imitation is to be shifted *forward* in each case, — generally one beat, possibly a little more or less. The vacant space that consequently intervenes between the end of the motive and the beginning of the Imitation, must be very carefully filled out, with close attention to the rule of par. 35*a*, i.e., *with strictly analogous material.* The interval of Imitation will be almost entirely optional, depending somewhat upon the current of the "intervening tones."

*2) In every case, both parts must be thus carried on, to the next accented beat, — with strictly analogous material.   For this purpose employ

        Exercise 6*B*, Nos. 4, 5;

        Exercise 7*A*, Nos. 3, 7, 10, 12, 18, 22, 24.

EXERCISE 10.

Manipulate a number of motives in **Stretto-imitations,** according to par. 36.

This work is almost purely *experimental ;* the possibility of obtaining one or more acceptable stretti is to be tested patiently, in each of the seven different intervals of Imitation and at different rhythmical distances.   The Imitation will, of course, always be shifted *backward,* and tested at each succeeding beat of gradually increasing proximity to the beginning of the motive.   The Stretto-imitations in parallel motion (Ex. 86, No. 1), and in Contrary motion (Ex. 86, No. 6), are both to be tested; occasionally that in Augmentation also (Ex. 86, No. 8).   Unessential melodic changes (in quantity of interval) may be admitted, to a reasonable extent.

For this purpose use any motives of Exercise 6*B*, Nos. 2–8, or of Exercise 7*A*. Also a few of the original motives invented in Exercise 1*B*.

DIVISION TWO.

THE INVENTION-FORMS.

INTRODUCTORY.

37. Polyphonic styles of composition are divided into three classes, distinguished chiefly by the degree of severity with which the principles of polyphony, or contrapuntal writing, are applied; namely: the **Invention**, the **Fugue**, and the **Canon**.

In the Canon the utmost rigor of thematic treatment prevails. In the Fugue, the contrapuntal methods are applied with less insistence, but with reference to certain *specific* conditions, peculiar to this class. In the Invention, the polyphonic principles (Imitation, etc.) are applied in a *general* way only, with much freedom of detail; and with almost, if not quite, equal regard of the broader considerations of form (structural design), and of general external effect.

The " Invention " (a term adopted from one of the musical practices of the 17–18th centuries) is, then, the simplest and least constrained of the three principal classes of Polyphonic Form.

38. The factors which enter into the construction of an Invention are: (1) The Motive; (2) The Imitations or recurrences of the Motive.; (3) The Contrapuntal Associates; and (4) The Episodic passages (including the Cadences).

THE MOTIVE.

a. The Motive is a brief melodic sentence, calculated to be (and adopted as) the basis and source of the evolution, construction (or " invention "), of the polyphonic composition in view. It is the " theme " of the structural task.

To this end, it should be simple and regular in its harmonic design, and faultless in melodic formation; but, at the same time, sufficiently characteristic and suggestive to invite manipulation, and to sustain interest. For this reason, *somewhat* striking melodic features may be admitted, and *moderate* rhythmic irregularities are appropriate, if not necessary, — hence the frequency of the *tie*, in effective Motives.

Review, very minutely, as a test of these details, the formation of all the Motives given in Exercise 6*B* (2–8) and Exercise 7*A*.

The *length* of such a thematic sentence concerns mainly the theoretical distinction made between

a **Figure** (a small group of about 3 to 6 tones),

a **Motive** (at least a measure long, compounded of 2 or 3 " figures," and with a
    more or less indefinite cadential impression), and

a **Subject** (in complete Phrase-form, with a definite cadence).

Some of the " themes " of Exercises 6 and 7 are, properly speaking, *Subjects*,
though the generic term " Motive " will be applied to all alike, for convenience.
Par. 113 may be briefly referred to.

The most important rule for the Motive is, that its first tone, or
tones, should impart an unmistakable *Tonic* impression : —

See Exercise 6*B*, Nos. 2, 3, 6, 8, — *beginning* with the Tonic note; also Exercise 7*A*, Nos. 1, 4, 5, 6, 7, 9, 12, 13, 14, 15, 21, 23, 24. Further, Exercise 7*A*, Nos.
2, 3, 8, 10, 11, 17, 22, 26, — beginning with the *Dominant* note, followed immediately,
or soon, by the Tonic. In Exercise 7*A*, Nos. 19 and 25, the Tonic note follows
quite late, but the Tonic impression is clear. Exercise 7*A*, No. 18, is misleading,
as the Tonic note is entirely absent. In Exercise 6*B*, Nos. 5 and 7 begin upon the
Mediant, followed soon by the Tonic, — this is perfectly clear. Exercise 7*A*, No.
16, is again misleading, because of the long absence of the Tonic, after the initial
Mediant (which imparts the impression of *e* minor, instead of *G* major). Exercise 6*B*,
No. 4, begins with the lower neighbor of the Tonic, and is entirely clear. Exercise
7A, No. 20, is misleading, because the upper neighbor of the Mediant, though unaccented, imparts a *B♭* major impression where *F* major is intended.

The Imitations, or Thematic Components.

b. The Imitations, or successive recurrences of the Motive, constitute the so-called *thematic* texture of the polyphonic fabric. Compare
par. 38*d*, and review Ex. 69, Note *2). The details of this factor are
given in Chapter IV.

The Counterpoint.

c. This term is applied (possibly a little loosely) to all the passages
that are invented as contrapuntal associates of the motive, upon each of
its successive Imitations or recurrences. See par. 34.

The Episodic Components.

d. To all those portions of the polyphonic fabric where the *motive
is not present* in either part, or is represented by only *one of its fractional
figures*, the term Episodic passage is applied. The necessity for such
elements in effective polyphony, as a foil to the thematic portions, is

obvious; for the monotony of persistent motive-imitation must be relieved from time to time. But it is equally manifest that episodic passages should, as a rule, be neither too frequent nor too extended; and that they must be in close keeping with the character of the thematic portions.

For the latter reason, the episodes are usually derived (1) directly from the motive itself, by using *some fraction of the same;* or (2) indirectly, by utilizing the whole or some portion of any of the *contrapuntal associates of the motive;* or, possibly (3), an *entirely new figure* may be adopted, on condition that it be conceived strictly in the spirit of the motive, or of the general context, and *that it reappear* at intervals during the composition. Finally (4), it is also possible that an episodic passage, after beginning in touch with the motive, may, by gradual and consistent stages, develop into a more or less independent character, — though it can scarcely be justified in becoming quite *foreign.* For illustrations of the episodic components, see Exs. 89, 90, 91.

CHAPTER V.

THE TWO-VOICE INVENTION.

39. An Invention may be constructed, like any homophonic composition, according to the design of the so-called Part-forms, or Song-forms. But it is somewhat inconsistent with the polyphonic style to check the current of thematic development with the emphasis necessary for the Cadence of a genuine and well-defined **Part;** * and it is, therefore, more common for the structural design of Inventions to consist in a kind of group-form, or chain-form, the several divisions of which may most appropriately be called " SECTIONS."

a. The **Section** of polyphonic designs differs from the **Part** of homophonic forms in being, as a rule, less regular and definite in character; in terminating with a *brief,* and less distinct, form of cadence; and in maintaining less obvious formative relation (with regard to general melodic design) to its fellow-divisions. For these reasons, the number of Sections, also, is entirely optional.

b. Generally, each successive Section undertakes a somewhat different method of manipulation, or the development of some special resource

* See the author's " *Homophonic Forms of Mus. Comp.*," par. 70, par. 72*b*.

of the Motive.   But, notwithstanding the comparative independence thus effected, it is necessary to preserve a *certain measure* of logical connection and relation between the Sections, and therefore it is cus- tomary to revert, from time to time, to some structural feature of an earlier Section; thus the *idea*, at least, of the Homophonic designs* prevails in the polyphonic designs as well — especially in the Inven- tion, which, in contents and purpose, is more closely akin to the ordi- nary (homophonic) Song-forms than are the more advanced grades of polyphony.

THE FIRST SECTION.

40.   The 1st Section, or " Exposition," of the Invention, will exhibit, as a rule, all of the structural factors enumerated in par. 38.

a.   The **Motive** may be first announced by either the upper or (more rarely) the lower of the two parts; generally it appears *alone*, though it is sometimes accompanied by a few unimportant auxiliary tones, the better to establish chord, key and rhythm.

Compare BACH, 2-voice Inventions, Nos. 1, 3, 4, 8, with Nos. 7, 13 — the first measures of each.

b.   The **first Imitation,** in an Invention, is almost always made in the *octave;* though occasionally the *fifth* is chosen, or some other inter- val which adjusts itself readily to the harmonic design, — *any* interval being permissible.

In BACH, 2-voice Inventions, Nos. 1, 3, 4, 7, 8, and 13, the first Imitation is in the lower 8ve; in No. 10 it is in the 5th; in BACH, English Suite No. 6, 2nd movement of the " Prélude," it is in the 4th; the same in BACH, Partita II, 3rd movement of the " Sinfonia " (3-4 time).

c.   The details of the Exposition up to this point have been thor- oughly exemplified in the work of Exercise 7, etc.   The next step in the development of the thematic design is, usually, another immediate recurrence of the motive, in the first (i.e., leading) part, as re-imitation of the preceding announcement.   The interval of this new Imitation is optional, though 8ve or 5th is the most usual.   Meanwhile the other

* *Idem*, par. 73*b*, par. 81*a*.

(second) part continues its movement, as contrapuntal associate of the Motive, according to par. 35. See, also, par. 41*a*. For example:

Ex.
87.

Par. 40*a*.

Counterpoint.

Par. 40*b*.

M. (Im. in 8.)

M. (Re-im.)

BACH.

Par. 40*c*.
*1)

etc.

Counterpoint.

*1) This "Counterpoint" to the second recurrence of the Motive closely resembles the first contrapuntal associate (measures 3-4). It is so natural and tempting to adhere thus to the first Counterpoint, that the student must be reminded of the *monotony it involves*, and be warned against making it a rule. The recurrences of the *Motive* provide amply for the necessary condition of consistency and symmetry; the equally necessary condition of variety devolves largely upon the contrapuntal associates, which may assume more or less different forms at the successive recurrences of the Motive. On the other hand, to guard against excess in this respect, it is advisable to adhere to a certain counter-motive during two (or three) consecutive announcements of the Motive, *and to return, from time to time, in the following Sections, to such former Counter-motives* (i.e., "counterpoints").

See further: BACH, 2-voice Invention No. 1, first six beats; the second recurrence of the Motive (meas. 2) is a Re-imitation in the 5th. The same is the case in No. 7, first six beats (Ex. 91). In No. 8, measures 1-3, it is in the 3rd.

d. What follows, after this second recurrence (i.e., the third announcement) of the Motive, cannot be determined in detail, but only with reference to the *general purpose* of the entire first Section, which involves the following contents: —

The announcement of the Motive ;

The Imitation and successive recurrence, as necessary thematic basis ;

The exhibition of variety (episodic and otherwise);

A modulation into the key in which the Section is to terminate;

The establishing of this key; and

A palpable Cadence in the same.

e. Perhaps the most imperative condition, at the juncture reached in the above example, is that of *variety.* This may be obtained, (1) by substituting the principle of the *Sequence* for that of Imitation, — i.e., reproducing the Motive once or twice in the *same* part instead of the opposite part; or (2) by dropping the thematic thread, and proceeding *episodically.*

The first alternative, the **Sequence** (see par. 41*c*), is illustrated in the following :

*1) The Motive, instead of being again imitated in the other part, reappears as Sequence in the *same* part, upon the next lower step. *The first tone is omitted,* in order not to disturb the smooth termination of the preceding announcement. A clue to the impulses which led **Bach** to choose this particular interval of Sequence, will be found in par. 41*a.* See also par. 40*g.*

*2) This "Counterpoint" differs from the preceding ones. Review Ex. 87, Note *1). It is retained during the following Sequence.

See also **Bach,** Well-temp. Clavichord, Vol. II, first 11 measures of Prelude 10; — Motive of 2 measures, accompanied briefly by auxiliary tones; followed by imitation in the 8ve; then a re-imitation, again in the 8ve; then a Sequence, a third above, — the "Counterpoints" constantly differing, up to this point; then another Sequence, a third above, — the "Counterpoint" as before, but in a lower octave.

The second alternative, the **Episode** (see par. 38*d*), is illustrated in the following:

*1) In the original (French Suite No. 5, "Courante"), a number of auxiliary tones accompany the first announcement of the Motive; they are omitted here.

*2) The "Episode" is interpolated already after the *first* Imitation; it is derived from the Counter-motive in the upper part (2nd measure), which is retained (or imitated) in the lower part in a somewhat modified form, and accompanied by a new contrapuntal figure in the upper part.

Examine, also, **Bach,** 2-voice Invention No. 10, first 6 measures, and endeavor to trace the derivation of the episodical passage; **Bach,** English Suites, No. 1, "Bourrée I," meas. 1–8; English Suites, No. 2, "Prélude," meas. 1–4; English Suites, No. 4, "Prélude," meas. 1–6. Further:

*1) This counterpoint, at the 2nd recurrence of the Motive, corresponds exactly to the Counter-motive of the first Imitation (meas. 2).

*2) The derivation of this episodic passage is not as obvious as in some examples, but nevertheless *palpably* in close keeping with the preceding thematic portions. The figure marked *a* may be accounted for in two ways, as shown by the two slurs: either as part of the Counter-motive, in contrary motion, or (the lower slur) as imitation of the ending of the Motive; *b* bears close *general* resemblance to the Motive, though the indicated derivation may appear tortuous; it embraces three beats, and is reproduced in slightly modified Sequence; *d* is derived from *a*; its modified Sequence, *e*, is admirably utilized in launching the next recurrence of the Motive. See par. 41*b*.

f. On the other hand, these specific modes of obtaining variety are sometimes not resorted to until the alternating Imitations have been extended still farther.   For illustration :

*1) Auxiliary tones (par. 40*a*). — **2)*   Up to this point, the development is not only exclusively thematic but consists in the unrelieved *alternate Imitation* of the Motive. This must be regarded as very exceptional, and illustrates how, even in the polyphonic style, the determination to realize a clear structural design may sometimes overrule the more specific thematic conditions of the texture; it is the prevalence of "form" over "thematic development." The counterpoint is uniform in the lower part, but is diversified in the upper part at each successive Imitation, excepting the last one.   What follows, as Episode, is easily demonstrated.

*3)   The conduct of the lower part effectively illustrates the application of the *brief rest* (par. 10, which review).

See par. 22*d*, last clause; Ex. 90, meas. 4 and 6.

See also, **Bach,** 2-voice Invention No. 8, meas. 1–5 (four announcements of the Motive before the texture becomes episodic).

In No. 1 of the 2-voice Inventions, the Motive is announced five times (the 5th time in Contrary motion) before the alternative of the " Sequence " is adopted; and no less than ten consecutive announcements are made before an " Episode " is introduced.

Further, **Bach,** 4th French Suite, " Gavotte," meas. 1–3.

g. The **modulatory design** of the First Section of an Invention corresponds to that of the First Part in homophonic forms, namely: if in *major,* the Section generally terminates in its *Dominant* key; if in *minor,* usually in its *Relative* (major) key. Exceptionally, these relations may be exchanged (i.e., the Dominant key from minor, and the Relative key from major). Or some other next-related key may be chosen; especially the Relative of the Dominant, — rarely the Subdominant keys.

The influence of this modulatory purpose will probably be evinced as soon as the original key is sufficiently established; generally during the first or second episodic passage; or during a line of sequential announcements of the motive.

In Ex. 88, the latter is clearly illustrated; in measures 7–8 (of the entire Invention) the lines of *d* minor waver, and in measures 9–10 the transition into *F* major is complete. In Ex. 91, precisely the same course is pursued: measures 1–3 are in *e* minor, measures 4–5 in *G* major. See also **Bach,** 2-voice Invention No. 1; measures 1–3 in *C* major; during the following sequences of the Motive (in contrary motion) in the upper part, the digression into *G* major is initiated, and is confirmed in the following (5th) measure.

And the remainder of the Section consists, probably, in a comparatively brief confirmation of the new key, and a cadence in the latter. For example:

Ex. 92. (Exs. 87 and 88, cont.)

*1) This example must be studied in connection with Exs. 87 and 88. The " Counterpoint," here, differs from the preceding ones; it is retained for the next announcement, and then, again, new forms are invented. Review Ex. 87, Note *1).

*2) This announcement of the Motive is an Imitation of the last Sequence in the upper part (Ex. 88); it is followed by a similar line of Sequences, but not in regular interval-succession, as before.

*3) Compare Ex. 91, Note *3).

*4) The "cadence-formula." See par. 40*h*.
*5) See also Ex. 93, No. 2, end.

When the Section is extended to an unusual length, the corresponding breadth of design will probably induce (or necessitate) *transient*
modulations into various next-related keys; and the prescribed modulatory aim of the whole may not assert itself until the Section
approaches its cadence. In this case, further, the cadence is apt to be
proportionately stronger.

See **Bach,** Well-tempered Clavichord, Vol. II, Prelude 10, first twenty or thirty
measures;—to be analyzed solely with reference to the changes of key.

h. The **Cadences** of polyphonic Sections are generally, as implied in
par. 39*a*, much less decisive than those of homophonic forms, both in
harmonic and rhythmic respect. Still, they assume the aspect of the
Perfect cadence (only excepting a few rare instances where the formal
purpose demands the effect of a Semi-cadence), and, therefore, the
distinctive traits of the former are usually preserved, — *especially as concerns the lower part* (the Bass).*

But the *rhythmic* interruption (or pause) is brief; so much so as to
create the impression of an Elision;** for the thematic thread is taken
up so promptly that the cadence-group of one Section is, almost always,
at the same time the initial group of the next.

For illustration (from **Bach**):

* "Homophonic Forms," par. 3, par. 6. ** Idem, par. 60.

*1) This cadence is much less distinct than the preceding ones, because of the instability of the lower (Bass) part, and its culminating upon an *Inversion* of the Tonic harmony. But the weight of the upper part, resting for some time upon the Tonic note, is sufficient. — *2) Here, again, the lower part is hasty, though its final tones are strictly cadential. — *3) This cadence, on the contrary, is unusually strong, being the final cadence of the entire Invention. *It is permissible thus to add auxiliary tones, at any cadence.* In Nos. 3 and 5 the leaps in the upper part are equivalent to two distinct part-progressions (Exs. 15, 19), and give to the cadence the strength of 3-part texture. — *4) The lower part proceeds immediately with the Motive.

The material of the cadence is very likely, in view of its special object, to be *episodic*, and may even be entirely independent of all anterior figures. It is, however, also possible, by ingenious treatment, to interweave thematic figures with the cadence, — especially when more than two parts are used.

See **Bach**, W.-t. Clav., Vol. I, Fugue I, measure 19; — cadence on 3rd beat, during thematic announcements (in Stretto) in Tenor and Alto. See also Ex. 96, Note *1). Ex. 116, last measure.

ADDITIONAL GENERAL PRINCIPLES.

41*a***. Influence of harmonic bent.** In determining the progressive conduct of polyphonic parts, the **harmonic and modulatory inclinations** must be respected, and even anticipated.

If the harmonic progression (or, in other words, the choice of the next chord) is self-defining, or perhaps even imperative, — as, for instance, at certain urgent Dominant or Second-dominant chords, which demand resolution, — *then this, the* **Harmony,** *will dictate the movement of the parts; and, if necessary, the unessential licences of Imitation* (par. 28) *will be summoned, to fit the thematic intention to this harmonic need.*

Should the harmonic progression not be self-defining, but optional, — as, for instance, after any Tonic chord, — *then the* **thematic** *design will supply the impulse and determine the choice of chord and key;* and either the Motive, with or without unessential modification, or the Episode, will be chosen, as appears most convenient. Review par. 11, par. 18, and the last clause in the directions to Exercise 6*B*.

b. **The Episodes.** It would be very wrong to assume that the above episodic passages (Exs. 89, 90, 91) proceeded from a deliberate intention, on **Bach's** part, to use just these particular fragments of thematic material, in just this manner. His purpose was a far broader one; and the episodes, while responding first of all to the demand for variety, are simply incidents in the realization of that purpose.

In general, then, the episode is rather an accidental *consequence* than an *aim;* and its details, — chosen, as they may be, from a myriad of equally consistent possibilities, — are influenced by the broad harmonic conditions noted in par. 41*a*, and determined by such comprehensive considerations of Form as those specified in par. 40*d*.

It is true, however, that the *beginner* must work along narrower lines, until his range of experience widens toward the master's standard. And the student will therefore, for a time, plan his episodic passages as more or less mechanical derivations from foregoing thematic premises; making generous use of the Sequence (par. 41*c*); **not pausing long to choose, but accepting the first reasonable suggestion;** and meanwhile analyzing the methods of great polyphonic writers (as found in the given citations) with the most penetrating scrutiny, — thus enriching his experience both by experiment and by observation.

As already observed, the number and variety of episodic deductions from anterior thematic figures, is practically unlimited, and the difficulty lies, not in *finding* a derivative, but in *choosing* from among the well-nigh infinite range of possibilities. So that the student who is at first apprehensive of not knowing what to do, will soon experience the still more real embarrassment of deciding what *not* to do; and this latter consciousness is, in fact, the most trustworthy sign of progress in thematic musical thought. For among so many possible deductions, many grades of excellence will, of course, be represented ; some episodic forms will be more appropriate, ingenious, and pregnant than others.

But, though the student may for awhile not succeed in finding the best forms, or even fairly good ones, the simple determination to adopt this deductive process, in his labors with the problem of musical composition, is, in itself, meritorious and wise. For such logical processes contribute *invariably*, at least in some degree, to the unity and stability of the musical structure. And as the student's experience increases and his judgment matures, he will more and more readily and unerringly select the better and best forms. At all events, *this* dependence is vastly preferable to relying upon chance, or upon that most delusive of resources, personal inspiration, for the answer to the vital and constantly recurring question, " What next ? " Eminent and indispensable as the impulse of emotional or intellectual ardor ("inspiration ") becomes to the *advanced* scholar and to the master of tone-texture, it is fraught with delusion and distraction to the *beginner*.

c. **The Sequence.**   One of the most essential details of effective polyphony is the Sequence.   It is the chief, if not the only efficient, safeguard against the most characteristic danger that besets the polyphonic style, — that of purposeless rambling, or the uncertain, discursive pursuit of a vague thematic scheme.

The Sequence imparts at least *regularity and symmetry* to the operations of thematic development; and, while particularly important in the more vagrant episodic components, is even freely used in the thematic passages themselves (par. 40*e*).   Hence, the pupil may fall back upon Sequences at almost any time, and drift with them until some higher structural condition asserts itself.   *The number of Sequences should, however, be limited to two or three* (i.e., three or four presentations of the figure at a time, in all).   A larger number is permissible only *when the figure is small.*   See also par. 21*f*.

d. **Unusual species of Imitation,** with Essential changes (par. 29, 31), are very rarely employed in the *first* Section, excepting the simplest variety of Shifted rhythm (par. 31*c*, second clause), and Contrary Motion ; and even the latter should, as a rule, be deferred to the second, or a still later, Section.   Both Augmentation and Diminution, excepting when applied to *fragments* of the Motive, are almost entirely inappropriate in the *two-voice* Invention.   The Stretto is most valuable in the later course of a polyphonic form.

EXERCISE 11.

A. Analyze the following specimens of the First Section of the 2-voice Invention. The contents of each group or measure must be defined, either as Motive, Counterpoint, or Episode; and when the latter, every figure must be accounted for:

> Bach, 2-v. Inv., No. 1, meas. 1–7.
> Bach, 2-v. Inv., No. 8, meas. 1–12.
> Bach, 2-v. Inv., No. 10, meas. 1–14.
> Bach, 2-v. Inv., No. 3, meas. 1–12.
> Bach, Well-t. Clav., Vol. I., Prelude 14, meas. 1–12.
> Bach, English Suites, No. 4, " Prélude," meas. 1–12.
> Bach, Partita (for clavichord), No. 2, " Sinfonia," 3rd movement (3-4 time), meas. 1–20 (cadence in Dominant key).
> Bach, Partita No. 3, " Fantasia," meas. 1–31 (largely episodic development of first half of Motive; cadence indefinite).

B. Take Motive No. 6 of Exercise 6*B*, and elaborate it into a moderately brief **First Section,** according to the above directions (par. 40, 41). Review par. 22*a* and *d.*

N. B. Begin this, and each of the following examples, on a separate sheet, leaving ample space for the continuation dictated in Exercises 12 and 13.

> The same with Motive 6 of Exercise 7*A.*
> The same with Motive 5 of Exercise 6*B.*
> The same with Motive 4 of Exercise 6*B.*
> The same with Motive 3 of Exercise 7*A.*
> The same with Motive 4, or 11, or 2, of Exercise 7*A.*

C. The same with one major and one minor *original* Motive, — one measure, or a little more, in length, invented strictly according to par. 38*a.*

THE SECOND SECTION.

42. The Second Section of an Invention must be conceived mainly as a continuation of the development of the Motive and its resources, initiated in the First Section. Its structural factors correspond to those of the latter (par. 38), but their arrangement is generally less systematic. The general requirements are as follows :

a. The new section may begin after the cadence of the foregoing has had its full rhythmic value, or it may follow immediately, after an elision. See par. 40*h*, second clause. It may begin with an announcement of the *Motive* (either alone, or with a contrapuntal associate) ; or with an *episodic* member. The former is the most natural and most common. Ex. 93, Note *4).

b. A certain degree of independence is desirable, and therefore the Second Section, while adhering to the spirit and general character of the First, may contain some distinctive traits; these may be obtained, either by adopting for the new section some special resource of the Motive (for instance, Imitation in contrary motion), or by inventing more striking and characteristic counterpoints than those of the First Section, or by introducing new episodic members. In this way, too, necessary provision may be made for sustaining interest. See Ex. 94, Note *2).

c. At the same time, it is desirable (though not indispensable) to institute some points of *manifest resemblance,* or even exact confirmation, between the sections, by reproducing some portion of the preceding section, — of course *in a different key,* and, if possible, *with inverted parts* (i.e., changing the former upper part to the lower, and *vice versa*). Review par. 39*b*. *And see pars. 55 and 56.*

This parallelism of design is strikingly illustrated in the 1st 2-voice Invention of Bach; — the last five measures of the Second Section (measures 11–15 of the entire Invention) almost exactly corroborate the last five measures of the First Section (measures 3–7); but they are transferred to the next higher step; the former upper part becomes the lower, and its contrapuntal associate is partly reconstructed, — near the end of the section.

d. The *modulatory aim* of the Second Section is, generally, the *Relative minor* from a major beginning, or the *Dominant* key from a minor beginning. In a word, the first two cadences are usually made in the keys most closely allied to the original key, that is, the *Dominant* and the *Relative;* in a *major* Invention the *Dominant* cadence comes first and the Relative next; in a *minor* Invention the *Relative* comes first, and then the Dominant. Other related keys may, however, be substituted. Review par. 40*g*, and *h.*

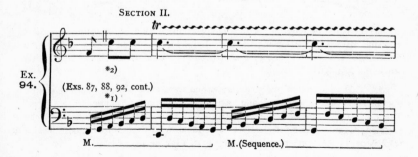

SECTION II.

Ex. 94. (Exs. 87, 88, 92, cont.)

*1) First review Exs. 87, 88, 92. The Second Section begins, after an elision, with the Motive in the lower part; it is followed, not by an Imitation, but by a Sequence, thus confirming the general structure of Section I, which was very largely sequential (par. 42c).

*2) This contrapuntal associate, upon one tone, is an obvious lapse of contra-puntal energy; it is a temporary and intentional subjection of "contents" to "form." The trill, however, lends vitality to the tone; and, altogether, it contrasts with the preceding Counterpoints sufficiently to individualize its Section (par. 42b). This is emphasized by its recurrence, in the lower part, a few measures later.

*3) Here the Contrary Motion of the Motive appears for the first time. It is reproduced in the prevailing sequential manner.

*4) Unessential change in quality of intervals; comp. par. 28*b*, *c*; Ex. 70*A*, with Notes.

*5) This counterpoint corresponds to one which appeared near the end of the First Section (par. 42*c*). Review Ex. 92, Note *1).

*6) Comp. Ex. 91, Note *3).

*7) Here the original motion of the Motive is re-adopted. The counterpoint in the lower part is unusually powerful and characteristic. During this the movement into the Dominant key is effected (par. 42*d*).

*8) The derivation of the Episode is apparent.

*9) See par. 20*c*.

EXERCISE 12.

A. Analyze the following specimens of the Second Section, defining, as before, every element; particular attention must be given to comparison of each with its foregoing First Section:

> Bach, 2-v. Inv., No. 1, meas. 7–15.
> Bach, 2-v. Inv., No. 7, meas. 7–13 (symptoms of an additional cadence in the 9th measure).
> Bach, 2-v. Inv., No. 3, meas. 12–24 (M. apparently "reconstructed" by addition of 3 introductory tones; par. 42*b*.)
> Bach, Partita No. 3, "Fantasia," meas. 31–66.

B. To each of the examples of a First Section, invented in Exercise 11 *B* and *C*, add a Second Section, according to the above directions. *Review par.* 41 *a*, *b*, *c*, *d*.

THE THIRD (AS FINAL) SECTION.

43. If the Invention is to embrace but three sections (perhaps the most common number), the Third Section (or final one) tends to regain and re-establish the original key. This will determine its general modulatory design, which, like all terminal sections of musical form, is very likely to include a more or less positive presentation of the *Subdominant* keys.*

a. Whether the Third Section is to constitute the climax of the form, the definite and intentional culmination of the progressive development within the preceding sections, or not, it is at least more subject than these to the demand for *increased interest;* and therefore the most attractive and ingenious methods of manipulation should be enlisted. These may consist in the more striking (possibly hitherto

---

* "*Homophonic Forms,*" par. 94*d*.

untried) species of Imitation; or in more characteristic and effective counterpoints, or in more elaborate episodic passages; or, perhaps best of all, in one or more forms of *Stretto-imitation* (par. 36); or in all of these together.

b. Care must be taken, however, not to diverge too widely from the prevailing character of the foregoing sections; and while it is by no means necessary to return to the beginning and corroborate the main contents of the First Section, as is done in the Third "Part" of the tripartite Song-forms * (see par. 49*a*), it is still desirable to employ some method of confirming one or the other of the preceding sections. Review par. 42 *b* and *c.*

See **Bach**, 2-v. Invention No. 1. The parallelism between Sections I and II, already cited, is again exhibited in almost exactly the same manner in the Third Section, which, in measures 19–20, copies measures 3 and 4 (in Section I), and measures 11 and 12 (Section II), — both parts in the Contrary motion of their former contents.

c. The final cadence is made in the original key, and, as a rule, with more emphasis than the intermediate cadences, — frequently strengthened by auxiliary (inner) tones. See Ex. 93, No. 6.

d. Sometimes, however, this cadence is evaded, by using the chord of the VIth step instead of the Tonic, in which case a brief **Codetta** is added. For illustration:

* "*Homophonic Forms*," par. 81*a*, 91.

*1) The Third Section begins, after an elision, with the M., again in the lower part ; see Ex. 94, Note *1). It immediately modulates down into the Sub-dominant key; see par. 43; also Ex. 57, No. 1 (par. 19*d*). — *2) The counterpoints, in this section, differ almost constantly from those of the foregoing sections; see Ex. 87, Note *1). But observe Note *5). — *3) This " counterpoint " agrees with the preceding one. — *4) Comp. Ex. 91, Note *3). — *5) These two measures *exactly* confirm measures 5 and 6 of the First Section (Ex. 87), in both parts. — *6) Here the expected perfect cadence is evaded, by substituting the VI for the I (par. 43*d*) ; what follows is a *Codetta*, in which, again, the Contrary Motion of the M. happens to be employed, as in Ex. 94, Note *3). — *7) Unessential change in quantity of intervals ; par 28*b*.

ADDITIONAL SECTIONS.

44. If the Invention is to be extended to four, or perhaps even more, sections, the above details of Section III will need to be modified :

(1) With regard to the adoption of the most effective and interesting resources of thematic development, which, in this case, are more likely (though not certain) to be deferred to the final section ; and

(2) With regard to the *cadence*, which will be made in some other related key, — preferably in one of the Sub-dominant keys, — thus also influencing the general modulatory design.

The conditions of individuality and confirmation (par. **42** *b* and *c*) are valid, as before ; while those of par. 43 *a*, *b*, *c*, and *d* refer, in any event, to the *final* section.

EXERCISE 13.

A. Analyze the following *miscellaneous* examples, as before:

Bach, 2-v. Invention No. 1, meas. 15 to end.

Bach, 2-v. Invention No. 7, meas. 13 to end (possibly four Sections in all, as intimated in Exercise 12*A;* brief Codetta).

Bach, Partita No. 3, "Fantasia," meas. 66 to end (four Sections in all, the third one cadencing, very exceptionally, in the original key).

Bach, Partita No. 2, "Sinfonia," 3rd movement (3-4 time); meas. 20 to end (3 Sections in all; Section II largely episodic; Section III very similar to II, but shorter, and in different keys).

Bach, English Suites, No. 4, "Prélude," meas. 12–20 (Section II, cadence in original key; the auxiliary inner tones may be ignored).

Bach, English Suites, No. 2, "Prélude," meas. 1–55; one long Section, with an occasional very vague intimation of cadential purpose. In meas. 47–51 a Codetta is added, with modified repetition in the following 4 measures. The prevalence of the principal key is owing to the Divisions that follow. The auxiliary tones may be ignored. The remainder of this example is cited in par. 67, which may be briefly referred to.

B. To each of the examples invented in Exercise 11*B*, and continued in Exercise 12*B*, add a third (as *final*) section, according to par. 43. *Review par.* 41 *a, b, c, d.*

C. To the *original* examples extended in Exercise 12*B*, add a *third and fourth* section (par. 44).

D. Write two *complete* Inventions, one in minor and one in major, with original (short) Motives; the number of sections optional, but neither less than two nor more than five.

THE INVENTION IN TWO–PART SONG–FORM.

45. While the "sectional" form is most consistent with the character of such polyphonic compositions as the above, representing the continuous development of an adopted thematic germ, it is nevertheless possible to cast them in the mould of some *homophonic* design, like the Two- or Three-Part Song-forms.

When this is done, the treatment of the "Sections" must be modified to conform with the more definite specific conditions of the "Parts." Review par. 39*a*.

This will probably affect the *extent*, which is usually greater in the "Part" than in the "Section"; and there is generally a marked distinction in the character of the *cadences*. As stated in par. 40*h*, second clause, and illustrated at the beginning of Exs. 94 and 95, the "Section" commonly ends with an *elision;* i.e., the cadence-chord (or *end*) of one section is at the same instant the beginning of the next.

This is more rarely the case in the " Part," which is likely to have a firmer, more decisive (i.e., *longer*) cadence-interruption.

Further, a certain predominance of the *structural* idea over the details of thematic texture will also be evident, when the Part-forms are adopted, and this will influence the general character; it may lead to greater freedom of contrapuntal treatment, in favor of the distinctive conditions of the homophonic style; a more definite melodic character, more regular succession of 4-measure phrase-groups, or even distinct period-formations may prevail.

46. The primary grade of the Two-Part Song-form. This differs, when applied to the Invention, but little from a Two-section design, the main details of which are given in par. 40 and par. 43; i.e., the First Section stands for Part I, though possibly extended slightly beyond the limit of the ordinary " Exposition," and ends with a somewhat stronger form of cadence (par. 40*h*). The Second Part may be a trifle longer; it should exhibit the traits of confirmation explained in par. 42*c;* and must close with the perfect cadence in the original key, possibly followed by a Codetta.

This form is illustrated in **Bach,** 2-v. Invention No. 8. The First Section, or " Part" (already analyzed), embraces the first 12 measures, — a regularity of design suggestive of the group of 3 phrases; it closes with a distinct perfect cadence in the Dominant key. Measures 12–14 (beginning of Part II) correspond to the beginning of Part I, with inverted voices; measure 15 is a new episode; the following 4 measures are a sequence of these, with inverted voices; measures 20–25 are thematic, but new in treatment, involving sequential announcements of the M. in *Contrary motion ;* measure 26 to the end exactly corroborates the last 9 measures of Part I, but transposed one fifth lower, in order to close on the original Tonic. See par. 48*a*, second clause.

See further, **Bach,** 2-v. Invention No. 10. Part I closes in measure 14 (already analyzed as Section I); Part II in measure 30, with an evaded cadence, followed by an extension of 3 measures.

THE GENUINE TWO–PART FORM. THE FIRST PART.

47. In the genuine (broader) Two-Part Song-form,* the First Part may be still more extended; possibly (though somewhat rarely) embracing *two sections*, the first of which fulfils the conditions of an " Exposition," with a comparatively light cadence, while the second one carries out the modulatory design, closing with a strong perfect cadence, — always in the *Dominant key* (whether major or minor). More com-

* *Homophonic Forms*, par. 71–73, 78.

monly, however, these details are all contained in one single (long) section, which in some cases (e.g., in old Dance-forms) assumes the character of a Period or Double-period.   See par. 45, last clause.

The First Part is very frequently *repeated;* generally with " 1st and 2nd ending," the second one with a more complete check of the rhythmic movement.

In the following examples the First Part only is to be analyzed, but with great minuteness: **Bach,** English Suite No. 1, "Bourrée I;" the First Part bears many evidences of regular Double-period form, parallel construction; it contains 16 meas ures, of which measures 9–12 corroborate measures 1–4 almost exactly.   It is repeated.

Bach, French Suite No. 3, "Allemande"; the thematic germ is unusually small, only a figure of 4 tones; a perfect cadence is made on the Dominant, in the 10th measure, and a Codetta follows; a very light cadence in the Relative major key, in measure 6, appears to divide the First Part into two sections.   The Part is repeated.

Bach, French Suite No. 4, "Gavotte"; the Motive is small (5 tones); the form of Part I is clearly a " parallel period "; it is repeated, with two endings.

Bach, French Suite No. 5, "Courante"; Part I is evidently a parallel Double-period of 16 measures, with sufficiently obvious semi-cadences every 4th measure· the Contrary motion of the M. occurs in measure 7; the evidence of *three-voice* writing in measure 8, and the auxiliary tones in measures 1 and 16, may be ascribed to the influence of the structural idea; they do not affect the actual two-voice style. The cadence is extended by a fragment of the Motive.   The Part is repeated.

Bach, Partita No. 2, "Allemande"; Part I contains two sections, the first one closing in measure 6 on the original Tonic.   The copious auxiliary tones assume sometimes the importance of a third part; but, as intimated above, they do not seem to affect the prevalent two-voice texture; some of them represent merely a device of notation.

Bach, Well-temp. Clavichord, Vol. II, Prelude 10; Part I is one long section, suggestive of Phrase-group form; it closes on the Dominant, and is repeated, with two endings.   Same work, Vol. II, Prelude 8; Part I, 16 measures long, suggestive of large period-form.

The Second Part.

48. The Second Part of a genuine Two-Part Song-form is usually much more distinctly individualized than any " section " of the smaller forms.   Its thematic basis may be defined in the following ways:

a. Most commonly, the *same Motive* (that of the First Part) is employed in Part II.   It may preserve its original form exactly; or may possibly be slightly modified or reconstructed (as already witnessed in **Bach,** 2-voice Inventions, No. 3, meas. 12–13; and No. 7, meas. 13–14).   Usually the Motive is announced first alone, or accompanied only by unessential auxiliary tones, as at the beginning.

In this case (when the same M. is retained) the characterization of the Part devolves largely upon the contrapuntal associates, which may be new and more striking than in Part I.

The condition of confirmation still demands fulfilment, as shown in par. 42c. This is most effectually realized by the very common device of *ending the two Parts with the same member,* — extending through an optional number of measures (from one up to ten or more). The member thus employed must reappear in a different key (Part I closing, probably, on the Dominant, and Part II on the Tonic *); and frequently the voices are inverted.

The Second Part may also consist of two (rarely more) sections, and is sometimes repeated.

See **Bach,** Well-temp. Clavichord, Vol. II, Prelude 8; Part II begins with the original form of the M., but the counter-motive is entirely new and characteristic in rhythmic form; it reappears in measures 3, 16, 17, and 18 of the Second Part; in measure 12 another new counter-motive appears, confirmed in the next measure. Measures 5–7 of Part II corroborate measures 3–5 of Part I (inverted voices, and somewhat modified); and measures 9–13 closely follow measures 6–10 of Part I (voices not inverted). The last 5 or 6 beats of the two Parts are identical, except in key.

Bach, Partita No. 2, "Allemande"; Part II uses the M. unchanged; it embraces two sections (like its First Part), cadencing in the 6th and 16th measures. The last 4 measures of the two Parts correspond, but in different keys and with inverted voices. Part II is also repeated.

Bach, French Suite No. 4, "Gavotte"; Part II uses the M. of the First Part, but much more persistently than the latter, and often in Contrary motion. There are no obvious traits of parallelism between the Parts. Both are repeated.

Bach, French Suite No. 5, "Courante"; Part II very similar to Part I in form and contents; the M. is retained without change, the form is well-defined Double-period; Contrary motion again appears, this time in measures 8 and 9; the final Phrase (4 measures) corresponds almost exactly to the ending of Part I, excepting the transposition. Both Parts are repeated.

Bach, English Suite No. 1, "Bourrée I"; Part II contains two sections, separated in measure 8; the M. is *slightly altered* from its original form and length; from measure 13 to 22 the polyphonic character relaxes notably, — the sequential successions and repetitions in the upper voice (though thematic) and the simple rhythmic accompaniment in the lower, lend a lyric effect to the passage that contrasts well with the rest. The Second Part ends in measure 24; a 4-measure Codetta, with nearly exact repetition, follows. Part II is repeated.

Bach, Well-temp. Clavichord, Vol. I, Prelude 17 (entire). The M. consists of two similar measures, of which, now and then, only one measure is used. Part I contains two sections, separated in measure 9; the auxiliary tones, the lyric quality of the M., and its general treatment, impart a somewhat homophonic complexion to

---

* *Homophonic Forms,* par. 75.

the whole Prelude. (See par. 83.) Part II utilizes the same M., and adopts a very similar mode of treatment, so that the Parts are more than ordinarily parallel, throughout; measures 26–33 correspond closely to measures 10–16 (extended one measure) with inverted voices. A Codetta of 10 measures follows.

Händel, Harpsichord Suite No. 16, "Gigue" (entire); Part I, a 6-measure Period; Part II contains two sections.

b. Quite frequently the *Contrary motion* of the M. is adopted as thematic basis for the Second Part. *It should be derived from the original M. in the manner defined in par.* 29*a* (Exs. 72 and 73), and must then be shifted (transposed) to the key or harmony with which Part II is to begin, — possibly with such modifications as may facilitate its adjustment. Comp. Ex. 74, Note *4), entire. When this is done it is likely, though by no means certain, that the Contrary motion will be held in abeyance during the First Part.

The new form of the M. may either extend to the very end of Part II, or it may be exchanged for the original motion in the later course of the Part; or the two forms of the M. may alternate, more or less regularly, throughout.

This device is a characteristic feature of the so-called Gigue-form (par. 51), in connection with which it will be more fully illustrated.

See **Bach,** Well-temp. Clavichord, Vol. II, Prelude 10. The M. of Part I (already analyzed) appears at the outset of the Second Part, but in *Contrary motion, and extended by sequence to four measures* (double its original length). In this new form it appears twice in the First Section (ending in measure 24 of the Second Part), and again twice at the beginning of the Second Section; the last announcement is followed by a recurrence of a long passage from Part I (measures 33-55, corresponding closely to measures 23–48 of the First Part, with inverted voices for a short distance); during this parallel passage the original motion of the M. naturally reasserts itself. The cadence falls in measure 55, but is evaded (by a VI, — par. 43 *d*), and a Codetta is then added.

Bach, English Suite No. 5, "Allemande"; M. of one measure in upper part, lower part auxiliary; the original motion of M. recurs near the end.

c. In somewhat rare instances a *new Motive* is adopted for the Second Part. Though thus quite independent, it should be intimately related in general character to the first Motive. As before, the new thematic form may be retained throughout the Second Part; but it is much more likely that the first Motive will reappear, near the end, — possibly in *alternation* with the new one; more rarely in *conjunction* with it, when, be it by accident or design, they harmonize. For illustration: The First Section partially shown in Ex. 90, after being continued in a very

similar manner up to its cadence (E♭ major), in the 15th measure, runs
on as follows :

*1) Compare the new M. with the first one (Ex. 90); they are strictly kindred,
though actual similarity is avoided. Observe, further, that the new M. is introduced
during (*across*) *the cadence* (par. 40*h*, final clause).

*2) The peculiar notation of *a* (♮) is owing to Bach's conception of this 2nd
beat as Dominant harmony of *c* minor, with *a* as ascending passing-note. Comp.
par. 20*b* (and *c*).

*3) First half of the Motive. The parts cross here, briefly.

*4) A few measures later the first M. recurs (see Ex. 98).

See also **Bach,** French Suite No. 3, "Allemande."   The M. of Part II, like that of Part I (already analyzed), is very brief; though strongly suggestive of the first M. in Contrary motion, it is really *new* (as its own Contrary motion, further on, proves). The Part has two sections, separated in the 4th measure; its perfect cadence is evaded in the 10th measure (by a VI), and a brief Codetta, for which Contrary motion is exclusively utilized, follows. This Part is even more persistently the-matic than Part I, containing scarcely an episodic note. It is repeated.

EXERCISE 14.

A. Write a complete 2-voice Invention (M. original), in the primary grade of Two-Part Song-form (par. 46). *Review par.* 41 *a, b, c, d.*

B. A complete Invention (in major) in broad Two-Part Song-form, according to par. 47 and 48*a, both clauses.*

C. A complete Invention (in minor), with Contrary motion of the M. in Part II, according to par. 48*b.*

D. A complete Invention (mode optional), with a new M. in the Second Part, according to par. 48*c.* A Codetta may be added to each Part. *See par.* 54.

The Invention in Three–Part Song–form.

49. In all Three-Part forms there is, in addition to the above two Parts, a more or less distinctly marked *return to the beginning*, and con-sequent recurrence of the essential thematic contents of the First Part or Section ; it is the fulfilment of this structural condition which devolves upon the Third Part.*   This affects, primarily, the *cadence of the Second Part,* which should be made upon the Dominant of the original key, and may therefore influence the later modulatory and thematic design of the Part.

The Primary Grade.

a. The primary grade of the Three-Part Song-form, when applied to the Invention, will resemble the Three-section design, explained in par. 40–43, with the significant exceptions, however, that the Third Section is not to be, as there, merely the continuation of its predecessors, but must represent the *Return of the original key, and must reproduce a por-tion of the early contents of Section I* (perhaps no more than one or two measures) ; and that, consequently, the Second Section must be so con-

---

* *Homophonic Forms,* par. 81.

ducted, near its end, as to lead to this result.   (Compare par. 43*b*.)
For example :

*1) With reference to the uncertainty of definition, compare par. 39*a*. The Motive is unusually long, and might be called a "Subject" (par. 38*a*).

*2) **Bach,** 2-voice Invention No. 2.

*3) This cadence is very indefinite; hence the impression of "sectional" form, and the distinction "primary grade" of the tripartite design.

*4) This measure and the following 7 correspond exactly (excepting the transposition) to measures 3–10 of Section I, but with inverted parts; one sequential measure follows, and then the last measure of the Second Part, leading to a brief but definite Dominant ending.

*5) The upper part corresponds to the conduct of the lower at the end of Part I.

*6) The purpose of this Third Section to reproduce the initial members of the First Section, though somewhat indistinct, is nevertheless sufficiently obvious to establish the tripartite design.

Furthermore, Ex. 96 is completed as follows :

Ex.
98.

(Ex. 96 cont.)
Meas. 19.

Episode *2)

Part III.

Dom.

Motive 1.
(See Ex. 90.)

*3)   *rall.* . . . .

M. 1.

*1) First half of Motive 2.

*2) This second member of the Episode (which began in the 17th measure) is less closely related to the M. than the foregoing.

*3) Up to this point the Third Part agrees *exactly* with the initial members of Part I (see Ex. 90). It is a much-abbreviated recurrence of the latter.

See also **Bach,** Well-temp. Clavichord, Vol. I, Prelude 14. Part I (already analyzed) closes in measure 12 with a strong Dominant cadence; in the Second Part many auxiliary tones are used, but the impression of essentially 2-voice polyphony is not disturbed; the Dominant semi-cadence in measures 18–19 indicates the termination of Part II; and the following tones are, under these circumstances, a sufficiently evident return to the beginning, — though no more than one measure is reproduced, and that with inverted voices. This somewhat vague Third Part is very brief, closing in measure 22 ; a Codetta, corresponding to the beginning of Part II, follows.

THE GENUINE THREE–PART FORM.

50.   In the genuine (broader and more clearly defined) Three-Part Song-form, the details of Part I correspond to those given in par. 47, which review; and the conduct of Part II corresponds to all the details of par. 48 *a*, *b*, and *c*, — excepting such as concern its *cadence*, which, in the Three-Part design, *must be made on the Dominant*, or, at all events, upon such harmonies, and in such a manner, as to prepare for and lead decisively into the recurrence of the first measures (as beginning of Part III).

a.   As before, the thematic basis of the **Second Part** may be :

(1)   The *same Motive* (usually with new, and more or less characteristic, counter-motives), — par. 48*a*, first and second clauses ;

(2)   The *Contrary motion* of the original Motive, as in the " Gigue " form (see par. 51) ; or

(3)   A *new* Motive, — par. 48*c*.

b.   The object of the **Third Part** is, as usual, to re-establish the principal key, and *to re-announce the original Motive and its Imitation as they appeared at the outset*, in a sufficiently accurate manner and through a sufficient number of measures to identify itself as the corroboration of the First Part.   In some cases, where the design is broad, the parallelism extends through a large portion of the Third Part (perhaps with inverted voices, and occasional modifications), or even to the end, —excepting, of course, the necessary change of modulation and cadence. But more commonly it is limited to the first two or three measures, and the remainder of the Part is then elaborated independently, and, as climax of the form, as ingeniously and effectively as possible.   Review par. 43*a*, which has peculiarly direct bearing upon " Part III."

When the Second Part has used the Contrary motion of the Motive, the original motion is resumed at the beginning of Part III, and is then either retained to the end, or, far more effectively, the two forms of the M. subsequently appear in more or less regular alternation, or even in conjunction (as Stretto). And precisely the same principles apply when Part II is based upon a *new* motive (as in Exs. 90, 96, 98).

See **Bach**, 2-voice Invention No. 3; Part I (already analyzed) closes in measure 12; Part II contains two well-defined sections, closing in measures 24 and 38; between the last cadence and the beginning of Part III (end of measure 42) a brief passage intervenes, which, though largely thematic, serves the purpose of a Re-transition,* or returning passage; Part III corroborates the first 4 measures of the First Part exactly, transposes and inverts the following four, then resumes the original line (transposed), but cadences on the VI (par. 43*d*); a Codetta follows. Throughout the Second Part the M., as already seen, is reconstructed by the addition of three preliminary tones; this form recurs once, in the Codetta.

Bach, French Suite No. 2, "Air"; the M. (one-half measure) is announced in the upper part in a somewhat imperfect form, and imitated in slightly altered Contrary motion; Part II *begins* with Contrary motion, but otherwise maintains the original motion; it has two well-defined sections, of 4 measures each; Part III (the last 4 measures) is vague in effect, though the structural purpose is clear; during the first 2 measures the lower voice agrees almost exactly with the upper voice at the beginning of Part I.

Bach, French Suite No. 4, "Air"; Part I largely episodic; the Contrary motion of the M. prevails in the Second Part, which contains two sections; Part III corresponds very closely to the First, — transposed after one and one-half measure, without other changes.

EXERCISE 15.

A. Write a 2-voice Invention (M. original) in the primary grade of the Three-Part Song-form (par. 49*a*).

B. An Invention (in minor) in genuine Three-Part Song-form, according to par. 50: in Part II the same M., but with new and characteristic contrapunʳal associates. *First review par.* 41 *a–d ; and see par.* 54.

C. An Invention (in major or minor), employing the Contrary motion of the M. in the Second Part.

D. An Invention, with new M. in Part II.

The "Gigue."

51. The adoption of the **Contrary** motion of the Motive as thematic basis for the Second Part (already touched upon, in par. 48*b* and par. 50*a*), is so common in the " *Gigue* " as to constitute a partly, though not definitely, distinctive trait of that old Dance-form ; and the term " *Gigue-form* " is therefore often applied to a polyphonic Invention thus designed, irrespective of its character. On the other hand, many ex-

---

* *Homophonic Forms*, par. 90*c*.

amples of the old-fashioned *Gigue* may be found in which the Second Part uses the original Motive, or a new one, as in ordinary forms.

The design of the whole is usually the Two-Part (more rarely Three-Part) Song-form, with repeated Parts. The most common measure is $\frac{6}{8}$. Review par. 48*b*. For illustration, see —

Bach, French Suite No. 2, "Gigue"; M. two measures in length, imitated at once in Stretto; Part I is divided into two sections by a brief but decisive cadence in the 23rd measure (Relative key); Part II uses the Contrary motion for 20 measures, when two announcements in original motion lead to a Dominant semi-cadence; Contrary motion is then resumed, though the next (last) section is largely episodic; the evaded form of the cadence occurs 10 measures before the end. Two-Part form, each Part repeated.

Bach, French Suite No. 6, "Gigue"; Part I has two sections, terminating respectively in measures 8 and 16; an episodic Codetta of 8 measures is appended, based upon a motive suggestive of the Diminution of the original M. (par. 31*b*); Part II uses Contrary motion, chiefly in the lower part, and with extensive episodic interruptions; its first section ends in measure 10, and its second one 5 measures from the end; the final measures are a partial recurrence of the former Codetta. The preponderant episodic portions, throughout this Gigue, seem to be based upon an additional (auxiliary) Motive, or several Motives, generated out of the 3rd measure. Compare par. 52*a*.

Bach, English Suite No. 1, "Gigue"; M. of 1 measure, imitated in Stretto; Part I contains two sections, and a Codetta of 4 or 5 measures; Part II begins with a curious version of the M, — the first half only in Contrary motion, the second half as before; this version alternates with the original form during the First Section (5 measures), and again during the Second Section, which is its almost exact sequence; a Third Section follows, and the added Codetta corresponds exactly to the former one.

Bach, French Suite No. 4, "Gigue"; in the 4th and 5th measures, and once or twice later, the notation represents *three*-voice texture, but the effect is distinctly that of auxiliary tones; Part I has but one section, followed by a Codetta (measure 22) beginning with a quaint modification of the M. (in the lower part), — compare par. 33; Part II employs Contrary motion throughout its two sections, up to the Codetta (7 measures from the end); the Codetta begins with one announcement of the M. in Contrary motion, not included in the former Codetta, and then reproduces the latter in its full length, with inverted parts.

Bach, English Suite No. 5, "Allemande"; in the Second Part a modified form of the Contrary motion is adopted; there are occasional brief intimations of 3-voice texture; the original motion of the M. recurs near the end.

Bach, English Suite No. 4, "Gigue"; here also, as in the preceding examples, there is an intimation of 3-voice texture (in measures 5–8 only); the lower part, during measures 1 and 2, though thematic enough to simulate a genuine Imitation, is nevertheless only *auxiliary*, — the M. is $1\frac{1}{2}$ measure in length, and its first real Imitation begins with the last tone in measure 2; the last 5 measures of Part II correspond to the ending of Part I. Each Part is repeated.

The Invention with Two (or more) Motives in Alternation.

52. A second (new) Motive may appear not only at the beginning of the Second Part, as specific basis of the latter (par. 48*c*), but may be introduced and developed *in closer connection and alternation* with the first, or principal, Motive.

a. Such an additional thematic germ may be so unimportant in character and extent as to subserve, chiefly or entirely, the episodic purposes, in which case it is to be called an *Auxiliary Motive* (or Figure), rather than "2nd Motive."

An example of this kind has already been seen in **Bach,** French Suite No. 6, "Gigue"; and others will be cited later.

b. When the new M. is more nearly or completely co-ordinate with the principal (first) one, it may appear at the beginning of the second (possibly a later) section, and become its thematic basis. Or it may enter into the polyphonic texture still earlier,—during the First Section, or Part,—and be utilized thereafter throughout the Invention, in more or less constant *close alternation* (not simultaneous conjunction) with the principal Motive.

As already stated (par. 48*c*), the new M. must, while asserting a certain measure of distinct individuality, still be conceived in intimate consistency of character with the first Motive.

For illustration, see **Bach,** 2-voice Invention No. 13:

Ex. 99.

Motive 1.   Motive 2.

The first (principal) M. is used during 2 measures; the 2nd M. during the rest of Part I (up to measure 6); the same arrangement prevails, very nearly, during the First Section of Part II (measures 6–13); in the remainder of Part II (up to measure 18) the 2nd M. appears alone, somewhat modified; in Part III (measure 18 to the end) the two Motives are employed, in closer alternation.

Bach, Well-temp. Clavichord, Vol. II, Prelude 23:

Ex. 100.

BACH.

Motive 1.   M. 2. (Auxil.?)

The 1st M. appears only at the beginning of Part I, with one Imitation, partly in Contrary motion; the 2nd M., which, but for its domination, would be regarded merely as an auxiliary figure, supplies the basis of development up to measure 8, after which fragments of M. 1 lead to the cadence (measure 12); Part II extends to measure 37; its First Section, ending in measure 17, is episodic, but derived from M. 1; an independent episode follows, suggesting a *third* M. (compare par. 52c); in measure 23 the second M. again asserts itself, and continues some time, though fragmentary; measures 29–32 closely resemble the episode of the foregoing section; Part III (measure 37 to end) is much like the First Part, but the 2nd M. is absent. There are several evidences of 3-voice texture, but scarcely enough to be conclusive.

The whole example belongs, more accurately, to the Prelude-class (Chap. IX). And the same is true of **Bach,** Well-temp. Clavichord, Vol. II, Prelude 13, in which the following contrasting thematic members are discoverable:

Ex. 101.

Motive 1 (introductory).   Motive 2 (principal).

Of these, **Motive 2 appears to be the more essential and important.** The design is 3-Part Song-form; Part II contains three well-defined sections; in the first one the two Motives are announced in conjunction (simultaneously); Part III resembles Part I very closely, but is abbreviated. A coda of 8 measures is appended.

Händel, Clavichord Suite No. 7, "Andante," employs the following Motives:

(Comp. Ex. 99.)

Ex. 102.

Motive 1.   M. 2 (in Sequences).

The design is 3-Part Song-form, Part III somewhat vague and abbreviated.

Händel, Clavichord Suite No. 16, "Allemande," is a very clear exposition of the following, in almost constant close alternation:

Ex. 103.

Motive 1.   Motive 2.

The design is 2-Part Song-form, each Part containing two sections, and repeated. The thematic development is unusually regular and perspicuous.

c. More rarely, *three* Motives participate in the development of an Invention; either (1) as the respective thematic basis of three successive *sections*, or (2) in closer and more constant *alternation with the first* (*principal*) *M.*, or with each other, in any order.

An illustration of the first of these methods is found in **Bach,** Well-temp. Clavichord, Vol. II, Prelude 4 (3-voice polyphony, and therefore to be reviewed in minuter detail in Chap. VII); a different M. is employed in each one of the first three Sections (beginning in measures 1, 17, 27), the first announced in the upper, the second in the inner, and the third in the upper part.

The second method is illustrated in **Bach**, Well-temp. Clavichord, Vol. II, Prelude 17 (belonging properly to the "Prelude"-species, Chap. IX); the following Motives appear, in measures 1, 2, and 7:

Ex. 104.

Motive 1.

Motive 2.   Motive 3.

Besides these, there are meagre evidences of additional brief auxiliary Motives. The principal M. (No. 1) is each time accompanied by a body of auxiliary tones, almost equivalent to two extra voices, but their unessential quality is nevertheless entirely obvious; the remainder of the texture is two-voice. The form is sectional (par. 39); each of the four Sections begins with the principal M., and employs both of the others generously, and with considerable regularity of design (M. 2 occasionally in Contrary motion). Section 2 begins in measure 17, Section 3 in measure 34, Section 4 in measure 50. The latter has quite a definite semi-cadence in measure 63, suggesting a possible fifth Section from that point to the end. The episode in measures 52–59 is based upon the first contrapuntal associate of M. 3 (measure 7), which is so prevalent that it might be regarded as a 4th Motive.

THE LYRIC INVENTION, WITH A LONG THEME.

53. The 2-voice Invention may, exceptionally, be based upon a thematic sentence of greater length than the ordinary Motives, seen in the above examples. Such a lengthy theme is very likely to represent the regular 4-measure Phrase, or even 4- to 8-measure Period-form, with a correspondingly definite melodic design, usually distinctly *lyric in character*, and with a *well-marked semi-cadence* (upon either a Tonic or Dominant chord).

Obviously, so extended a Motive cannot be announced (imitated) effectively very often in the course of an ordinary Invention, at least not at its full length; and therefore the development, while none the less strictly polyphonic, will necessarily be more largely *episodic* than usual; and in general the structural idea and considerations of " form " will prevail almost constantly over the thematic purposes (compare par. 45, last clause). The episodic interludes will probably be derived from some figure or figures of the large Motive, though they may be independent. (Compare par. 38*d* and par. 41*b;* see also par. 42*c.*)

See **Bach,** 2-voice Invention No. 14; the theme is announced in the upper part and extends into the 4th measure; it consists of a figure two beats in length, which alternates with its Contrary motion, excepting in the 3rd measure; the lower part is "auxiliary" in character, though it is again employed as "counterpoint" to the Imitation of the theme (in measures 6–8); measures 4, 5, and 9–16 are episodic, derived directly from the germinal figure of the theme; one more announcement of the entire theme, in the lower part (in shifted rhythm), leads to the concluding cadence. The entire design appears to embrace but one long section, as Phrase-group.

Bach, Well-temp. Clavichord, Vol. II, Prelude 24; theme of 4 measures, announced in upper part and imitated immediately in lower part, with different counterpoint; an Episode follows, based during 4 measures upon a new auxiliary figure, and then for 4 more measures upon a figure from the second contrapuntal associate (measure 7); the Second Section begins in measure 17, announces the theme four times in unbroken succession, using two *former* and two *new* "counterpoints"; it then becomes episodic (measure 33), the lower part corresponding to the upper one of the former Episode, during 4 measures, while the following 4 measures are a new Episode; the Third Section (measure 41) announces one-half of the theme, first in the upper, then in the lower part; an Episode follows, 8 measures of which correspond very nearly to the first Episode (excepting in key); the remaining measures (53–59) are new Episode and cadence. A Coda is added, containing one announcement of the theme, and a few effective thematic fragments.

Bach, Well-temp. Clavichord, Vol. II, Prelude 6; Two-Part Song-form and 5-measure Codetta; theme extending into the 5th measure; both Parts are largely episodic, — especially Part II, — but constantly in close touch with the contents of the theme.

Bach, Well-temp. Clavichord, Vol. II, Prelude 15; Two-Part Song-form; theme 3 measures long, appearing in a modified form of Contrary motion in Part II (compare par. 51); the extensive episodic passages, which contribute to the Prelude-like character of this Invention (see Chap. IX, par. 83), are strictly congruous, if not of thematic derivation. The last six measures of the two Parts correspond.

THE STUDENT'S ATTITUDE TOWARD THE PRESCRIBED TASKS.

54. In working out the required Exercises in these grades of 2-voice Polyphony, the student need harbor no. fear that he may imitate the given authoritative examples of **Bach** too closely, and thus perhaps unconsciously acquire the unwelcome habit of conceiving and writing in the somewhat antiquated manner of these old-fashioned compositions. The propagation of this particular style — the multiplication of pieces for which our modern ears have but little sympathy — is not the *aim* of the student's present labors; it is simply the exercise of contrapuntal discipline within the dominion of these forms, as a *means* to an end, —

an end which may be as modern and original as the student (or the listener) could desire.

There is but little likelihood that the pupil will wholly escape the influence of modern musical thought, especially if he be observant (as successful students invariably are), alert to recognize and to appropriate the acquisitions of recent times, whether in the polyphonic or in the homophonic domain of musical creation.

Polyphony is merely *a product, resulting from the employment of the contrapuntal method;* and this *method* may be applied in dealing with any phase of musical style, romantic, classic, dramatic, or archaic. The distinction rests mainly, perhaps, upon the choice of *harmonic basis*, out of which all Polyphony must emerge, just as well as Homophony (par. 11); for this harmonic element it is which has grown "modern," leaving former simpler customs of harmonic progression behind. The distinctive contrapuntal "method" adopted for the presentation of the harmony is, however, not thus subject to the changes of time; Polyphony is the embodiment of the same principle in the twentieth century as in the fifteenth; but its character and complexion will differ, as the harmonic material becomes richer and more pliable.

There can be no excuse for writing an unattractive Invention in our day, on the ground that it must be produced by contrapuntal methods. Nothing is devoid of interest in which the operation of a quick imagination is discernible; and nothing discloses, from the proper point of view, a more powerful and constant stimulus to the imaginative faculty, than the *contrapuntal methods* of tone-association.

Brief reference may be made to par. 72 and par. 82. And the following effective specimens of the modern Invention for two parts should be thoroughly analyzed:

Rubinstein, Prelude, op. 24, No. 2; 3-Part Song-form; in Part I the Motive, 4 measures long, appears twice, followed by an episode (measures 9–16); Part II (measure 17) announces the M. once, in lower voice; a long and brilliant episode follows (measures 21–52), based wholly upon the last measure of the M.; in measures 35–36 the figure is somewhat concealed among auxiliary tones; a second episode (measures 53–60) is based on the first measure of the M.; a strong Dominant cadence occurs in measure 60, followed by an extraordinary organ-point, as Re-transition into Part III; the M. is announced twice in Part III (measures 77–84); from this to the end is episodic Coda, based on first member of the Motive.

Chopin, Étude, op. 10, No. 4; 3-Part Song-form; the M. lies in the upper part, measures 1–4; the texture is largely episodic, though all derived directly from the M.; there is an auxiliary *harmonic* accompaniment almost throughout, but the whole is distinctively 2-voice Invention-form (Prelude-species, par. 83).

EXERCISE 16.

A. Write two examples of the " Gigue "-form (par. 51), one in major and one in minor. Review par. 41 *a, b, c, d*, and par. 54.

B. An Invention, in optional form, with two Motives in close alternation. Par. 52*b*.

C. An Invention in three Sections, with a separate Motive for each section, — returning to the first M. near the end. Par. 52*c*.

D. An Invention with a longer theme, of lyric character. Par. 53.

The Natural Species of Double–Counterpoint.

55. Double-counterpoint is a *process;* but the term is generally applied to the product resulting from it. The counterpoint is said to be " double " when the added voice (i.e., the contrapuntal associate) presents perfect agreement with the given voice or Motive, *in two different relations to the latter.* These two relations always imply, in Double-counterpoint, the distinction of *register*, and refer to the agreement of the added part **both above and below the given part ;** or, in a word, the counterpoint is " double " when the parts admit of *inversion.*

a. The inversion of the parts is effected by transferring either part toward *and beyond* the other (shifting it up or down, as the case may be) ; thus, the upper part may be shifted down, *past* the lower ; or the lower part shifted up ; or each may be shifted so that they exchange registers. See Exs. 105, 106, 107.

b. When one of the parts is shifted just an *octave* (or possibly two octaves), while the other part remains where it was, it is obvious that no essential change in their harmonic relationship takes place, because each retains its original series of letters (or tones), and the association or union of the melodies is actually the same as before ; the only difference being that their respective registers have been exchanged. Each contrapuntal interval is simply inverted, and the octave-inversion of an interval, as has been amply tested, is practically identical with the original interval. For illustration :

(*a*), the Original Counterpoint.

Ex. 105.

later:

6 3 2 3 etc.

*1) At *b* the two parts are inverted, the original upper part becoming the lower, and the lower the upper. The original upper part remains where it was, and the lower is shifted upward *one octave, beyond the other.* That no essential change takes place in the harmonic relations of the parts, is easily verified by comparing the contrapuntal intervals.

The result would be precisely the same if the lower part were to remain, and the upper part shifted down an octave:

Ex.
106.

Inversion of Original Counterpoint.

Or if *each* part were shifted one octave (possibly two octaves) towards and beyond the other:

Ex.
107.

*1) Here the original lower part is shifted up one octave, and the upper is shifted down two octaves.

c. Further, the same result is obtained (without essential change) when the Inversion of the original counterpoint is *transposed.* In this

case each voice is shifted toward (and past) the other in such a manner
that the *sum of the two shifts equals an octave;* for instance, if the
upper voice is shifted down a 5th, the lower must be moved up a 4th;
or one a 3rd and the other a 6th; or one a 2nd and the other a 7th.
For example :

*1) The upper part is shifted down a 7th, the lower up a 2nd (or 9th, which is
the same thing); the original counterpoint is thus transposed bodily, as Inversion,
from *C* major to *d* minor. That no other change than simple "inversion" has taken
place, is shown by the first contrapuntal interval (a 3rd, becoming a 6th in the
Inversion). See Ex. 86, Note *6).

*2) The inverted form does not need to be enchained with the original counter-
point, as chances to be the case in Ex. 107; it may occur and recur at any later
moment in the form.

56. Such Inversions as these, in the octave or in intervals equalling
an octave (or two or more octaves), are so common, so nearly inevitable
in contrapuntal writing, and the product is, as has been shown, so likely
to be exactly equivalent to the original, that this — **the Inversion in**

the Octave — is called the Natural species of Double-counterpoint. Its feasibility is almost a foregone conclusion, and therefore all good contrapuntal association is, in a sense, naturally double-counterpoint.

57. No specific rules can be given for natural Double-counterpoint. The best method is to write the counterpoint as usual, and then simply *test* the effect of inverting the parts; any lurking discrepancies can thus easily be detected and removed. The following general points may, however, be borne in mind:

(1) The Original counterpoint should be as perfect and free from irregularities as possible.

(2) Some caution should be exercised in the use of the chord-5th, for certain irregularities that are permitted with it in the *upper* part become objectionable in the *lower;* this refers particularly to skips to or from the chord-5th, during a change of harmony. Compare par. 17*d*, last clause; (Ex. 50*B*, No. 2, the last measure, would be much worse in inverted form). See also par. 62.

A curious instance of characteristic disregard of this rule is seen in the following. Its undeniable peculiarity is palliated by broad considerations, that will become obvious to the more advanced student:

*1) The *c♯* in the lower part is the 5th of the chord (I of *f♯* minor). In the Inversion, the chord-5th *f♯*, also, is unpleasantly prominent in the upper part.

(3) If the two parts are kept within an octave (from each other), the shifting of either part a single octave suffices to effect Inversion. If the parts diverge more than an octave at any point, however, it will be necessary to shift each voice an octave (or either voice two octaves) in order to obtain Inversion throughout; and so on.

58. Frequent unconscious use has already been made of natural Double-counterpoint in the preceding exercises. Systematic application of it may hereafter be made, in the Invention, in many ways that will suggest themselves to the student. For instance:

In the sectional form, any later section may correspond exactly (or nearly) to some foregoing section, but with inverted voices, **and, of course,** in a different key.

Or, in the 2-Part Song-form, a portion, or the whole, of the Second Part may be an inverted reproduction of the First, in the proper key. This is strikingly illustrated in **Bach**, Well-temp. Clavichord, Vol. I, Fugue 10, to which brief reference may be made; the entire Second Part (measures 20–38) is an Inversion of Part I (measures 1–19) in a different key; the necessary modulation is made in measure 29, first beat (compare with measure 10).

Or, in the 3-Part Song-form, Part III may corroborate Part I in the same manner.

See **Beethoven,** Pianoforte Sonata, Op. 10, No. 2, *Finale*, measure 87 (*ff*) to 106.

Beethoven, Violin Son., Op. 30, No. 1, *Finale*, Var. V; meas. 1–8, inverted in meas. 9–16; meas. 17–24, inv. in meas. 25–32.

EXERCISE 17.

Write a number of 2-voice Inventions, applying the principle of natural Double-counterpoint, according to the suggestions in par. 58.

CHAPTER VI.

THE CONTRAPUNTAL ASSOCIATION OF THREE MELODIC PARTS (VOICES).

59. Review the definition of Polyphony given in the Introductory Statement (page 1).

The " harmonious " association of three co-ordinate melodies must necessarily be controlled by the conditions of **chord-structure** to a far greater and more manifest extent than that of only two voices, — for which latter a schedule of euphonious **intervals** was found to suffice.

For this reason 3-voice Polyphony exhibits a much more evident harmonic character than the 2-voice; and the chief difficulty in its successful manipulation consists *in respecting and enforcing the control of the Chord-forms, without fettering the individual parts* and interfering with that independence and melodic smoothness which is, in true Polyphony, as significant a requisite as that of unanimous action.

60. The chord-forms, i.e., any combination of three or four 3rds, with or without inversion, afford the necessary consonance or general "harmony" of effect. But an excess of this harmonic (i.e., homophonous) effect must be counteracted, by modification (through inharmonic adjuncts) sufficient to *disguise the chords, as such,* and create the impression of *individual voice-movements* within the channels marked off by the chord-tones. The problem of genuine and effective Polyphony for more than two parts is, concisely stated, that of achieving this impression of independent melodic progressions, and *still preserving sufficient evidence of the chords* to ensure a harmonious result.

Technically considered, this is secured by the employment of Suspensions, Passing-notes (accented and unaccented), and occasional Neighboring tones or Appoggiaturas, as disguising adjuncts of the predefined chords, as evidences of freedom and elasticity in a movement whose *general direction* is dictated by an underlying stern principle of harmonic necessity. But the *manner* and the *extent* of the use of these inharmonic (dissonant) factors must be vigilantly guarded, and tempered by due consideration of the demands of euphony and harmony. Review par. 17*b*.

· Details of Three–Voice Polyphony.

61. *a.* This imparts a corresponding degree of importance to the harmonic idea, and greatly emphasizes the rules of *chord-succession* given in pars. 18 and 19, which must be carefully reviewed.

b. Of the three parts, *two will very likely co-operate temporarily according to the rules of 2-voice polyphony* given in Chapter II; and the remaining (third) part *aims to secure some essential tone which*, with the essential tones already present, *completes some legitimate chord-structure.*

This rule is merely stated for the convenience of the student, who, as beginner, can scarcely expect to conduct *three* independent parts successfully, all at once, but will need some such division of the labor as the rule indicates. He must observe that no attempt can be made to intimate *which two* of the three parts will be chosen thus to form the temporary basis of the contrapuntal fabric, or *how far* the choice each time extends; for that depends upon conditions that are either self-evident, or follow as a matter of course out of later details, — especially par. 64. And in any case the rule does not refer to a certain pair of voices *throughout*, but implies a *temporary* choice, liable at any moment to be exchanged for another pair. The ultimate consideration is, after all, that the three parts together must represent, in their simultaneous *essential* tones, some legitimate *chord-form.*

Hence, in the preliminary draught of the three-fold melodic association, the intervals of the 3rd, 6th (8ve, etc.), will govern the choice of simultaneous essential tones, as shown in pars. 14 and 15. For illustration:

Ex. 110.

d-f-(a). c-e-(g). c-(c)-e. f-(f)-a. (b)-d-f. e-g-(b). a-(a)-c.

*1) Assuming (arbitrarily, simply by way of illustration) that **Bach** defined first
the conduct of the two higher parts, it will be seen that they conform exactly to the
rules of 2-voice counterpoint, and represent, in their essential tones, *fragments of
successive chords,* whose *absent intervals* afford the staple out of which the additional
(3rd) part is constructed.

*2) The notes of the lower part correspond to the letters in parenthesis, and
represent, in nearly every case, the tones which *complete the chord-structure.*

Further :

Ex.
111.

*1) Assuming, as above, the small notes to represent the added (3rd) part, the
same process may be traced. See also **Bach,** Well-temp. Clavichord, Vol. I, Fugue 3,
measures 1–7.   Here the process of adding first one part to the given motive, and
then a third to these two, is actually employed; the upper and inner parts of measures 3–4 become the inner and lower parts in measures 5–6, with transposition and
very slight change; to these a new part is added, above.   See par. 66*a.*

Vol. I, Fugue 13, first 6 measures; the same, in every particular.

Vol. I, Fugue 18; the lower and inner parts of measures 3–4 become inner and
upper parts in measures 5–6, with transposition, while a third part is added, below.

Vol. I, Fugue 23 ; the same.

Vol. II, Fugue 16; the same (measures 5–8 increased to three parts in measures
9–12).

Vol. II, Fugue 23; the same (measures 5–8 increased to three parts in measures
10–13).

c. As stated in par. 60, second clause, the harmonic points thus
definitely fixed as basis for the conduct of the additional (3rd) part,

should be so modified or disguised by means of auxiliary tones, unessential neighboring and passing-notes (*inharmonic* tones, in a word), as to counteract the impression of simple chord-succession.   This device is omitted in Ex. 110, but plainly seen in Ex. 111, No. 2; and may be verified in the other given illustrations, also.

But this is not all; the insertion of passing-notes must not be adopted as a device to this end alone, or the texture will, after all, amount to no more than "embellished harmony."   A higher purpose — that of *independent melodic progressions* — must dictate the employment of such inharmonic tones; and while the progressions must necessarily be governed by the chord-contents, their independence must be ensured by sufficient evidence of **thematic purpose.**   Review, in this connection, par. 17*b*, (pars. 13*i*, 21*b*); also par. 7.

d.   Of the purely mechanical means of obtaining voice-independence, none is more efficient and indispensable than the **Tie,** which advances in importance in proportion to the number of polyphonic parts associated.   Review thoroughly par. 22*d*, and par. 9, entire.   For example:

*1) Some of the ties in this sentence result in positive *dissonance*, by producing **Suspensions;** at other places, on the contrary, the tie simply modifies the *rhythm* of its part, without influencing the consonant effect.   See also Ex. 57, No. 6 (ties in lower part); Exs. 58, 59, 60; Ex. 111, Nos. 1 and 2; Ex. 113.

e. The greater the number of parts employed in a polyphonic complex, the greater the likelihood and necessity of *indirect coincidence*
between a certain pair of them, — to counteract the danger of exces-
sive dissonance from the independent movements of so many individual
parts.   This is probably most frequently exhibited in the prevalence of
parallel movement in 3rds or 6ths, between two of the three (or more)
voices, — a trait which is strikingly common in the best examples of
Polyphony, and affords the surest guaranty of smooth and euphonious
effect.   The limit of such a parallel series of 3rds or 6ths can be
defined only by a perfect understanding of the momentous principle
stated in par. 60, and of the "spirit of Polyphony" in general.   Sometimes (as if to redeem the independence of the parts, or perhaps for
thematic reasons) the line of parallel 3rds or 6ths is *disguised* by some
means; for instance, in Ex. 112 the inner part is obviously defined in
parallel 3rds with the upper, from measure 4 to 8; but by embellishment, first in one part and then in the other, their indirect coincidence
is completely veiled.   See further:

Ex.
113.

*1) Measure 1, beat 2, — 6ths between outer parts (up to first pulse of next
beat); beat 3, — 6ths between inner and lower parts (again up to first pulse of next
beat); measure 2, beats 1 and 2, — 3rds between outer parts, *disguised by the omission
of alternate 16ths in upper part* (again the parallels extend into the following beat,
modified by transferring the last tone to the higher octave); beat 3, — 3rds between
inner and lower parts. See also Ex. 57, No. 6; Ex. 111, No. 2.

Of similar (though far inferior) efficiency is that variety of indirect
coincidence in which two of the parts *reciprocate* in the embellishment
of chord-tones that lie a 3rd apart, — both using the same tones, but in
contrary direction.   Thus:

1.

Ex.
114.

Bach uses this device so rarely, as compared with his employment of parallel 3rds and 6ths, that it may justly be regarded with suspicion, as a *polyphonic* factor. See **Beethoven,** Pianoforte Sonata, op. 106, first movement, measures 55–61.

f. All *general* rules of contrapuntal association (as those of par. 17 *d* and *e ;* pars. 18, 19, 20) apply alike to every variety of polyphonic texture, regardless of the number of parts employed. The rule in par. 17 *f,* with reference to conducting the parts in contrary (opposite) directions, applies to polyphony for three and more parts also, but with certain modifications. It is evident that all three (or four) parts cannot move at the same time in different directions ; but it is possible (1) to hold one part level, while the other two are respectively ascending and descending (or even moving in parallel direction) ; (2) to carry one part, at least, in contrary motion with the other two, so that one descends while two are ascending, or vice versa. It is wise to conduct the two *outer* parts in opposite directions, as a rule, and to avoid parallel movement in all three parts at once.

Of peculiar value in 3-voice polyphony is the device of modulatory Substitution expounded in par. 19*c,* which is to be thoroughly reviewed.

62. The conduct of the **lowermost part** is of increased importance in 3-voice polyphony, because of the more pronounced harmonic character of this species of writing (par. 59), and the consideration due to those forms (Inversions) of harmony in which the *chord-fifth* lies lowermost (i.e., the 6-4 chords).

It is, of course, impossible (and needless) to shun this chord-form altogether; but vigilance must be exercised in the treatment of all *obvious* 6-4 chords.   Former rules apply strictly; see par. 18*h*.   To recapitulate :

a. Avoid *leaping* to, or from, a bass tone which is manifestly the 5th of the momentary chord, — excepting in *chord-repetitions.*

b. Avoid a *succession* of chord-fifths in the lowermost part (i.e., 6-4 chords) when both represent *Consonant* forms of harmony ; if either of them is an *imperfect* 5th, or the inverted form of any *Dissonant* harmony, the succession is good.   This grave error is most easily checked **by avoiding parallel perfect 4ths with the Bass,** in the conduct of any upper part, when the 4ths are both *essential* intervals (par. 14).

c. Avoid any very conspicuous 6-4 effect, excepting when the harmony is Tonic.   Avoid, hence, *beginning or ending a Section* upon a 6-4 chord.   As a rule, the lowermost part should not be announced (or re-announced after a rest) upon the 5th of the momentary chord; nor should it discontinue (pass into a rest) after a tone which is evidently the chord-fifth.

d. These rules may be said to apply to all 6-4 chords *excepting that of the Tonic;* the latter is largely, if not entirely, exempt.

For example :

63. The **rhythmic conditions** of 3-voice Polyphony are identical in principle with those of the 2-voice, as detailed in par. 22, which review.

a. The chief rule is stated in par. 22*a :* the three voices participate, with a certain regularity of alternation, in sustaining the adopted rhythmic movement (of ♪-notes, ♪-notes, — or whatever the *prevailing uniform rhythm* may be).   *Rhythmic diversity* between the parts being, as repeatedly emphasized, the principal means of instituting voice-independence, it is evident that its importance, and the necessity **of its** careful treatment, increase in proportion to the number of **parts** engaged.   Review, very thoroughly, par. 22 *a* and *d.*

Quite frequently the same rhythm will be given to *two* of the parts simultaneously; but this similarity must never be carried very far (best not more than 2, 3, or 4 beats), before being *transferred to another pair*, or abandoned temporarily in favor of one part alone. See Ex. 114, No. 2, No. 3; Ex. 113; Ex. 111, No. 1.

One of the three parts may run on in *uniform rhythm* almost indefinitely, if sufficient provision for diversity is made in the remaining two parts. See Ex. 110 (Soprano); Ex. 113 (Bass); Ex. 114, Nos. 2 and 3.

As a general rule, the most definite and constant aim is, *to assign to each of the three parts, temporarily, a different rhythmic movement*, i.e., different tone-values; not obstinately, but as an ever-conscious preference. This, and the maintenance of a smooth, uniform, *collective rhythmic effect*, satisfy, together, all the rhythmic demands of polyphonic texture.

See Ex. 110, — different values in each of the three parts; Ex. 111, No. 2, — during almost every beat the three parts have different values; Ex. 112, the same; Ex. 113, measure 2. This may best be verified by careful analysis of the given references.

Finally, the exchange of one rate of rhythmic movement for another (faster or slower) may, of course, be effected within the same Invention without confusion, if care be taken to preserve good balance of total effect (by regularity of recurrence, — on the principle of par. 22*e*), and a perfectly clear impression of the *fundamental* metric design. See **Bach,** 3-voice Inventions, No. 15 (alternating $\flat$ and $\natural$-movements); No. 2; and Ex. 117, with context (par. 70).

b. The **Rest** enters into the rhythmic design of Polyphony more significantly when three or more parts are used than when there are but two. Review par. 10, and par. 22*d*, last clause.

In general, *short* rests, interspersed promiscuously through the polyphonic texture, are of inferior value, and often rather injure than improve the effect. It is far more judicious to interrupt the conduct of one of the three parts by a *longer rest, for a whole measure or more*, so that a decided and noticeable change of volume results.

A part may be thus definitely discontinued (1) at any *cadence;* or (2) at any point in the course of a Section where the part reaches a tone that has *no special obligation* or tendency to fulfil, — especially when it is any interval of the Tonic harmony; and, as a rule, only at an accented beat or the accented fraction of a beat; rarely, if ever, after any dissonant tone that demands resolution.

In 3-voice Polyphony, generally no more than one part should rest at a time (unless it be very briefly) ; hence, another part must not be discontinued until the absent part has fairly recommenced; in other words, the extremities of a discontinuing and recommencing part should overlap noticeably.

After a protracted pause, the part may recommence with an announcement of the Motive.   This is the most appropriate and effective method, but is by no means essential.

c. Further, **the part should recommence, after a rest, on an unaccented beat ; or, still better, on a fraction of the beat,** as a very general rule.

For illustration of all these points, see Ex. 112, inner part; Ex. 113, lower part; Ex. 114, Nos. 2 and 3 ; **Bach,** 3-voice Inventions, No. 1, measure 13 (Bass), 15 (inner part), 16 (lower part pauses directly *after* inner part recommences, overlapping one beat), 17 (brief rest in upper part).   3-voice Invention No. 2, — in measures 5 and 6, the outer parts pause *together* during the last beats ; this is unusual, but the reason is obvious ; the irregular acceleration of the rhythm in the inner part (contrary to the fundamental principle, par. 63*a*), is fully justified by its *recurrence, or sequence,* in the following measure, and again, at intervals, throughout the Invention.   Compare pars. 22*e* and 21*f.*   In this same Invention, measure 4 from the end, the lower part discontinues precisely as the upper part recommences, i.e., without overlapping ; this is least confusing when, as here, the parts in question are so distant from each other that their extremities cannot be confounded.   In nearly or quite all of these cases, the rule of par. 63*c* is illustrated conclusively.

LEADING PARTS.

64. It is extremely difficult — for the beginner, almost out of the question — to lead *three* polyphonic parts abreast, and preserve the individuality of each part as if it were alone.   Before this supreme command of simultaneous part-leading shall have been acquired, the student must adopt some method of systematic division of the labor, by centering his attention upon first one and then another *single* part for a time. This is entirely feasible and justifiable, because it is consistent with the processes of polyphonic texture, that **a certain one of the three (or more) parts temporarily takes the lead,** — the other parts meanwhile deferring to the "Leader," as simple contrapuntal associates, **until some other part, in its turn, assumes the lead.**

The choice of temporary "Leader" may be made arbitrarily; but it is far more likely to determine *itself*, as a matter of course, out of the natural conditions and exigencies of the progressive development.   For example, that one of the three parts which has charge of the *Motive*

invariably assumes the leadership for the time being; and, during episodes, that part takes the lead which pursues the most obvious and
important thematic purpose, — as, for instance, the projection of a line
of *Sequences*, the pursuit of some significant imitatory process, or any
other definite and far-reaching melodic or structural aim.

Further, it is precisely the same with the question "how long" a
part may assert the leadership, before abandoning it to some other part;
it depends upon the conditions which determine the *choice* in the first
place; it may be a measure or several measures, or possibly only a
single beat.

In any case, the leading part should be written down *alone*, as far
as it is to extend; it is then comparatively easy to return and "fill out"
the remaining parts.

This idea is closely allied to that expounded in par. 61*b*, which
review.

See **Bach,** 3-voice Invention No. 1; during measure 1 the upper part "leads";
during measure 2, the inner part; measures 3, 4, and 5, the lower part; measure 6,
the inner; measures 7 to 9 (beat 3) the lower part "leads," first with its Sequences
and then with the Motive; measures 9 (beat 3) to 10 (beat 3), the inner part; measures 10 (beat 3) to 11 (beat 3), the upper; *meanwhile*, during the first half of measure
11, the lower part claims the lead, and maintains it to the end of the measure; and
so forth. The student is to continue the analysis to the end of the Invention,
with reference to the "leading parts."

SUMMARY.

65. *a.* The simultaneous *essential* tones should constitute some
chord-structure; and the chords should succeed each other according to
the fundamental conditions of chord-progression.

b. The problem of good Polyphony for more than two parts is, to
preserve an equipoise between the *Consonance* of the chord-forms and
the *Dissonance* involved by independent part-conduct.

c. Ties are invaluable in effective Polyphony.

d. Parallel movement in 3rds or 6ths is the most legitimate and reliable guaranty of smooth and euphonious voice-association. At the
same time, a certain degree of *Contrary motion* should be maintained.

e. The lowermost part must be so conducted as to avoid conspicuous or faulty 6-4 chord effects.

f. The rhythmic requirements are, to *diversify the tone-values* of the several parts, but to maintain a generally uniform *collective* rhythmic effect.

g. *Rests* — especially of palpable extent — are invaluable in effective Polyphony for more than two parts. After a rest, the part should re-enter upon an *unaccented* fraction or beat.

h. In the execution of a multi-voice polyphonic texture, it is necessary to concentrate the attention upon a certain *single* part, as *temporary "leader,"* — the choice and extent depending upon thematic conditions.

EXERCISE 18.

A. Analyze minutely, with regard to the above regulations of 3-voice Polyphony:

> **Bach,** 3-voice Invention No. 1, meas. 2–5; 10–14.
> **Bach,** 3-voice Invention No. 3, meas. 4–9.
> **Bach,** 3-voice Invention No. 4, last 7 measures.
> **Bach,** 3-voice Invention No. 6, meas. 2–10.
> **Bach,** 3-voice Invention No. 8, meas. 2–7.
> **Bach,** 3-voice Invention No. 12, meas. 3–10.
> **Bach,** 3-voice Invention No. 13, last 12 measures.
> **Bach,** 3-voice Invention No. 14, last 8 measures.

B. To some of the (corrected) examples of two-part counterpoint made in Exercises 7, 8, and 9, add a third part, — above, below, or between (or all three successively), as appears most convenient or effective. Begin the third part about one beat later than the second, — as a rule, upon an *unaccented fraction* of the beat (compare par. 63*c*). At least *one tie* is to be introduced, in the added part, if possible.

C. Extend the Stretto examples made in Exercise 10, to 3-voice Stretti.

CHAPTER VII.

THE THREE–VOICE INVENTION.

66. The structural conditions of the 3-voice Invention coincide exactly with those of the 2-voice Invention. *Review pars. 37, 38, 39.*

a. Three polyphonic parts are distinguished, in *instrumental* music, as Upper, Inner, and Lower.

In writing for three solo instruments (string or wood-wind), the compass and register of the parts depend upon the instruments chosen. If a *keyboard* instrument is employed (Pianoforte, Harmonium, Organ), the compass is practically unlimited, though it is most consistent with the spirit of polyphonic music to confine the movements of the parts to the three and one-half octaves in the center of the keyboard;

and, while *each* of the three parts is entitled to nearly or quite this entire range, and while adjacent parts may occasionally *cross*, good balance must be preserved, (1) by avoiding too wide divergence of the *outer* parts from each other, and (2) by conducting the Inner part, as a rule, *closer to the Upper* than to the Lower part.

If *vocal* parts are chosen, they should be adjacent voices (Soprano, Alto, and Tenor, or Alto, Tenor, and Bass), and the compass and register will be defined accordingly. Further, the treatment of vocal parts constantly calls for more limitation (in every respect), and more careful consideration, than that of instrumental parts. This species of writing is, however, *not to be chosen at present.*

b. The "Sectional" form is, here again, the most fitting. Its details correspond to those given in Chapter V; but there are a few additional considerations, naturally involved by the additional voice, which call for special explanation.

The First Section, or Exposition.

67. Review par. 40.

a. The Motive — which is likely to be a trifle less ample in compass, and less lively in rhythmic character, than the foregoing ones — may be announced in either one of the three parts, most commonly in the inner or upper part.

b. Unless occupied with the M., the *lower* part, at the beginning (seldom any other voice), is generally utilized as an *auxiliary accompaniment,* of quiet, unpretentious character, and of optional length, — though usually discontinued several beats before it (as legitimate third voice) is to announce its Imitation of the Motive.

See **Bach,** 3-voice Inventions, Nos. 4, 10, 12, 13, 2, — first few measures of each. The more exceptional method of passing immediately out of the auxiliary melody into the Imitation of the Motive is seen in **Bach,** 3-voice Invention No. 1, measure 3; the abrupt change of rhythm, and the leap of an octave into the first tone of the Motive, serve, however, to identify the latter. See, also, 3-voice Inventions, Nos. 6, 7, 8, 11, 14.

c. The *first Imitation* of the M. may follow in any voice, — generally in the next higher or lower one (i.e., the *neighbor* of the first voice). The interval of this first Imitation is optional; but very positive preference is given to that in the 5th. The necessity of accurate and natural adjustment, expounded in par. 35*b* (which review, thoroughly), is here again to be respected, especially when any other Imitation than the 8ve is chosen. Any *unessential* modifications (pars. 28*b*, 30 *a* and *b*) which serve this important end, are permissible.

Bach, 3-voice Inventions, No. 1, first Imitation in the 4th; No. 2, in the 8ve; Nos. 4, 6, 7, 8, 10, 11, 12, 13, 14, first Imitation in the 5th.

d. The *second Imitation* (third announcement) of the M. is most likely to be made in the remaining part; though in many instances the latter does not begin its imitatory function until the first two parts have announced the M. several times (Ex. 116); or, as is the best and most common procedure, until they have interpolated one or more *episodic measures,* — not only for variety, but as a means of achieving some necessary or desirable modulatory purpose.

The interval of Imitation is here again optional, but nearly always *the 8ve of the first announcement* is chosen.   See, again, par. 35*b*.

Bach, 3-voice Inventions, No. 1; first the upper, then the inner, then the lower part takes the M., in regular succession; the same in No. 2 and No. 12. — In No. 6, the order is inner, upper, and lower part, in regular succession; the same in No. 8. — In No. 4, the M. appears first in the upper part, then in the inner; then *an episode of one measure intervenes,* before the last part takes up the Motive; the same in No. 11 and No. 14; No. 13 similar. — In No. 7, the upper part has an additional (3rd) announcement of the M. before the absent (lower) part follows with its legitimate Imitation; the same in No. 10.

e. As concerns the rest of the Section, — the episodic passages, the modulatory design, and the cadence,— review par. 40 *d, e, g,* and *h.*

For general illustration :

Ex.
116.

*1) Auxiliary part.

*2) From this point on, a very distinct intention of omitting the first tone of the original M. is exhibited; these two versions of the Motive — with and without the initial accented tone — actually participate in the development, throughout the entire composition (Well-temp. Clavichord, Vol. II, Prelude 19).

*3) The lower part does not appear with its Imitation of the M. until the upper and inner parts have announced it four times. The upper part has the M. at the same time, in parallel thirds; such *double announcements* are not uncommon (see measure 6).

*4) The derivation of this episodic passage is somewhat indirect, but manifestly consistent.

*5) Here the M. appears to be *divided* between the inner and upper parts. Such interaction of the parts is, naturally, very exceptional, though not without occasional justification. See **Bach,** 3-voice Invention No. 1, second measure from the end; M in Contrary motion, announced by the upper part, but, after one beat, taken up without interruption, and concluded, by the inner part.

EXERCISE 19.

A. Analyze the following Expositions:

Bach, 3-voice Invention No. 1, meas. 1–11.
Bach, 3-voice Invention No. 4, meas. 1–8.
Bach, 3-voice Invention No. 8, meas. 1–7.
Bach, 3-voice Invention No. 10, meas. 1–11.
Bach, 3-voice Invention No. 12, meas. 1–9.
Bach, 3-voice Invention No. 13, meas. 1–21.
Bach, 3-voice Invention No. 14, meas. 1–12.

B. Elaborate each of the following four Motives into a First Section, or Exposition; imitating the character and extent of those analyzed at **A.**

The pupil may choose any technical style, but he is advised to write for a *keyboard instrument,* — unless he may chance to be entirely familiar with the trio of strings, or some other *ensemble.* The choice of *vocal* parts must be deferred for a time.

Begin each example on a separate sheet, and leave ample space for its completion in the next lesson.

First review pars. 21; 28; 41 (thoroughly); 60; 61 entire (especially *d, e*); 62; 63; 64; and 65 (thoroughly):

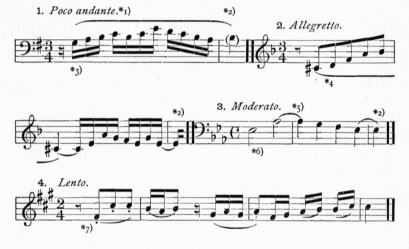

*1) *Poco andante,* — with gentle, but quite palpable, motion. The tempo must always be taken into consideration, as it affects, very directly, the question of euphony, — the number, extent, and quality of *dissonant combinations;* see par. 65*b.* The more rapidly these pass by, the less objectionable they are; and conversely. See also par. 14.

*2) The final tone is optional, both as to pitch and duration.

*3) This M. is to begin in the inner part, with auxiliary Bass. *It may also be manipulated an 8ve higher,* beginning in the upper part.

*4) Beginning in the inner part, with or without auxiliary Bass. Also a *5th higher* (in *a* minor), as upper part.

*5) The prevailing rhythm should be quarter-notes.

*6) As lower part, — without auxiliary tones above.

*7) As upper part. Also a *5th lower* (in *b* minor), as inner part.

C. Write two Expositions, one in minor and one in major, upon *original Motives;* or upon Motives chosen at option from the list given in Exercise 7*A.*

The Remaining Sections.

68. The details of the further development and conclusion of the sectional form correspond exactly to those given in pars. 42, 43, and 44, *which review thoroughly.*

a. Contrary motion of the M. is a peculiarly valuable resource, and should be freely used in these remaining sectionş. *Stretto*-announce-ments (for two, or for all three, parts) are most desirable in the later Sections. Perhaps an Imitation in Augmentation (or Diminution) may be successfully introduced in the *3-voice* Invention, though these unusual forms of Imitation are most likely to be applied to a *portion* only of the Motive. Compare 41*d*.

b. The student should conceive this present Exercise chiefly **as an effort to discover and apply as many of the latent resources of his Motive as possible.** Therefore, he should employ the Motive (entire or in part) almost constantly, test-ing every form of presentation which the chapter upon "Imitations" (Chapter IV) designates, or which his own imagination may suggest, and introducing compara-tively few and brief episodic passages. In pursuing this interesting and profitable course of thematic experiment to a satisfactory conclusion, the number of Sections may be increased to any reasonable extent (see par. 68*c*) ; and each Section, in turn, may be devoted more or less exclusively to testing some certain (untried) resource of thematic presentation (compare par. 39*b*) ; this will tend to *individualize* the several Sections, while, on the other hand, the necessary unity and consistency of form may easily be restored by establishing points of *similarity and corroboration* between the Sections (par. 42*c*). See —

Bach, 3-voice Invention No. 1, meas. 11 to end.
Bach, 3-voice Invention No. 4, meas. 8 to end.
Bach, 3-voice Invention No. 8, meas. 7 to end.
Bach, 3-voice Invention No. 12, meas. 9 to end.
Bach, 3-voice Invention No. 13, meas. 21 to end (new and more characteristic counter-motive than in Section 1).
Bach, Well-temp. Clavichord, Vol. I, Prelude 18 ; Motive in the upper part with full auxiliary accompaniment ; imitated in lower, in the 8ve ; Section 1 closes in measure 5 ; the last Section (measures 18–27) is largely episodic, but derived strictly from the Motive ; the last 3 measures are a Codetta.
Bach, Supplement (Peters ed. 1959), page 68, — called " Fuga," but belonging to the lower range of " Invention ";-forms ; irregular voice-texture.
Bach, Organ Comp. (Peters ed.), Vol. VI, No. 29, *second* division, $\frac{3}{8}$ time ; two Motives, in close alternation, — M. 1 in upper part, measures 1–3 ; M. 2 in upper part, measure 4.—Vol. VIII, No. 7.
Händel, Clavichord Suites, No. VII, Presto-movement of the " Ouverture "; largely episodic.

c. Sometimes the design of an Invention is extended to embrace an unusually large number of Sections, or even Parts. The result is either a **Large Group-form** * ; or, less frequently, the middle Sections are approximately equivalent to a " Trio," followed by a broad *Da capo* of all the anterior ones (quasi **Song-form with Trio** **).   In such long lines of development it is almost indispensable to introduce *complete episodic Sections*, often of quite distinctly homophonic character, based more upon harmonic figuration (in the prevailing rhythm) than upon thematic recurrences.   Compare par. 45, last clause ; and par. 84.

For illustration of this rare design see —

Bach, English Suite No. V, " Prelude "; very broad sectional design; Section 1 extends to measure 40, and is largely thematic; Section 2 (to measure 52) is entirely episodic, and almost suggestive of a new (auxiliary) motive, — par. 52; Section 3, to measure 71, is again thematic, but largely *two*-voice texture; Section 4 is episodic, and closes in measure 81 with a semi-cadence; Section 5 resembles Section 2, but is longer (to measure 105), becoming strictly thematic, and, in its last six measures, corresponding to the end of Section 3; Section 6 resembles Section 4, and closes with a Dominant semi-cadence in measure 117; Section 7, from there to the end, is a *literal* recurrence of Section 1 (i.e., a *da capo*).

Bach, " Ouverture à la manière française " (Peters ed., 208, No. 1), first number, second tempo ($\frac{6}{8}$ time), is very similar; Sections 1, 3, 5, 7 are thematic; 2, 4, 6 episodic ; Section 7 is a *da capo*, abbreviated at the beginning.   The first tempo (¢ time) is an Introduction, balanced by a Postlude of corresponding character; they belong to a different species of polyphonic form, and are not to be analyzed here.

Bach, Partita No. IV, " Ouverture," second tempo ($\frac{6}{8}$ time); 5 sections, the final one of which (last 26 measures) reverts to nearly every characteristic trait of the foregoing sections, and, during its last 11 measures, practically reproduces the First Section (transposed).

Bach, English Suite No. IV, "Prelude"; 14 comparatively brief sections, Nos. 13 and 14 a literal *da capo* of Nos. 1 and 2.   The texture is largely *two*-voice, especially during the thematic passages; but unmistakable evidences of multi-voice counterpoint exist. — See, further, par. 71.

EXERCISE 20.

A. To each of the Expositions written as Exercise 19*B* add the concluding sections, — preferably not more than two or three in number.   Review again pars. 19*c*, 61 *b, d, e,* 63, 64, and 65.

B. Conclude the original work begun in Exercise 19*C*.

OTHER STRUCTURAL DESIGNS.

69. *a.* **The primary Two-Part Song-form.**   Review pars. 45 and 46 ; and analyze the following examples very thoroughly : —

* *Homophonic Forms*, par. 115.
** *Ibid.*, par. 117.

Bach, 3-voice Invention No. 14; Part (or Section) I, already analyzed, closes in measure 12, with a very distinct Dominant cadence; Part II (to the end) is characterized by abundant *stretti.* — **Bach,** Well-temp. Clavichord, Vol. I, Prelude 23; Part (or Section) I terminates in measure 6, Part II in measure 15 (somewhat indefinitely); a Codetta, with evidences of four-voice texture, follows. — **Bach,** Partita No. 1, " Praeludium "; M. of one and one-half measures, — possibly two measures; Part I ends in measure 14. — **Bach,** 3-voice Invention No. 15; two Motives in close alternation, in different rhythms; the Counter-motive is retained throughout, in Natural Double-counterpoint (compare par. 58); Part I ends in measure 14.

b. **The genuine Two-Part Song-form.** Review pars. 47 and 48; and see —

Bach, 3-voice Invention No. 6; Part I embraces two Sections, closing respectively in measures 11 and 18. — **Bach,** Well-temp. Clavichord, Vol. II, Prelude 9; several Motives, — No. 1 in measures 1–8, No. 2 in measures 9–12, No. 3 in measures 13–15, and No. 4 in the Second Part (measures 8–10, etc.); Motive 1 recurs at the beginning of Part II; Part I closes with a long Codetta (measures 18–24), which recurs at the end of Part II (measures 19–27) with its two Phrases in reversed order, and followed by a 4-measure Coda. — **Bach,** French Suite No. 3, " Courante."

Händel, Suite No. VIII, " Allemande "; largely 2-voice texture. — **Händel,** Suite No. IV, " Gigue "; two Motives in close alternation (upper part, measures 1 and 2, respectively); Part II begins with the *second* Motive, — not with Contrary motion of the principal Motive (par. 51.) — **Bach,** Partita No IV, " Gigue "; Part II is based upon a new Motive, which proves, after 6 measures, to be a *Counter-motive to the principal Motive of Part I,* in connection with which it appears once (or twice); the last 8 measures of the two Parts correspond. — **Mozart,** " Gigue " in *G* major (Cotta edition, No. 22); Part II begins with a fragment of the original Motive, answered by the same fragment in Contrary motion; the two Parts are very similar in contents; a Codetta of 5 measures is added to the whole. — **Bach,** English Suite No. 2, " Allemande "; the M. of Part I appears first in the upper part, curiously confounded (on the 4th beat) with one of the lower auxiliary tones, — compare the simple form as it occurs in the lower part in measures 6, 7; Part II has, apparently, a new Motive throughout, but careful scrutiny reveals its origin in the *modified Contrary motion* of the first Motive.

c. The conventional **Gigue-form,** with Contrary motion of the M. as basis of Part II. Review par. 51, and see —

Bach, French Suite No. V, " Gigue."
Bach, English Suite No. III, " Gigue "; the original motion of the M. recurs once, at the very end.
Bach, English Suite No. V, " Gigue."
Bach, English Suite No. VI, " Gigue."
Bach, Partita No. II, " Capriccio."
Bach, Partita No. III, " Gigue."

The above superb illustrations of the 3-voice Invention-species are to be analyzed with more than ordinary attention and minuteness.

Bach, Organ Comp. (Peters compl. ed.), Vol. I, Sonata No. I, 2nd movement; M. one measure, upper part, followed by another measure of episodic extension (related to par. 72*c*); Part II, after 5 measures' exposition of the Contrary motion, corresponds closely to sections of Part I, but in *different order*, with inverted voices, and (partly) transposed. To be minutely analyzed.

Bach, Suite, Peters ed. 214, No. 3, "Gigue."

Bach, Suite, Peters ed. 214, No. 5, "Gigue"; M. 3 or 4 beats, in lower part; curious insertion of auxiliary tones, before Imitation in each of the other higher parts.

Bach, English Suite No. III, "Allemande"; M. one measure, lower part.

d'Albert, Pianoforte Suite, op. 1, movement 5 ("Gigue," — excellent example).

Händel, Suite No. VIII, "Gigue."

Händel, Suite No. VIII, "Courante"; largely harmonic in general character, and at times definite 4-voice texture; the original motion of the M. recurs in measures 18 and 19 of Part II.

Händel, Suite No. XIII, "Gigue."

d. **The primary Three-Part Song-form.** Review pars. 49 and 49*a;* and see —

Bach, 3-voice Invention No. 10; Part (Section) I closes, a little indefinitely, in measure 11, as already seen; Part II embraces two Sections, closing respectively in measures 22 and 25; in measure 26 a vague, but probably sufficient, intimation of "the return to the beginning" (the distinctive condition of a "Third Part") is recognizable.

Bach, Well-temp. Clavichord, Vol. II, Prelude 3, second tempo ($\frac{3}{8}$ time); Section I ends in measure 10; Section II, based chiefly upon the Contrary motion of the M., closes in measure 17; the remaining (Third) Section is sufficiently indicative of a recurrence of the early contents of Section I to represent the 3-Part form.

e. **The genuine Three-Part Song-form.** Review par. 50, and see —

Bach, French Suite No. 1, "Gigue"; Part II, based on the Contrary motion, terminates 7 measures from the end, upon a strong Dominant semi-cadence; what follows is a very obvious (though somewhat disguised) Third Part, or recurrence of the beginning; it opens with several stretto Imitations, in the original motion, and, in the second measure, in Contrary motion (upper voice); the last two measures correspond to the ending of Part I.

Bach, Well-temp. Clavichord, Vol. II, Prelude No. 5; M. one measure long, with an episodic extension of one well-contrasted lyric measure, which reappears at the beginning of Parts II and III, but does not participate essentially in the thematic development; Part I has a Codetta of 4 measures; Part II begins with the Contrary motion, but utilizes the original motion also; its ending, and the announcement of Part III, are very distinct; the latter diverges into the Sub-dominant key, in its 3rd measure, and thereafter follows almost exactly the line of Part I, transposed, of course, to the principal key.

Bach, Well-temp. Clavichord, Vol. II, Prelude 21; based throughout upon three brief Motives (announced in measures 1, 9, and 13, respectively), — see par. 52; Part II is 16 measures in length; Part III begins very definitely; a curious series of double-announcements of the principal Motive, in simultaneous original and Contrary motion, appears in measures 12 to 7 from the end.

Bach, Peters ed., Supplement (No. 1959), page 63.

In the following examples of the 3-part Song-form, the Third Part is a more or less accurately *transposed recurrence* of the main contents of Part I : *

Bach, Well-temp. Clavichord, Vol. I, Prelude 9 ; M. 7 beats long, followed by an episodic (lyric) extension; the first Imitation is in measure 3 (lower part); Part I ends in measure 8 ; Part II ends in measure 14 ; Part III is a nearly exact transposed recurrence of the First Part, ending, with an evaded cadence, in measure 22, and followed by a brief Codetta, or plagal extension.

Bach, Well-temp. Clavichord, Vol. II, Prelude 4 ; Part I, closing in measure 17, manipulates the principal M. (upper part, measures 1–5; lower part, very much modified, measures 5–7) ; Part II begins with a new (2nd) Motive, two measures in length (inner voice), which is carried through the first of its Sections (to measure 27) ; in measure 27 a third Motive appears (1½ measures, upper voice), derived from the auxiliary Bass at the beginning; this is retained to the end of Part II (measure 33) ; see par. 52c ; Part III (measure 33) is, for 7 measures, a transposed recurrence of the first 7 measures of Part I, with the M. transferred to the inner voice ; thereupon it *returns to the beginning and reproduces these 7 measures in the original key*, with slight changes. The remainder of Part III embraces the following factors : Measures 45–49, an episodic passage, largely sequential; measures 50–55, a transposed reproduction of the Second Section of Part II ; measure 56 to end, a reproduction of the last 7 measures of Part I, the upper and inner voices inverted. See, again, par. 58.

Bach, Well-temp. Clavichord, Vol. II, Prelude 19 ; Part I is analyzed in Example 116 ; Part II begins with Contrary motion of the M., and uses it freely during its two Sections ; Part III (measures 22–30) is an almost exact reproduction of Part I, but transposed, and with inner and upper voices inverted (par. 58) ; a Codetta of 3½ measures is added.

Bach, Well-temp. Clavichord, Vol. II, Prelude 22 ; the M. is 5 measures long, announced first in the inner part, and associated with contrapuntal fragments from its first members; an " Auxiliary figure" appears in measure 7 (inner part), which assumes vital importance in the total development; see par. 52a ; Part II embraces three Sections, beginning respectively in measures 16, 24, and 42 ; Part III (measures 55–70) is an accurate reproduction of Part I, transposed, and with inverted inner and upper voices (par. 58) ; a Coda is added, the last 6 measures of which correspond to the ending of Section 2 of the Second Part.

70. A very effective variety of the 3-Part Song-form is obtained, on the basis of the idea expressed in par. 48*a* (second clause), by introducing *in Part II* a *Counter-motive in more animated rhythm.*

a. This implies that the original Motive should be of a rhythmically quiet or stately form, with correspondingly quiet counterpoint during Part I.

---

* *Homophonic Forms*, par. 110.

The characteristic Counter-motive of Part II may be nothing more than an ordinary contrapuntal associate, in shorter note-values. But it is not unlikely that its figures may be generated, by Diminution, out of parts of the Motive itself : and, in either case, it should be treated to a certain extent as an " Auxiliary motive," i.e., recurring, entire or in part, from time to time (freely modified, if necessary), in order to avoid the impression of desultory rambling. For example (**Bach,** 3-voice Invention No. 7):

Ex.
117.

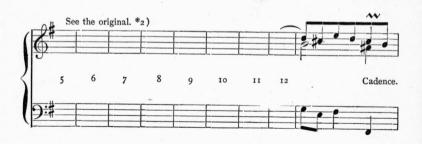

*1) The irregularity of rhythm at this place (16th-notes upon the *accented* beat only) is balanced and justified by the recurrence of the same figure two measures later; compare par. 22e.   Further, the 16ths are called forth by the purpose of connecting the inevitable $d\sharp$ and $d\natural$ as smoothly as possible. — *2) The First Part runs on thus in a fundamental rhythm of 8th-notes, interrupted three times as in measure 3.

*3) This figure of four tones is the evident thematic germ of the new, characteristic Counter-motive in animated movement, which begins abruptly at the outset of Part II.   The figure was doubtless conceived and adopted by **Bach** as the Contrary motion of the first member of the principal Motive, in Diminution. — *4) The peculiar "cross-relation" between the inner and lower parts here ($d\sharp$–$d\natural$) is justified by the structural joint (or light cadence) at the first beat; compare par. 19d, and Ex. 57, especially Note *7). — *5) This Counter-motive agrees with the preceding one throughout, but skilfully transposed to correspond to the interval of Imitation adopted for the M. in the upper part (the 5th); therefore, the contrapuntal calculation is identical, and harmonious union is assured. — *6) From here on the animated contrapuntal figure is transferred impartially from one voice to another. — *7) The animated rhythm is maintained, without a check, to the cadence of Part II, which is made with much emphasis upon a Dominant chord, in measure 37 (see Ex. 118). The 2nd Section of the Part begins (measure 25) with the *Contrary motion* of the animated Counter-motive (modified unessentially to conform easily to the altered conditions); this reveals more clearly the origin of the figure indicated in Note *3). The original is to be thoroughly analyzed, up to measure 37.

b. If the characteristic Counter-motive in quicker rhythm is to distinguish Part II especially, it will be abandoned at the beginning of

Part III, and the latter will *resume the original fundamental rhythm,* — possibly only for a few measures, however; for the animated rhythm is quite likely to assert itself again, either in the later course of Part III, *or in the Coda or Codetta,* which, in such definite structural designs as these, is almost indispensable. The first of these alternatives is illustrated in the continuation of the above example (**Bach,** 3-voice Invention No. 7), thus:

*1) At the beginning of Part III the original rhythm of 8th-notes is resumed, abruptly; but after two measures the characteristic Counter-motive reappears. As a rule, the original rhythm should have *more* time than this, to re-assert itself.

*2) The rhythm of 16th-notes is carried on without interruption, up to the cadence-beats. There is no Codetta in this instance.

See also — briefly, and solely with reference to the *rhythmic* design of the three Parts and Coda — **Bach,** Well-temp. Clavichord, Vol. I, Fugue 19; Part I, measures

1–20; Interlude, measures 20–22 ; Part II, measures 23–42; Part III, measures 42–49 ; Coda, to end.

The Song–form with Trio.

71. As intimated in par. 68*c*, an extension of the sectional line of development to an abnormal length is not unlikely to resolve itself into that broad homophonic design of three Divisions, the third of which is a more or less exact " Da capo " (recurrence of the first), thus isolating the second Division somewhat, — like the " Trio " of certain dance-forms.

See **Bach,** English Suite No. VI, " Prelude," *allegro*-movement. The Introduction of 37 measures is not to be analyzed at present. Section 1 extends to the 11th measure ; Section 2 utilizes the Contrary motion of the Motive ; Section 3 (measures 20–49) is preponderantly two-voice texture, and contains several effective episodic passages, more in the style of harmonic figuration than polyphonic development; this closes with a strong Tonic cadence in the principal key, and terminates the First Division. The following five sections constitute the Middle Division or " Trio " (up to measure 110) ; Section IV (measures 49–61) is mainly episodic, and suggests the presence of an Auxiliary Motive ; Section V (measures 61–76) reverts emphatically to the principal M., and contains a reminiscence of Section III ; Section VI (to measure 90) begins with a novel treatment of the M., and then (measure 80) corroborates the main contents of Section IV ; Section VII (to measure 106) begins with a new form of treatment, but soon runs into the current of Section III, to which, especially during its last 6 or 7 measures, it bears close resemblance ; Section VIII (to measure 110) is a brief Re-transition. The remaining three sections (measure 110 to the end) are a *literal* recurrence of Sections I, II, and III, i.e., the First Division.

Bach, English Suite No. II, " Prelude." This is preponderantly *two*-voice texture, and its First Division has already been analyzed in Exercise 13*A*. The Middle Division (measures 55–110) begins with an episodic passage, based upon a new (Auxiliary) Motive which distinctly governs the Division, though the principal M. asserts itself from time to time,— somewhat analogous to par. 48*c*; in measure 87 a 4-measure Section occurs, corresponding exactly (excepting in key) to the Codetta of the First Division ; it is immediately repeated, with transferred register and other unessential changes; in measure 95 the Auxiliary M. again resumes its sway, and leads to an unusually impressive cadence in measure 110, in the Relative key,— followed immediately by the literal reproduction of the First Division, as " Da capo." It is almost certainly only an accidental coincidence that the three Divisions should each contain the same number of measures (55).

EXERCISE 21.

A. Write a complete example of the 3-voice Invention in 2-Part Song-form (broad design, par. 69*b*), employing the same Motive in Part II, chiefly in the original motion (par. 48*a*). An original M. is to be used, — preferably in major.

B. An example of the 3-voice Invention in the 2-Part Song-form, as "Gigue" (par. 69c), — Contrary motion of the M. as basis of Part II.   Original M., preferably in minor, and $\frac{6}{8}$ time.

C. Two examples (major and minor, but in different species of measure from each other and from those above) in the 3-Part Song-form, par. 69 *d* and *e.*   Thematic basis of Part II optional.   Motive original.

D. An example (preferably major) in the 3-Part Song-form, with characteristic counter-motive in animated rhythm during Part II, — par. 70 *a* and *b.*   Either Motive 3 of Exercise 19*B* may be used, or an original one of similar stately character.

DISTINCTIONS OF "STYLE" IN THE INVENTION.

72. Distinctions of *Style* are necessarily less definite in polyphonic than in homophonic composition; not only because Polyphony is, in itself, so characteristic a "style" as to counteract the assumption of other specific style-distinctions, to a large degree; but also because the peculiar restrictions of polyphonic writing render it difficult to realize all the essential details of certain (especially the conventional) styles.

But the *broader* distinctions of style may, nevertheless, be exhibited definitely enough in an Invention (or any other polyphonic form for at least three voices), as far as these distinctions rest upon the choice of *tempo, mode, rhythmic character,* and similar general qualities; or upon the *melodic character of the Motive;* and it is therefore entirely feasible, as it is desirable, to distinguish at least three broad divisions of polyphonic style, namely:

a. The **Light** or Spirited style (with its kindred qualifications, *sprightly, joyous, vigorous, brilliant, capricious, flowing,* etc.).   The chief characteristics of these species are a comparatively brief Motive, of lively, flowing, gay, or rhythmically capricious (distinctly individualized) character; fairly rapid tempo; probably (though by no means certainly) the major mode; and general brightness and vivacity of expression.

For example: **Bach,** 3-voice Inventions, Nos. 8, 6, 1, 10, 14, 15; Well-temp. Clavichord, Vol. II, Prelude 5.

b. The **Serious** style (with its kindred qualifications, *grave, somber, stately, pathetic,* etc.), characterized mainly by a Motive of stately or even heavy character, generally brief; quiet or moderately slow tempo; generally the minor, though not infrequently the major, mode; and subdued, dignified expression.

For example: **Bach,** 3-voice Inventions, Nos. 4, 9, 13; Well-temp. Clavichord, Vol. I, Prelude 18; Vol. II, Preludes 9 and 17.

c. The **Lyric** (melodious) style; characterized by a M. of distinctly melodious nature, and generally of considerable length, — often in regular (4-measure) Phrase-form; graceful, flowing tempo; major or minor mode indifferently; and unusual definiteness of structural design.

For illustration: **Bach,** 3-voice Inventions, Nos. 7, 12, 3, 2 (the last-named is to be thoroughly analyzed; it is largely episodic); Well-temp. Clavichord, Vol. II, Prelude 4.

d. Another, scarcely less genuine, variety of the Lyric class, is distinguished by a *brief Motive*, or simple thematic Figure, out of which (1) the broader lyric sentences are sometimes constructed, by sequential combination; or which (2) enters still more incidentally into the lyric texture, apparently as a mere figural accompaniment (or auxiliary Figure) derived from the successive *harmonies* that underlie the principal melodic lines.

This is clearly illustrated in **Bach,** 3-voice Invention, No. 11, which is to be carefully analyzed; the thematic Figure of four (or five) notes stands at the beginning of the principal melodic part, but its connection with the latter is thereafter, almost constantly, purely incidental; the lyric sentences are *built upon,* not *derived thematically from,* this Figure. The character of this Invention is distinctly lyric; its form is Sectional.

See further, briefly: **Bach,** Well-temp. Clavichord, Vol. I, Preludes 9 and 17; Vol. II, Prelude 21.

e. These distinctions of Style must be adopted and applied in a very general sense only. It is as impracticable as it is obviously undesirable, to coerce a polyphonic composition into such definite agreement with the essential conditions of "Style" as is found in some free homophonic structures. Consequently, even the analytic definition will often be found doubtful and difficult, because the related phases overlap so widely that both styles may be distinctly represented in the same composition; a lyric Invention may incline toward either the light or the serious style; and even these extremes may touch, — a serious Invention may contain vivacious episodes, and vice versa.

Furthermore, the number of parts employed influences the style to a certain extent; two-voice texture is most appropriate for the Light styles, three-voice for the Lyric, and four- (or more) voice for the Serious. Examples in two-voice texture have been cited in pars. 51 and 53. *Three-voice* texture is the only kind that may be adapted to all three styles.

Finally, in an Invention expressly designed to represent one or another of these styles, the *episodic passages* are apt to predominate somewhat, both in extent and character; for the relief from strict thematic treatment which they afford contributes to the realization of the specific purposes involved. And, in general, the structural (formal) details advance proportionately in significance, and are defined more distinctly than in the more neutral varieties of polyphonic development. Compare pars. 45 and 53.

Exceptional Species of the Invention.

73. *a.* The Invention in **Contrary motion** ("per moto contrario"). In this species the Motive appears throughout in nearly, or quite, *regularly alternating* original motion and Contrary motion.

See **Bach,** *Prelude* of the "Preludio con fughetta" for Clavichord, in *e* minor (Peters ed. 200, No. 7). The *thematic* texture is exclusively two-voice, but an auxiliary third part is frequently introduced. — **Bach,** Organ Comp. (Peters ed.), Vol. VII, No. 58, measures 1–7, 11–18, 22–28; in measures 32–40 a similar association of the original M. with its *Diminution* and Contrary motion is effected.

b. The Invention with an **Independent Lower part.** The thematic manipulation is restricted, largely or wholly, to the inner and upper parts; and the Bass *accompanies* these, chiefly as an auxiliary contrapuntal associate. The latter may (1) be based upon some more or less characteristic figure, usually reiterated regularly, as in *harmonic figuration;* or (2) it may be a *Running part,* in a uniform rhythm of two (or more) notes to each beat.

The first species is most common in Organ music; the peculiar difficulties and limitations of Pedal-technique render it often expedient to assign certain adapted figures to the Pedal-part, either quite independent of the Motive, or as a modified (simplified) form of the latter.

In either case it is absolutely necessary to preserve a certain (if not constant) *uniformity of melodic delineation* in the independent Bass; especially when it is a running part, which must be prevented from deteriorating into a "rambling" part by consistency of formation, — i.e., by frequent *recurrences,* sequential or otherwise, of the leading figures. Review par. 17*c.* For example:

Ex.
119.

*1) The Pedal-part is based upon this independent M. throughout.

*2) Here the Pedal has, *constantly*, a simplified form of the first member of the principal Motive. For further illustration:

See **Bach,** 3-voice Invention No. 5; there are several brief thematic figures, the principal one of which is first announced in the upper part (one measure long); the form is Sectional, the style Lyric; during the last $8\frac{1}{2}$ measures, the inner part corresponds exactly to the upper part of the First Section. The Bass is an independent auxiliary part throughout, in uniform harmonic Figuration.

Bach, Well-temp. Clavichord, Vol. I, Prelude 24; the Bass is an auxiliary running part in 8th-notes, with two or three brief interruptions; the consistency of its formation is noteworthy; the M. of the two other voices is one measure long, first announced in the inner part, and imitated mostly in stretto; in Part II the original M. is abandoned, and in its place the modified *Diminution* is adopted as thematic basis, resulting in greater rhythmic animation throughout the Part.

Bach, 30 Var. for the Clav. in *G* major; Var. 2.

Bach, Organ Compositions (Peters compl. ed.), Vol. I, Sonata No. IV, 1st movement; the form embraces 3 Sections, with Coda, and an independent Introduction; the M. is 6 measures long, first announced in the inner part; the Pedal-part (Bass) is entirely independent of the thematic voices; Section 3 (measure 25 from end) is wholly episodic, but corroborative of the foregoing Sections.

The same Sonata, 2nd movement; Pedal entirely independent; design embraces 9 brief Sections; principal M. of two measures, announced by the upper part, carried through first 2 Sections (measures 1–11); an auxiliary M., one-half measure in length, is adopted as sole basis of Section 3 and (in Contrary motion) of Section 4; Section 5 (measures 22, 23) is episodic; the remainder is practically a reproduction of the foregoing, transposed, — Sections 6, 7, and 8 corresponding closely to 2, 3, and 4, extended by a 9th Section based on the principal Motive (last $5\frac{1}{2}$ measures).

The same Sonata, 3rd movement; 4 Sections and repeated Codetta; M. 8 measures; the Pedal takes the M. twice, — as regular third announcement (measures 21–27), and again near the end, — in a *simplified form*, convenient for pedal-technique' otherwise the Bass is independent.

Bach, same Volume, Sonata No. I, last movement; 2-Part Song-form, "Gigue"-species; the Pedal has occasional fragments of the M., but is chiefly independent; Part II, after 15 measures devoted to the exposition of the Contrary motion, corresponds to the latter portion of Part I, but transposed, and with inverted voices (par. 58).

The same Sonata, first movement; 2-Part Song-form, closely corresponding structure; M. 1½ measures; the Pedal is independent, excepting a very few imperfect imitations of the principal figure of the Motive.

Mendelssohn, Pianoforte Capriccio, op. 5, middle Division (measures 135–290); M. 8 measures, upper voice; running Bass during Part I; M. in Contrary motion and running *upper* voice during Part II; after 28 measures (3 complete announcements) the M. appears in sequential succession, *each time contracted* more and more at the end (up to the *ff,* where another complete announcement is made); in Part III the original motion of the M., and the running Bass, are resumed.

Mendelssohn, *Prelude* (Pfte.), op. 35, No. 4; 3-Part Song-form; Part I, Double-Period with Codetta; Motive, 2 measures; Part II is based upon a *new* M. of 2 measures, in stretto Imitations, but also announces the principal M.; Part III like I, but abbreviated to Single Period with Codetta, and extended by a Period taken from Part II, and brief Coda; the Bass is a running auxiliary part throughout, and consists in strictly uniform harmonic Figuration.

EXERCISE 22.

A. Write a complete 3-voice Invention, with consideration of the essential conditions of the *Spirited Style* (par. 72a), and the *Serious Style* (par. 72b), as follows: Adopt the design of the 3-Part Song-form; develop the rapid M. during Parts I and III, and the stately M. during Part II; the second M. may be quite new (par. 48c), or it may be developed out of the first Motive by Augmentation (of a *portion* of the latter),— see par. 31a. This arrangement of movements reverses the rhythmic order given in par. 70a.

B. Write an Invention in the *Lyric Style,* according to par. 72c; mode, tempo, and form optional.

C. An Invention with a *Running Bass* (par. 73b).

D. An Invention for the Organ, with *Independent Pedal-part* (par. 73b).

CHAPTER VIII.

THE INVENTION FOR MORE THAN THREE VOICES.

74. As the number of polyphonic voices or parts is increased, the texture assumes a proportionately pronounced *harmonic* character; and the difficulty of preserving proper balance between the dissonances of friction, inevitable in the "independent conduct" of the parts, and the consonances indispensable to their "harmonious union," becomes more and more real and severe. Review par. 59, and par. 60.

Details of Four–Voice Polyphony.

75. *a.* As before, the sum of 4 parts may be successively accumulated by adding contrapuntally first a second voice, then a third, and finally the fourth voice, to the *leading part,* — in such order as appears most convenient, and generally in brief stages of about five or six beats at a time. Review, thoroughly, par. 61*b.*

b. Or, probably better and easier, the three other voices may be led more nearly, or exactly, abreast of the leading part, and of each other; their movements will then be controlled directly by the successive *harmonic structures,* or chords (i.e., the vertical clusters of essential tones, which are to represent the successive rhythmic pulses); and the vital condition of *voice-independence* must be satisfied at the same time by judiciously disguising these harmonic clusters. Review, thoroughly, par. 61*c.*

The choice between these two processes will probably be determined by individual disposition; some students will find the "cumulative" process easier, while others will prefer the "harmonic" one.

c. The importance of the *Tie,* and of *parallel movement in 3rds or 6ths* between two of the parts, is as great, here again, as in three-voice texture, and must not for an instant be lost sight of. Review, thoroughly, pars. 61 *d* and *e;* also par. 61 *f.*

d. The rules relative to the conduct of the *lowermost part,* to the *rhythmic conditions* of the polyphonic texture, and to the adoption of a **temporary leading part,** apply without modification also to the association of four contrapuntal parts. Review, thoroughly, pars. 62, 63, and 64; also the summary, par. 65. Especial care should be taken to avoid too great *density of texture.* To this end, it is wise to sustain the rhythm of at least one of the voices as much as possible, — as shown in Ex. 122 (Note *4); and, at all events, to avoid conducting all the parts together in (simultaneous) rapid rhythmic movement, or in any fashion that produces a "jumbled" rhythmic effect.

e. The condition which probably increases most in significance, in this fuller species of polyphonic writing, is that of the **Rest**; not only because the temporary cessation of one (or more) of the voices conduces to greater variety of volume, and to greater clearness of texture; but also because it facilitates, very materially, the manipulation of the whole. On the other hand, the indispensable discipline of strictly 4-voice Polyphony obliges the student (for a time, at least) to abstain from such frequent use of Rests, — especially protracted omission of one or another of the four parts, — as would reduce the present task to that of the 3-voice texture. Review, particularly, pars. 63*b* and 63c.

For illustration of the domination of the *harmonic* principle, and the methods of preserving voice-independence, etc.:

*1) Last tone of M. lengthened (par. 30*a*).

*2) Shifted rhythm (par. 31*c*).

*3) First tone of M. lengthened (par. 30*b*).

*4) Suspension.

*5) Parallel 6ths in upper, and 3rds in lower, voices (par. 61*e*).

*6) This line of Roman numerals indicates the harmonic basis; compare with par. 18 *a* to *c*.

*7) The Triad upon the Leading-tone (sometimes marked VII) is an abbreviated form of the Dominant 7th-chord.

*8) From the Well-temp. Clav., Vol. I, Prelude 7, measures 10–15; *the student is to continue the analysis,* up to measure 24.

*9) From the same Prelude, measures 36–38 ; *continue the analysis,* with extreme thoroughness and minuteness, to the end.

*10) The "chord-forms" are here indicated in letters, without regard to the accidentals (which are always determined by the key), or to the chord-names.

*11) All tones foreign to the prevailing chord-form are marked +; it will be observed that they invariably obey the law of inharmonic tones, and progress *conjunctly.* Compare par. 4*a*.

*12) These two beats illustrate admirably the fundamental rule of rhythmic relation of the voices (par. 65*f*).

Observe, also, how effectively the rhythmic movement of the other parts is restrained (by heavy notes) while one part is active.

*13) Indirect resolution of Suspension (Ex. 10).

*14) These beats illustrate a very effective *interaction of adjacent parts,* whereby one part appears to coöperate with its neighbor in furthering some melodic or thematic purpose of the latter ; in this instance the *descending scale* passes, without a check, from the Soprano into the Alto, and from that into the Tenor, describing a long and powerful line, and unifying the parts without impairing their independence. Compare Ex. 116, Note *5).

Analyze the following specimens of 4-part Polyphony ; very minutely, but only with reference to the *voice-conduct,* — not thematically :

Bach, Well-temp. Clav., Vol. I, Fugue 1, last 7 measures; Vol. I, Fugue 12, last 6 measures; Vol. I, Fugue 14, last 9 measures; Vol. I, Fugue 17, last 8 measures; Vol. I, Fugue 18, last 10 measures.

Bach, Well-temp. Clav., Vol. II, Fugue 5, measures 1–16; Vol. II, Fugue 9, measures 1–9; Vol. II, Fugue 23, measures 14–27.

THE FOUR–VOICE INVENTION.

76. Review par. 37. — When four polyphonic parts are used, they are always named Soprano, Alto, Tenor, and Bass, in analogy with the vocal quartet. Review par. 66*a*.

The structural designs are somewhat more limited, — in keeping with the other specific limitations of 4-voice Polyphony; hence, while any of the forms already enumerated may be adopted for the 4-voice Invention, the Sectional form is probably the most appropriate and effective.

The First Section, or Exposition.

77. *a.* The Motive must, as a rule, be brief, comparatively narrow in compass, and of quiet (or at least not too lively) rhythmic character. The following Motives are used by **Bach** for 4-part development:

See also Ex. 120, Nos. 1 and 2; and Ex. 122.

b. The first announcement of the M. may occur in any one of the four parts; and, as usual, one or two, or possibly all, of the other parts may supply *auxiliary* lines (either contrapuntal, or simply harmonic) until their turn comes to imitate the M. legitimately. Review par. 67 *a*, *b*, and *c*.

c. The order of Imitations at the beginning of a 4-voice Invention may be *regular;* i.e., each successive Imitation may appear in the part nearest (adjacent) to the preceding imitating voice; thus, after Soprano, in the Alto; after Bass, the Tenor; after Alto, either Soprano or Tenor; after Tenor, either Bass or Alto.

But this regularity of voice-succession is by no means necessary in the Invention, and the utmost freedom is exercised in the choice, both of the interval of Imitation, and of the voice in which the Motive is next to appear, — not only at the beginning, but through the entire Exposition.   Compare par. 67*d;* and see also par. 67*e.*

For illustration :

*1) Motive in Soprano; Alto and Tenor *tacent;* Bass auxiliary.

*2) Unessential modification of the M., corresponding to par. 33—(1), which see. This form recurs frequently, later on.

*3) Thus far the order of Imitation is regular, as concerns the part-succession, — Soprano, Alto, Tenor. In the following measure the M. appears again in the Alto, and during the next 3 (sketched) measures two other announcements are made, in upper parts, before the Bass announces its legitimate Imitation, in the 9th measure.

*4) Observe, here again, how carefully the inner parts are restrained in their rhythmic movement, by long notes, while the outer parts are active. The same disposition to preserve good balance of motion and to avoid "jumbled" rhythmic effects is evinced throughout. See Ex. 120, Note *12), second clause.

*5) From the *Prelude* of the "Preludio con Fughetta" in *d* minor, for the clavichord (Peters ed., 200, No. 6).

78. The remaining Sections of the 4-voice Invention are conducted in the usual manner. Review par. 68 ; and analyze the following Inventions, in sectional form, very diligently :

The remainder of Example 122.

Bach, English Suite No. I, "Prelude"; introductory cadenza of 2 measures ; M. given in Ex. 121, No. 3; Section I ends in measure 9, and is extended by a Codetta of 1½ measures; Section II closes in measure 16, followed by a similar Codetta ; Section III extends to 3rd measure from the end, and has the same Codetta, extended. (Compare last two measures with Well-temp. Clavichord, Vol. II, Prelude 19, end.) The texture is frequently 3-voice (compare par. 75*e*), and the register of the four parts is somewhat obscure, at times.

Bach, Toccata for Clavichord in *c* minor, measures 12–29; M. given in Ex. 121, No. 4. The rhythm is gradually accelerated.

Bach, Toccata for Clavichord in *f♯* minor, second tempo (3-2 time) ; M. chromatic, first announced in Soprano ; Bass has the M. once only, abbreviated.

Bach, Air with 30 Variations (Clavichord) ; Var. 16, second tempo (3-8 time) ; chiefly 3-voice texture.

Bach, Fantasia con Fuga in *a* minor (Clavichord), "Fantasia" (Peters ed. 208, No. 2) ; Section I, measures 1–12, is purely introductory, containing only allusions to the Motive; it is 5-voice texture, and harmonic in character, and recurs as Section IV (measures 31–42), transposed; recurs again, as Section VI (measures 69–80), transposed; and once more, as final Section (last 12 measures), as a nearly literal *da capo*. The M. is first announced in Section II (Soprano, measures 11–13, — given in Ex. 121, No. 2), and imitated, chiefly in stretto, during this and the next Section (to measure 31); in Sections V and VII (measures 42 and 80) the rhythm is more or less persistently animated, — somewhat after the manner of par. 70*a*.

Bach, Well-temp. Clavichord, Vol. I, Prelude 12; the M., 2 beats long, is announced by the Soprano, and then followed by a lyric extension (or episode) before an Imitation occurs, — in Tenor; the Bass is auxiliary, taking no evident part in the thematic announcements; the same is partly true of the Alto, also; there are three Sections, the last one containing (in measures 16–18) a fairly convincing indication of a return to the beginning, and thus imparting the impression of 3-Part Song-form (primary grade).

Bach, Well-temp. Clavichord, Vol. I, Prelude 4; M. one measure, Soprano part; the texture is largely 3-voice; there is a strong Dominant cadence in measure 14, which probably resolves the structure into a 2-Part Song-form (primary grade). The manipulation of this M. is extremely ingenious and instructive; unique *rhythmic* modifications, and the shifted rhythm, occur frequently; analyze carefully.

Bach, Toccata for Clavichord in *d* minor, measures 15–32; M. 3 beats, in Alto.

Bach, Fantasia con Imitazione, Peters ed. No. 216, Section II (¾ time); M. undergoes several modifications. Bach, Fantasia, Peters ed. 215, bottom of page 7 to page 10. Same volume, page 22, — first 4 measures introductory; M. in Alto, one measure. Bach, Fantasia, Peters ed. 1959, pages 94 to 97, — first 14 measures introductory. Same volume, pages 99–100 (C time).

Mendelssohn, *Var. sérieuses*, op. 54, Var. 10.

Bach, Organ Comp. (Peters compl. ed.), Vol. VIII, No. 8; independent **Bass** (par. 73*b*).

EXERCISE 23.

A. Write a 4-voice Invention, in brief sectional form, in minor; with an original Motive, patterned after those shown in Ex. 121. Especial reference must be made to par. 64 (Leading part); Ex. 122, Note *4) (sustained parts); par. 61*d* (Ties); par. 63 *b, c* (Rests). The Imitation in *Augmentation*, and also in *Diminution* (par. 31 *a, b*), are both available in 4-voice texture, and must not be neglected.

B. A 4-voice Invention, sectional form, in major.

OTHER STRUCTURAL DESIGNS.

79. Besides those in sectional form, occasional examples of the 4-voice Invention are found in the 2-Part or 3-Part Song-form. For example, see —

Bach, Air with 30 Variations (Clav.), Var. 4; M. of 3 notes, Soprano part; first Imitations in alternate original and contrary motion (compare par. 73*a*); definite 2-Part Song-form.

Same work, Var. 22; M. of 2 measures, first announced in Tenor, after 1½ introductory measures; definite 2-Part form.

Bach, English Suite No. I, "Allemande"; the M. of Part I is presented in a mode of notation peculiar to *keyboard*-instruments, and, as it represents harmonic *bulk* rather than individual tone-*lines*, scarcely justifiable in any other than these inferior grades of polyphonic writing; it appears thus, after 3 introductory beats,

and is imitated in this form without exception to the end of the Part; the Second Part has a *new* M., announced in Bass after two preliminary beats; the last 4 measures of the Parts correspond.

Beethoven, Variations, op. 120, Var. 24 (M. for each Part, somewhat free).

80. The fullness and weight of 4-voice Polyphony leave less opportunity for distinctions of *style* than were definable in 3-voice texture, and therefore the Serious or Stately style is almost the only consistent variety (par. *72b*).

a. But it is possible, by such use of *protracted rests* as will virtually reduce the texture to three voices, for a time at least, to realize the lyric, and even the moderately spirited styles. This is ingeniously illustrated in **Bach,** Clavichord Sonata (Peters ed. No. 213), No. I, " Gigue."

b. Another device, very common in the 4-voice Invention, and especially effective in the lyric style, is the adoption of a *brief thematic Figure*, which is carried through the several voices more as an incidental than as an essential motive, and merely enlivens what is actually a definite *harmonic* stratum. Compare par. *72d.* This was seen in **Bach,** Well-temp. Clavichord, Vol. I, Prelude 12, cited above.

See also **Bach,** Well-temp. Clavichord, Vol. II, Prelude 16; M. of 4 notes, announced at once in Soprano; its recurrences, often much modified, are recognizable more by the striking rhythm than by the melodic form; the first 3 Sections (4 measures each) are very similar.

Bach, Well-temp. Clavichord, Vol. I, Prelude 22; M. of 5 notes, Soprano, often extended by sequence, and at times contracted to 3 tones; 2-Part Song-form.

Bach, Well-temp. Clavichord, Vol. II, Prelude 1; the first $4\frac{1}{2}$ measures are an Introduction, containing only intimations of the M., which first appears in its legitimate form, in Bass, at the end of measure 5, where Part I begins; the texture is largely episodic; the design is 3-Part Song-form, with transposed Third Part (measures 20–29 corresponding closely to measures $4\frac{1}{2}$–$13\frac{1}{2}$, shifted one-half measure).

In organ music the association of three thematic parts with an *independent Bass* (pedal-part), as explained in par. *73b*, is effective and not uncommon, — especially in connection with the elaboration of a chorale melody (to be considered later on).

See **Bach,** Organ Compositions (Peters compl. ed.), Vol. V, Nos. 1, 14, 16, 38, 56, and others.

THE FIVE–VOICE INVENTION.

81. An Invention for 5 parts is naturally rare. When so elaborate a polyphonic apparatus is employed, it is mostly in the service of the higher grades of Polyphony. It is, however, easily possible to expand the 4-voice to an *ostensible* 5-voice texture, by the *occasional* addition of a 5th part, with entire freedom as regards register, though usually in thematic form. The M. should be brief, narrow in compass, and of ψuiet, if not heavy, rhythmic formation; the style will probably be lyric, or stately.

See **Bach,** Well-temp. Clavichord, Vol. II, Prelude 11; M. of 4 notes, Soprano, reproduced twice in same voice, in Contrary motion, before the regular Imitations begin. The design is genuine 3-Part Song-form; Part I ends in measure 16, and is followed by a complete *sequential reproduction*, before Part II appears (in measure 33). Texture largely 4-voice. *Analyze minutely.*

Bach, Organ Comp. (Peters compl. ed.), Vol. IV, No. 12. — Same Vol., No. 11, second Division (*Grave*); M. 2 measures, Soprano; observe, also, the frequent ascending scale-passage, in whole measures.

EXERCISE 24.

A. Write a 4-voice Invention in 2-Part Song-form; all details optional. Either an original Motive or one of the following may be used:

1. *Sosten.*

TENOR.

2. *Andante con moto.*

SOPRANO.

3. (Exercise 19.)

BASS.

B. A 4-voice Invention, in "Gigue"-form, moderately lively tempo, according to par. 80*a*.

C. A 4-voice Invention in Lyric or Serious style, with Incidental thematic Figure, according to par. 80*b*.

D. An Invention for 5 parts; form optional. Either the following or an original Motive:

Lento.

M.

M.

etc.

CHAPTER IX.

FREE POLYPHONIC FORMS. — THE INVENTION AS PRELUDE. — THE
FANTASIA, TOCCATA, ETC.

82. In a *genuine* Invention the principle of thematic Imitation prevails with little or no interruption; for though it represents the lower
grade of polyphonic writing (par. 37), it is nevertheless *Polyphony;* the
thematic development is of primary, the structural design of secondary,
importance. In Homophony this relation of qualities is reversed, —
the material subserves the Form.

But it is not always possible, or desirable, to separate these two
domains of musical thought absolutely, and many intermediate varieties
exist, in which a mixture (or the alternation) of the two ruling purposes
is exhibited. Thus, the Invention may very gradually deteriorate from
its original polyphonic rank, — as the thematic treatment becomes more
and more loose and free, and the episodic passages more extended and
independent, in the pursuit of some more and more marked *structural*
purpose, — until it becomes partly (at times totally) homophonic in
character and effect. And, on the other hand, a genuine homophonic
form may, by the interlineation of more or less assertive and extensive
imitatory passages, assume a partially (at times distinctly) polyphonic
character.

Examples of such intermediate grades have been quite frequently
cited in the preceding pages, and in some instances their classification
among the "Inventions" has been doubtful, — in exact proportion to
the increasing importance attached to all essentially structural (formal)
conditions. See, especially, pars. 45, 51, 53, 72, 80*b*.

It appears, therefore, that this primary division of the polyphonic
forms, for which the collective term "Invention" has been adopted,
embraces a number of subordinate varieties, inclining more or less positively toward the homophonic domain, and distinguished by certain
peculiarities of design or treatment.

THE PRELUDE.

83. As its name indicates, the Prelude was not, *originally*, a separate and independent composition, but always an adjunct of some

legitimate form (or of a collective set of pieces), in the inferior capacity of a preliminary or introductory movement.

The *inferiority of rank* thus involved is exhibited in many and vari-ous ways: either in looseness of form, or in freedom of technical detail, or both; in frequency, extent, and homophonic quality of episodes; in indifference to the number of parts,— the frequent employment of purely auxiliary tones or melodic fragments, and *free interchange of 2, 3, 4 (or more)-part texture;* or in a certain general superficiality and sketchiness of character, suggestive, in extreme cases, of a mere improvisation.

Such a form, consisting mainly in a free exposition of the principal harmonies of the key, perhaps with thematic allusions, may very appro-priately precede, and prepare the hearer for, the more definite design and thoughtful contents of the principal movement to follow.

The *degree* of inferiority depends mainly upon the function assigned to the Prelude; and likewise, while the species of texture (homophonic or polyphonic), and the general style (lyric, dramatic, brilliant, etc.), are almost entirely optional, they may be partly definable according to the character and quality of the principal movement with which the Prelude is connected.

a. The treatment of the Prelude is, as a rule, most serious when it precedes the **Fugue.** In this connection it is likely to be a genuine Invention, entirely (or largely) polyphonic. Generally it bears no other relation to its Fugue than that of *key;* — time, tempo, Motive, and character may be independent of the latter, though occasionally the M. of the Prelude is derived from the Subject of the Fugue.

The latter (thematic) coincidence does not appear in any of the 48 numbers of the Well-temp. Clavichord, excepting, perhaps, in Vol. I, No. 23 (*B* major), where a faint, probably accidental, resemblance between the first 4 notes of the Prelude and of the Fugue, may be traced. In the 6 numbers of **Mendelssohn's** op. 35, also, there is no thematic connection between Prelude and Fugue, save a brief coincidence in No. 4 (*Ab*). On the other hand, see **Rubinstein,** op. 53, where thematic connection is obvious between Prelude and Fugue in Nos. 1 and 6; and, more incidentally, in Nos. 3 and 4.

Generally the Prelude to a Fugue ends with a complete cadence on the Tonic, becoming thus a separate piece, virtually independent of its Fugue. In rare instances, however, especially when the Prelude is brief, and of a looser, more extemporaneous character, it closes with a *Dominant* semi-cadence, leading, as Introduction, into the Fugue.

See **Rubinstein,** op. 53, Nos. 1, 2, 4, and 6, — Dominant ending. In the Well-temp. Clavichord, and in op. 35 of **Mendelssohn,** the Preludes are independent.

The texture is distinctly polyphonic (i.e., *Invention*-species) in the following Preludes of the Well-temp. Clavichord, already analyzed: Vol. I, Nos. 4, 9, 12, 14, 18, 23, 24; Vol. II, Nos. 4, 5, 8, 10, 11, 19, 21, and 22; also No. 3, 2nd division.

The texture is of a less strict type, including more episodes, or definitely homophonic passages, in Well-temp. Clavichord, Vol. I, Nos. 17, 20; Vol. II, Nos. 9, 13, 17, 18. It is of a more general imitatory character (less definitely thematic) in Vol. I, No. 16; Vol. II, Nos. 1, 16. Prelude 11 of Vol. I is based upon *Sequence* rather than *Imitation*. For all of these the term *Prelude* (or Prelude-Invention) is more appropriate than " Invention " would be.

See also, **Bach,** Organ Comp. (Peters compl. ed.), Vol. II, Prael. 1; Invention, 3- to 4-voice, indep. Pedal, sectional.

Vol. II, Prael. 5; 2-Part Song-form.

Vol. II, Prael. 7; Invention, 4-voice, 2 motives (Pedal an indep., 3rd, motive).

Vol. II, Prael. 9; many motives, definite sectional form, ample confirmation, 4- to 5-voice.

Vol. II, Prael. 10; very similar to Prael. 9; 4-voice.

Vol. III, Prael. 1; long sectional form (ten Sections), free, but including genuine polyphonic texture (Secs. 5 and 8); confirmations, and Da capo.

Vol. III, Prael. 4; 3-Part Song-form.

Vol. III, Prael. 9; three divisions: Introduction, Invention (4-voice, 2 Sections), Transition into Fugue.

Vol. IV, Prael. 2; two motives, sectional.

Vol. IV, Prael. 3; three divisions: Prelude, Thematic section, Coda.

Mendelssohn, Organ Comp., op. 37, Prael. 1; Invention, elaborate thematic treatment; excellent illustration of *fragmentary* manipulation; 4-voice, long motive, sectional (quasi 3-Part Song-form).

Op. 37, Prael. 2; 3-Part Song-form, motive for each Part; distinctly thematic, but homophonic (lyric) *in character*.

Op. 37, Prael. 3; 4-voice, six Sections; a principal Theme with various counter-motives, in different (accelerated) rhythms.

b. The Lyric Invention, with a long, melodious Motive (pars. 53, 72c), belongs properly to the Prelude variety; and when the lyric purpose so overshadows the polyphonic that evidences of thematic imitation are faint, and incidental in effect, it becomes ultimately a **Prelude as Aria,** with, at most, occasional imitatory traits in the accompanying parts.

See **Bach,** Well-temp. Clavichord, Vol. II, Prelude 24, 14; Vol. I, Prelude 13, 8. The extreme limit of this design is touched in the following—almost distinctly homophonic—Preludes of the Well-temp. Clavichord: Vol. II, No. 12; Vol. I, No. 10 (with long Coda, as Toccata, — par. 84), No. 1 (simple chord-figuration); Vol. II, No. 3, first division (the same).

c. The **Chorale-Prelude** is an organ composition, designed to precede the congregational intonation of the opening chorale in the Lutheran and other Reformed church-services, chiefly in Germany. Hence its M. is derived recognizably from the first line of the chorale, and the treatment is usually distinctly, sometimes severely, imitatory, as in the Invention; though evidences of the freedom of design and treatment characteristic of the Prelude-species are seldom wanting, and sometimes so pronounced as to lower the Prelude to the rank of a mere Chorale-Fantasia, — especially in *practical* expositions, which are quite commonly actual polyphonic *improvisations*, i.e., made *extempore.*

Examples of this form will be cited in Chapter XI.

d. The Prelude as opening number of a **Suite** is more independent than any of the foregoing, and *may* be isolated, as well as any other number of the Suite. In this respect it resembles, and probably was the incentive to, the variety treated at *e* below.

It relates to the succeeding numbers of the Suite solely in point of *key;* and its texture may be selected, at option, from the whole range of Polyphony; very rarely, indeed, however, is it any more severe than the genuine Invention (**Bach,** English Suite No. I); most commonly it is of the looser fabric of the " Prelude "-species (as in **Bach,** English Suite No. VI, first 37 measures; **Bach,** Prelude to Suite, Peters ed. 214, pages 32, 33, — first 15 measures introductory); sometimes of a *general imitatory character,* without manifest thematic development (as in **Händel,** Suites Nos. V, VI, VIII; **Bach,** Sonata, Peters ed. 213, pages 4, 5; same volume, pages 20, 21); possibly still more nearly, or absolutely, homophonic (as in **Händel,** Suites Nos. I, III; **Bach,** Prelude to Suite, Peters ed. 214, pages 18, 19).

The Prelude as " Fantasia " is touched upon in par. 85.

e. The modern Prelude, as **isolated** piece. The propriety of the title Prelude is apparently cancelled by isolation, for its relation as " Prelude " to a subsequent movement is uncertain, if not utterly chimerical. But it is nevertheless possible to institute close analogy with the legitimate Prelude-form, by preserving such traits as distinguish the latter, or, at least, imply its origin in that early era of musical history which gave rise to the conventional Prelude. The modern isolated Prelude will therefore usually be found to exhibit some traces of this origin, in remnants of the polyphonic bearing of earlier centuries; in the presence of certain scholastic details which suggest (if they do not constitute) " imitation," " contrapuntal treatment," or other distinctive traits of the traditional Prelude; particularly in the absence of that dominating *romantic* expression, significant of the modern conception of music.   For example :

Mendelssohn, 3 Praeludien, op. 104 (No. 1, thematic, contrapuntal, but free, and not imitatory; No. 2, running parts; No. 3, elaborate figuration, quasi thematic).
Rubinstein, 6 Préludes, op. 24 (No. 1, elaborate running inner part; No. 2, already cited, Invention; No. 3, imitatory,—at times almost canonic; No. 4, Toccata; No. 5, elaborate figuration; No. 6, imitatory).
Beethoven, Praeludium in *f* minor (Peters ed. 142); thematic, quasi Invention.
Chopin, Prélude, op. 45; elaborate figuration.
Bach, Praeludium, Peters ed. 1959, page 67 (Invention).
Schumann, Praeludium, op. 99, No. 10; elaborate figuration.
Bach, Organ Compositions, Vol. VIII, No. 11.

Further, the title "Preludes" has been assigned by several modern writers to a series of 24 pieces in each of the 24 major and minor keys, partly in analogy with the design of **Bach's** Well-temp. Clavichord; and also partly because this device supplies the pianist with a piece (presumably brief, and either extemporaneous and sketchy in character, or of the traditional "prelude" consistency) in every key, and therefore *actually available*, if desired, as preliminary sentence to any number upon a concert-program,—as far as the relation of key is concerned.

This is the modulatory disposition of the 24 Préludes of **Chopin,** op. 28, several of which exhibit, furthermore, certain scholastic traits (Nos. 1, 3, 4, 5, 8, 12, 14, 15 —the persistent reiteration of $a^b = g\sharp$,—19, 21), while others are brief or extemporaneous (Nos. 2, 6, 7, 9, 10, 11, 16, 18, 20, 22, 23); and others, again, are lyric and definite enough in design to merit a more significant title (Nos. 13, 15, 17, 21, 24). See further:
Heller, 24 Praeludien, op. 81 (brief, rhapsodical, and extremely loose in respect of formal design,—with but few exceptions). **Heller,** 32 Praeludien, op. 119 (certain keys represented twice, or oftener). **Hummel,** 24 Préludes, op. 67 (all brief, and distinctly extemporaneous in design and effect).
Further: 2 Praeludien by **Beethoven,** op. 39 (Peters ed. 142); each is a modulatory study, the design being to describe the complete circuit of major keys, twice; —both are thematic, the first one (cited above) more definitely imitatory than the second.

The Toccata.

84. This is one of the earliest forms of instrumental music, and derived its name from the primitive mechanical act of manipulating the keyboard (*toccare*, to touch).   Originating thus, long before instrumental music had assumed any of its present definite structural designs, the early Toccata was a formless succession of figures and runs, some-

times purely harmonic, again imitatory and contrapuntal, often incoherent and indefinable.   It was the legitimate forerunner of the
Fantasia, but has retained its own title to the present day, and has
gradually developed into a somewhat more definite and characteristic
style, the basis of which is *the manipulation of a small Motive, or mere
brief Figure*, usually of but two or three notes,— possibly strictly polyphonic, as in the genuine Invention, — much more commonly, however,
only partly polyphonic, or even purely homophonic; generally in lively,
vigorous tempo.

  a. The Toccata as single movement:

  The Toccata as Invention is exemplified in **Bach,** Well-temp. Clavichord, Vol. I,
Prelude 22 (already cited); Vol. I, Prelude 15; Vol. II, Preludes 2, 6, 15, 23, and 7
(the last more graceful than the ordinary Toccata).   **Bach,** English Suite No. III,
" Prelude" (Figure of 3 tones, uppermost part; texture variable, from one to five
parts; broad sectional design, — par. 68*c*, — with *da capo*).
  Bach, Toccata con Fuga, Peters ed. 211, page 4, *Allegro moderato.*
  Bach, Organ Comp. (Peters ed.), Vol. III, No. 2, " Toccata"; No. 3, " Toccata"
(approaching the Prelude-species).
  It assumes the looser Prelude consistency in **Bach,** Well-temp. Clavichord, Vol. I,
Preludes 2, 5, 6, and 21 ; Vol. II, Prelude 3, first 24 measures.   **Bach,** Preludio con
Fuga, Peters ed. 211, pages 14–21 (two Motives, in close succession) ; same volume,
pages 28–31, *Allegro.*   **Bach,** Preludio con Fuga, Peters ed. 214, pages 4, 5 ; same
volume, pages 10, 11.   **Bach,** Toccata, Peters ed. 215, pages 19–21.   **Bach,** Organ
Comp., Vol. II, Prael. 2 ; Prael. 3 ; and Prael. 8. Vol. III, Prael. 5, and Prael. 7. Vol.
IV, No. 4, " Toccata" (encloses the Fugue, quasi as Prelude and Postlude).
  See further, **Schumann,** Toccata for Pianoforte, op. 7 (largely homophonic,
but with occasional Imitatory, and even distinctly thematic, passages).   Of kindred
texture and character is the last movement of **Beethoven's** Pianoforte Sonata, op.
54; and even the Finale of his Sonata, op. 26, might be called a Toccata.
  It is left to the student to inspect such other examples of the Toccata, both
homophonic and polyphonic, as he may find in published literature for Pianoforte or
Organ.

  b. The Toccata sometimes appears as *collective* form, of three, four,
and even more distinct divisions, or movements.   In this broader and
more elaborate design it usually comprises as many distinctions of style
as there are divisions, and is therefore a composite of Invention, Prelude, Toccata, Fantasia, — very frequently including also the higher
Fugue-species, — in apparently optional succession.

  See **Bach,** Toccata for Clavichord in *e* minor (Peters ed. 210, No. 1), three brief,
totally independent sections, the 2nd (¾, *Allegro*) a Double Fughetta, to be considered later; a Fugue follows, to which the Toccata may be considered to be a
" Prelude."   **Bach,** Toccata in *f♯* minor (Peters ed. 210, No. 2), four different, but

kindred, divisions: I, an introductory "Toccata"; II, a 4-voice Invention; III, a Fugue, connected with IV, a Double Fugue, by a curious sequential Interlude of 31 measures.   **Bach,** Toccata in *c* minor (Peters ed. 210, No. 3), very similar: Movement I, an introductory "Toccata"; II, a 4-voice Invention; III, a Fugue, connected by a brief Interlude with IV, a Double Fugue, followed by brief Coda.   **Bach,** Toccata in *d* minor (Peters ed. 210, No. 4), three divisions: I, a brief introductory "Toccata"; II, 4-voice Invention; III, Double Fugue, followed by a Coda.   **Bach,** Toccata con Fuga in *g* minor (Peters ed. 211, No. 1), four divisions: I, introductory Cadenza, three measures; II, Aria, 12 measures; III, an Invention, 2- to 4-voice; IV, a Postlude, 11 measures.   The "Fuga" which follows is entirely independent of the Toccata, excepting in key.   **Bach,** Toccata in *G* major (Peters ed. 215, No. 3), three movements: I, Toccata; II, 4-voice Invention; III, Fugue.   **Bach,** Organ Comp., Vol. III, No. 8, "Toccata"; four divisions (31 measures introductory Cadenzas).

THE FANTASIA.

85. This is of still less definite and definable form and consistence than the Toccata, though in many respects closely connected with the latter in origin and character.   It is, as its name indicates, a fanciful combination of tone-effects.   Irregularity of design, freedom of melodic and rhythmic treatment, and generally incoherent character, are therefore almost essential conditions of the species; at the same time, the domination of a central tonality, occasional concurrences of style (corroboration of former sections), and the evidences of at least a broadly consistent progressive design, cannot be wholly dispensed with.

The texture of the Fantasia, as a whole, is more likely to be homophonic than polyphonic, though the latter style is frequently adopted for certain sections, — probably in unconscious imitation of the technical conditions under which, centuries ago, the Fantasia came into existence.

For illustrations see **Bach,** Fantasia for Clavichord in *c* minor (Peters ed. 212, No. 1), already cited, as 2-voice "Invention."   **Bach,** Chromatic Fantasia, *d* minor (followed by a Fugue).   **Bach,** Fantasia in *g* minor (Peters ed. 215, No. 5), introductory Cadenza, 2 measures,—the rest a strictly polyphonic "Invention" in double counterpoint, to be analyzed later.   **Bach,** Fantasia e Fuga (Peters ed. 1959, page 80, 21 measures) ; same volume, pages 84, 85, — quasi "Toccata."   **Bach,** Clavichord Sonata (Peters ed. 213, No. 3), first movement; this bears no other title than the tempo-mark, *Adagio,* but it is a "lyric Fantasia," quasi "Aria."   **Händel,** Clavichord Suite No. 1, " Prelude,"—clearly Fantasia in consistency.   **Bach,** Fantasia con Fuga in *a* minor (Peters ed. 208, No. 2), already cited, as "Invention."   **Bach,** Organ Comp., Vol. III, No. 6, " Fantasia"; 4-voice Invention, or rather, Invention-group, 2 Motives, for successive Sections; treatment serious and strict; form very definite. Vol. III, Prael. 10; Vol. IV, Prael. 1; and Prael. 5.   Vol. II, No. 4, "Fantasia" (elaborate).

The Fantasia as more elaborate collective form,—like the broad Toccata,—is illustrated in the following :

Bach, Fantasia con Fuga in *D* (Peters ed. 211, No. 3) ; five movements, viz., Introduction, Toccata, Interlude (similar to Introduction), Double Invention, Postlude (similar to I and III),—followed by a Fugue. **Bach,** Fantasia in *a* minor (Peters ed. 215, No. 1) ; three movements,—Toccata, Invention, Toccata (similar to I). **Bach,** Fantasia con Imitazione (Peters ed. 216, No. 7) ; two movements, — Introduction and Invention. **Bach,** Organ Comp., Vol. IV, No. 11 ; three movements (the *" Grave"* already cited as 5-voice Invention).

General reference may also be made to the more modern, and almost wholly homophonic, Fantasias : **Mozart,** Pianoforte Fantasia (followed by a complete Sonata) in *c* minor (Cotta ed. No. 18) ; **Mozart,** Fantasia for Pianoforte in *d* minor (Cotta ed. No. 23) ; ditto in *c* minor (Cotta ed. No. 24) ; ditto in *C* major (Cotta ed. No. 25),—followed by a Fugue. **Mendelssohn,** op. 15.

MIXED FORMS, OF A GENERAL IMITATORY CHARACTER.

86. Finally, there is a very numerous class of musical forms which are neither definitely homophonic nor polyphonic, but a mixture of both ; partaking of the characteristics of the Invention, the Prelude, and the Fantasia, though not strictly to be classified as any of these.

Such mixed forms rest upon a *homophonic* basis, and therefore exhibit distinct harmonic and melodic traits, and, generally, well-defined form. The polyphonic elements are exhibited, side by side with these, and more or less sparingly, in *incidental imitations*, or a *general imitatory bearing*, quite different from that continuous thematic development of which Imitation is an essential factor,—the essential condition of the genuine Invention, as has been seen, and, in a higher degree, of the Fugue and Canon, as remains to be seen.

Many of the examples cited above, under the head of the Prelude, Toccata, or Fantasia, belong properly to this mixed class, though designated thus definitely by their authors, and, usually, approaching most nearly in general design the character of the form in question.

The most characteristic examples are to be found in some of the " Allemandes " and " Courantes " (more rarely in the " Bourrées," " Gavottes," " Minuets," and kindred dances) of the French and English Suites, and clavichord Partitas, of Bach. In these the " melody" is usually continuous, and sometimes as distinct as in purely homophonic writing ; the harmonic successions are everywhere clearly apparent, and the design is almost always regular. But fragments of *incidental* imitation are frequently introduced ; or, at least, the general impression of contrapuntal texture (partial voice-independence) is sustained, — despite the entire freedom exercised with regard to the number of parts employed, and the use of auxiliary tones.

See particularly, **Bach,** Clavichord Partita III, " Allemande " (decidedly polyphonic in general effect, though no evidences of systematic imitation exist) ; same

Partita, "Courante," "Sarabande," and "Burlesca." **Bach,** Partita IV, "Allemande" (quasi *Aria*); "Courante" (quasi *Invention*, — M. in contrary motion during a portion of Part II); "Aria" (general voice-independence, but little evidence of even incidental imitation, — the same is true of the following "Sarabande" and "Menuet"). **Bach,** Partita V, "Allemande" (quasi *Invention*; the M. evades strict definition, being rather of a rhythmic than melodic consistency). **Bach,** Partita I, "Allemande" (quasi *Toccata*, — occasional incidental imitations); "Courante" (quasi *Invention*, M. of one measure, in upper part, chiefly in sequential succession). **Bach,** Partita II, "Allemande," is a genuine *Invention*, already cited; the following "Courante" is quasi *Invention*, but the imitation is more incidental than essential; "Sarabande," — incidental imitations, chiefly in 2nd Part.

Bach, English Suite No. I, "Courante I" (a few faint traces of thematic imitation, and considerable incidental imitation; the form is unusually regular and definite, the melody of measures 4 and 8 being similar, in both Parts; the voice-texture is treated with great freedom). **Bach,** English Suite No. III, "Courante," — excellent example of incidental imitation, and general voice-independence, without a trace of *thematic* development. **Bach,** English Suite VI, "Allemande"; and the "Double" of the "Sarabande." **Bach,** French Suite I, "Allemande" and "Courante"; "Sarabande" (the first 5 measures of Soprano, in Part I, become the Bass in Part II, and again Soprano, 4 measures later); "Menuet I," similar. **Bach,** French Suite V, "Bourrée II"; French Suite VI, "Courante."

Händel, Suite for Clavichord No. I, "Allemande" and "Courante"; the texture is quite regular (3-voice, occasionally 4), but it is only of a general imitatory character, not definitely thematic. **Händel,** Suite III, "Allemande" and "Courante"; Suite IV, "Allemande" and "Courante"; Suite V, "Prelude," "Largo," and "Gigue." And so forth; the majority of **Händel's** clavichord pieces, excepting the Fugues, are replete with *incidental* imitations, but not strictly thematic.

Scarlatti (Peters ed. No. 277), Suite No. I, "Preludio," "Sarabande"; Suite II, "Courante," "Scherzo" (quasi *Invention*); Suite III, "Courante" (quasi *Invention*, several Motives, Large 2-Part form).

Mendelssohn, op. 7, No. 1, No. 2 (Nos. 4 and 7, — see par. 87), No. 6.

Mendelssohn, *Var. sérieuses,* op. 54, Var. 2, Var. 3, Var. 4 (quasi *Invention*). Also, Variations, op. 83, Var. 2.

Schumann, Jugend-Album, op. 68, No. 40 ("*Kleine Fuge*"), first 22 measures (quasi 3-voice Invention).

D'Albert, Pianoforte Suite, op. 1, "Allemande," "Sarabande," "Courante."

Brahms, op. 76, No. 8.

Arthur Foote, op. 45, No. 1, Invention; 2-voice; 3-Part form.

HOMOPHONIC FORMS WITH POLYPHONIC EPISODES.

87. A mixture of the polyphonic and homophonic styles, of still another kind, is obtained by introducing brief thematic imitations, or complete thematic sections, into a composition of distinctly homophonic character and otherwise unalloyed homophonic texture.

Such incidental polyphonic episodes may occur in the *course* of a homophonic design (as, for instance, during the Second Part of the Three-Part Song-form); or the form may *begin*, like an Invention, with genuine thematic imitations, which extend for a few measures and then gradually (or even abruptly) relax and yield to pronounced homophonic treatment; or, more rarely, the polyphonic texture may be adopted near the *end*, as a means of promoting interest or creating a climax, — or as basis of the Codetta. For illustration:

Beethoven, Pianoforte Sonata, op. 2, No. 1, "Trio" of the Menuetto (thematic throughout, quasi *Invention* of the "Prelude" consistency). Sonata, op. 2, No. 2, Finale, first 16 measures (a 3-Part form, in which Part II, measures 9–12, is imitatory). Sonata, op. 2, No. 3, Scherzo (thematic throughout, quasi *Invention*, "Prelude"-species). Sonata, op. 10, No. 2, Allegretto, measures 9–30 (Parts II and III, imitatory). Same Sonata, Finale, entire; broad 3-Part form, quasi *Invention* with homophonic episodes; thematic imitation almost constantly, but within the definite limits of a homophonic design. Sonata, op. 10, No. 3, Menuetto, Part II. Sonata, op. 22, Adagio, measures 34–45. Sonata, op. 27, No. 1, Finale, measures 106–131 (thematic imitation). Sonata, op. 28, Finale, measures 29–35; and measures 79–101 (thematic, M. of 4 measures, upper part). Sonata, op. 54, Finale, first 28 measures. Sonata, op. 109, Finale, Variation IV and Variation V. **Beethoven,** Variations, op. 35, Var. V, 2nd Part; Var. VI, 2nd Part. Variations, op. 120, Vars. IV, V, VI, IX, XI, XIV, XXX (portions of each). Variations in *A* (Righini-Theme), Var. VII, — 2-Part form, new Motive for Part II; Var. XXI, 2nd Part.

Mendelssohn, op. 7, No. 4 (partly thematic, almost throughout); op. 7, No. 7 (general imitatory character); op. 14, Principal Theme of Rondo; Prelude, op. 35, No. 3 (quasi Toccata, practically homophonic, but with numerous imitatory episodes). Organ Sonata, cp. 65, No. 5, Finale (Secs. I, III, and V are based upon a Motive of two measures; Secs. II and IV upon a new Theme, longer, and lyric, with more animated accompaniment). — See also, again, op. 37, No. 2.

ADDITIONAL MISCELLANEOUS EXAMPLES.

Schumann, *Papillons,* op. 2: No. 3; No. 9, Second Part.

Schumann, *Intermezzi,* op. 4: No. 1, measures 3–7, measures 17–24; No. 5, "Alternativo," imitatory throughout, with harmonic accompaniment (in figural form in Part III).

Schumann, *Symphonic Études,* op. 13: No. 1, measures 1–8; No. 8, thematic Imitation throughout (quasi 4-voice); No. 12, measure 37 ("animato") to 75, thematic Imitation, partly 2 Motives.

Schumann, *Waldscenen,* op. 82, No. IV; also No. III.

Schumann, *Kreisleriana,* op. 16, No. 5, measures 5–14.

Schumann, *Novellette,* op. 21, No. 1 (5-flat signature).

Schumann, *Romanzen,* op. 28, No. 3, measures 1–24; also "Intermezzo I," thematic Imitation throughout, quasi 4-voice.

Schumann, *Gigue,* op. 32, No. 2, 3-voice Invention, sectional.

Chopin, *Mazurka,* No. 32 (op. 50, No. 3), measures 1–9, 33–41.

Chopin, *Mazurka,* No. 41 (op. 63, No. 3), measures 1–10 from end.

Chopin, *Ballade,* No. 4 (op. 52), measures 134 (cadenza) to 145.

Chopin, *Scherzo,* No. 3 (op. 39), measures 59–98; Motive in Bass, measures 59–66, and repeated, in octaves; Imitation in inner voice, measures 75–82, and measures 83–90.

Chopin, *Étude,* op. 25, No. 11; the Motive (measures 1–2) pervades the entire Étude, with figural accompaniment; not strictly Invention, but *thematic,* and generally polyphonic.

Schubert, Pianoforte Sonata, op. 143, principal theme of the Finale.

EXERCISE 25.

A. Write two examples of the *Prelude* as Invention (minor and major, respectively), according to the general explanation given in par. 83, and with reference also to par. 86.

B. An example of the *Toccata* (in one or two movements), according to par. 84.

C. An example of the *Fantasia* (par. 85).

D. Two or more examples of the *homophonic Three-Part Song-form,* with imitatory episodes as indicated in par. 87. Use a different mode, different measure, and different style (par. 72) for each.

DIVISION THREE.

CHORALE-FIGURATION.

INTRODUCTORY.

88. The contrapuntal elaboration of the **Chorale** (the characteristic representative of German ecclesiastic song since the days of the Reformation) has always been regarded by serious German masters of the past three centuries as a most important and truly indispensable part of the academic discipline of the composer; and, while a portion of this conception may be due to religious enthusiasm, it is nevertheless a just and wise pedagogic view. There is, unquestionably, no field of contrapuntal training so reliable and wholesome, so stimulating to the determined student whose aims are serious and genuine, and, best of all, so many-sided and inexhaustible, as "polyphonic Chorale-elaboration," — or "Chorale-Figuration," as it is more commonly called.

For this reason, although its immediate practical utility may not be apparent (as available "composition"), its *very thorough* and conscientious exercise is warmly urged upon the student; particularly upon him who desires to master the Fugue and Canon, — forms which cannot (as a rule) be successfully realized with the comparatively limited contrapuntal technique that will have been acquired through the exercise of the Inventions only.   Chorale-figuration affords precisely the quality and degree of *supplementary technical discipline* required for the proper achievement of these higher polyphonic forms.

89. Chorale-elaborations are divided, according to their magnitude, and certain distinctions of treatment, into two classes known as the **Small Species** and **Large Species.**

CHAPTER X.

The Small Species of Chorale–Figuration.

90. In the small species the adopted chorale melody (called the **cantus firmus**) is placed in the uppermost part, as regular Soprano, and in its original metric condition, without extensions or interruptions. The exercises are to be written for the Organ, and therefore the lowermost part is for the Pedal keyboard, while the upper three parts are placed on two staves for the Manual keyboard (generally one, possibly two).

The student who is unfamiliar with the technique of the Organ must first obtain at least a general insight into the treatment of the Manuals and Pedals, before undertaking the present tasks.   The only information that can be given here is, that the compass of the pedals is, generally, as follows: and that the tones of two adjacent manual-parts should always be well within reach of one hand.

Elaborate Harmonization.

91. As the basis of this species of polyphonic texture is again mainly *harmonic* (see par. 75*b*), the student had best begin with experiments of a specifically harmonic nature, and make a number of chorale harmonizations, as ingeniously as possible and elaborately as desired, in ordinary 4-part writing (with or without Pedal-bass), after the manner of the following :

Bach, Organ Comp. (Peters compl. ed.), Vol. V, No. 36 (*analyze thoroughly*) end of No. 53; page 60, I; page 68, I; page 76; page 105. — Further, Vol. V, No.

27. — Vol. VI, No. 26 (5-voice). — Vol. VII, No. 53 (chorale melody extended by rests before and between the lines; imitatory, but not thematic).

THEMATIC ACCOMPANIMENT.

92. The number of parts ordinarily employed is four: the *cantus firmus*, two inner parts, and the Pedal bass.

a. The three lower (accompanying) parts — including the Pedal — are to be thematic; that is, *a Motive (or brief Figure of one or two beats) is adopted, and imitated in the usual manner, as contrapuntal harmonization, or Figuration, of the given chorale.* The cantus may be written in ♩-notes, with a thematic figure (below) in ♪-notes; or in ♩-notes, with figure in ♪ or ♪-notes. Or, these values *dotted* (⁶⁄₈ or ¹²⁄₈ time).

For illustration (beginning of a chorale):

*1) C. F. — the *cantus firmus*, or given chorale melody.

*2) The Motive, or thematic figure. In this instance it is only one beat long; in the next version it is a genuine "Motive," two beats in length.

*3) Imitation in contrary motion. Every conceivable device of Imitation may be freely used, in this polyphonic task.

*4) Or an 8ve lower; the Pedal-bass is generally kept fairly low, though it may cross the Tenor occasionally, without objection. See also Ex. 129.

b. The usual *harmonic* process must be pursued, more or less insistently, in defining the chord-basis of each beat or tone of the *cantus firmus;* but the *effect of the accompanying (figural) voices must be thoroughly polyphonic.*

Much liberty may be taken with the adopted Motive; as a rule, it should be present constantly, in some part, in some shape or other, — Ex. 124, Note *3); though it may, briefly, be replaced by episodic fragments, either derived from the M., or independent.

It is not necessary to have a separate chord for each tone of the *c. f.* The same chord may be held through two successive tones, or more; or the harmony may change within one *c. f.* tone. Modulations, both diatonic and chromatic, must be freely made, and may be as swift as is compatible with perfect smoothness.

The Pedal-part should be kept somewhat more quiet (sustained) than the inner parts. See also Ex. 124, Note *4).

The end of each "Line" of the chorale is designated by a ⌒; this, however, merely serves to mark the lines, *and is not to be respected,* in the Small species, — no check of the rhythmic movement is to occur, anywhere. At the same time, these final tones (⌒) should produce a certain cadential impression, and therefore they should, as a rule, be harmonized with some triad, in fundamental form.

At the end, the thematic rhythm runs on, a beat or so (usually in one or both of the inner voices), past the final *c. f.* tone. Or, better, the final tone may be expanded to a whole measure, or more, while the lower parts effect a plagal ending.

The following illustrations are to be analyzed very thoroughly and minutely:

Bach, Organ Comp., Vol. V, No. 22 (M. in Alto, one beat); No. 48 (M. in Tenor, one beat); No. 33; No. 32 (M. in Pedal, two beats); No. 5; No. 2 (M. in Pedal, two beats); No. 4, verse II (M. in Tenor, four beats); No. 47 (manuals only); No. 31 (M. in Pedal, four beats, divided into two definite figures; inner parts largely episodic).

Table of German Chorales, for Use During This Entire Third Division.

N. B. It is not obligatory to use the keys here given. The chorales may, sometimes must, be transposed to other, higher or lower, keys.

(*g* V)

(*g* V)
(or *d* V)

(d or D I)

(*D* I)
(or ♭ V)

(may end
here.)

18.

Same as 17, but in ₵-measure:

(either)

A similar transformation of any ₵-measure chorale into $\frac{3}{2}$ measure may occasionally be made.

EXERCISE 26.

A. Harmonize a number of the above chorales, according to par. 91. Write the chorale in ♩-notes, $\frac{4}{4}$ or $\frac{3}{4}$ time; limit the accompaniment to ♪- and occasional ♫-notes; employ organ-notation (3 staves, including Pedal-bass).

B. Two 4-voice thematic elaborations of No. 1 of the given chorales, with a Figure of one beat and two beats, respectively, according to par. 92 *a, b*.   Use $\frac{4}{4}$ time, and imitate closely the **Bach** examples.

C. The 4-voice thematic elaboration of two or more other chorales, in any keys, with a Motive one whole measure in length.   The end plagally extended. $\frac{4}{4}$, $\frac{6}{8}$, or $\frac{12}{8}$ time may be used.

INDEPENDENT PEDAL–PART.

93. Partly for the sake of effective variety, and partly on account of the limitations of pedal-technique, it is quite common to conduct the Pedal-bass independent of the inner thematic voices.   This is done (1) either by so modifying (simplifying) the Motive as to adapt it better to the character and technique of the pedals; or (2) by adopting an independent (auxiliary) figure for the bass, in *more sustained rhythm.*   See par. 73*b*; Ex. 119; and the following:

Bach, Organ Comp., Vol. V, No. 1; No. 13 (inner parts thematic, but largely episodic); No. 14; No. 16 (running Pedal-bass); No. 28 (entire Pedal-motive 3 measures long); No. 38 (very characteristic Pedal); No. 40; No. 46; No. 50 (Augm. of Motive, in Pedal; observe rhythmic form of *c. f.*); No. 54; No. 55 (Pedal-motive a simplified form of figural motive); No. 56 (M. in Pedal related, but longer); No. 4, Verse 3.

Brahms, "Choral-Vorspiel" (and Fugue) in *a* minor.

EMBELLISHED CANTUS FIRMUS.

94. Although it is characteristic of the present task to restrict the *c. f.* to the *exact form of the original chorale*, it is, nevertheless, both natural and desirable (especially in actual practice) to modify certain tones of the given melody by means of unessential passing- or neighboring-notes.

a. Such embellishment of the *c. f.* may be limited to *strictly unessential* auxiliary tones, introduced here and there in order to facilitate the thematic development, but not altering or obscuring the original chorale tones.   Or it may consist in occasional slight changes of the original even rhythm, by means of dots.   For example:

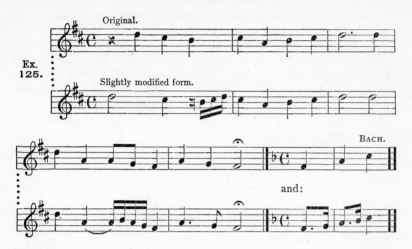

Bach, Organ Comp., Vol. V, No. 22 (already cited); No. 25 (Pedal indep.); No. 49 (ditto); No. 41 (*c. f.* embellished thematically, i.e., according to figural Motive; Pedal, simplified form of M.); No. 53 (compare with above Table of Chorales, No. 22; the modification of the *c. f.* oversteps, somewhat, the present limit. Compare, also, with reference to the *c. f.* only, the preceding and following numbers of Vol. V — Nos. 52 and 54).

b. Or the modification may extend to a *systematic ornamentation* of the chorale melody, involving all (or nearly all) of the original tones, and resulting often in a richly embellished form of the *c. f.*, to which the lower parts, though usually the-matic, appear to constitute a subordinate accompaniment. This variety of elabora-tion will be considered in detail further on (par. 107).

Motive Derived from Chorale.

95. The motive of the thematic accompaniment may be, and very frequently is, derived from the first line of the *c. f.;* usually by simple *Diminution* of the first group of (three or four) tones; or by unessential figuration of them. Thus:

More elaborate forms are shown in Ex. 128.

See **Bach.** Vol. V, No. 21 (contrapuntal associate retained throughout) ; No. 12 (ditto).

96. Finally, each of the three accompanying (figural) parts may have its own, separate, motive. Each should be sufficiently characteristic, especially in its rhythmic form, that of the Pedal-bass being naturally the most sustained ; and they are likely to differ in length. Each part announces its motive independently, and without necessary regard to regular association with the others.

In **Bach,** Vol. V, No. 9, the following 3 Motives are manipulated, more or less independently of each other :

Ex. 127.

In Alto.   In Tenor.   In Pedal-bass.

Analyze the whole number thoroughly, and see also **Bach,** Vol. V, No. 11 (less thematic than "figural"; Alto and Tenor appear to coöperate in announcing a composite motive, or figure, of one or two beats; the Pedal is independent, and not obviously thematic). — No. 17 (somewhat similar; inner parts coöperate; Pedal plainly thematic).

EXERCISE 27.

A. Write a 4-voice example, with Independent Pedal-part, according to par. 93. Select chorale from the table given in Exercise 26.

B. An example with *slightly* embellished *c. f.*, as in par. 94*a*.

C. An example with a Motive one measure long, derived from the *c. f. ;* par. 95.

D. An example with separate M. for each part ; par. 96.

THREE–VOICE ELABORATION.

97. When two parts only are added to the *c. f.*, they are most likely to be an inner and lower part for the *manual* keyboard ; though a Pedal-bass is of course possible.

The following specimens are all somewhat peculiar, especially those in which the *c. f.* is placed in a lower part, instead of in the Soprano. Analyze carefully :

Bach, Vol. V, No. 30 (*c. f.* in Soprano, slightly embellished ; running inner part ; Pedal independent). Vol. V, page 81 (Var. VI) — *cantus firmus* in *Pedal-bass.* Vol. V, page 86 (Var. IX) — *cantus firmus* in Pedal, *as inner voice ;* two motives.

FIVE–VOICE ELABORATION.

98. For this an Alto, two Tenors, and Pedal-bass are added to the *c. f.* The motive is apt to be brief, and rests may be freely used. See par. 81.

Bach, Vol. V, page 91 (Var. XI) — Pedal independent; strictly 5-voice, throughout. Vol. V. No. 42 (chiefly 4-voice; *c. f.* slightly embellished; separate M. for Pedal.)

MISCELLANEOUS. **Bach**, Vol. V, No. 4, Verse I (two motives together, Double counterpoint, in inner parts; Pedal employs motive 1 exclusively). — No. 6 (*c. f.* in *Alto*, slightly embellished; M. two beats, in Soprano; same simplified for Pedal). No. 24 (running Tenor, two alternating motives; Pedal independent; Alto uniform rhythm with *c. f.;* brief pauses between the Lines). — **Brahms**, *Choral-Vorspiele*, op. 122: No. 2 ; *c. f.* in Sopr., emb. ; 4-voice; indep. Pedal. — No. 5, *c. f.* in Sopr., 3-voice — fine example. — No. 6, ditto, 4-voice. — No. 8, elab. harmonization ; 4-voice, *c. f.* richly emb. ; each Part rep., with *c. f.* partly in Tenor. — No. 11, ditto ; 5-voice; *c. f.* in Sopr. ; end of each line extended by two-fold " echo." — No. 9 ; *c. f.*, in Sopr., richly emb. ; Ped. independent.

EXERCISE 28.

One or two examples each of the 3-voice and 5-voice chorale elaborations.

CHAPTER XI.

THE LARGE SPECIES OF CHORALE–FIGURATION.

FIRST VARIETY: INVENTION WITH CHORALE.

99. In this larger and more elaborate species, the thematic or figural voices are the chief, essential factors, while the chorale melody is (at least apparently) an incidental factor. The first Line of the *c. f.* is preceded by an introductory exposition of the Motive ; similar thematic Interludes occur between the Lines of the chorale ; and a more or less lengthy Postlude follows the final Line. Hence the chorale melody has the appearance of entering *incidentally*, when convenient, into the thematic texture, while the lower parts pursue the *imitatory development of the adopted Motive* (precisely as in the Invention), as aim and burden of the entire composition.

Of the Large Species there are several varieties, the first and simplest of which is called **" Invention with Chorale."**

Cantus Firmus in Soprano.

100. This — as in the Small Species — is the most natural, and probably most common, location for the chorale melody (*c. f.*).

a. The Motive is usually at least a measure long, often much longer. It may be invented "free," i.e., independent of the *c. f.*, and in that case it is wise to select some melodic progression (of two or three tones) that occurs frequently in the course of the chorale (as, for instance, the tone-repetitions in chorale No. 24 of the above table), and invent the Motive *as characteristic counterpoint to that figure;* this ensures its availability at these points, at least.

b. But it is somewhat more likely that the Motive will be *derived from the first Line of the c. f.,* — possibly, though rarely, from the last line, or even some other (striking) line of the chorale. The derivation may be simple, as shown in Ex. 126 (which see). Or it may be elaborate; for example, all the following motives (and many more) are derived by **Bach** from the first line of the same chorale:

*1) The rhythmic arrangement of the original tones is preserved, in this Derivative; i.e., the *accents* of the successive groups, regularly, represent the successive chorale notes (marked – – –). This is desirable, but not obligatory.

*2) Here the original tones are shifted a trifle; and at

*3) they are transferred to the higher octave.

*4) The remainder of the chorale line is vague, — probably intentionally abandoned.

It will be seen that, despite the freedom in choice and extent of *added* tones, the Derivatives all bear a distinctly recognizable relation to the original *c. f.* line; the latter "sounds out" plainly through the new array of tones. Observe the variety of measure ($\frac{12}{8}$, $\frac{3}{4}$, $\frac{6}{8}$, $\frac{4}{4}$, $\frac{3}{2}$).

c. Not infrequently, two or even three Motives are used (par. 52).

d. The introductory measures, or "Prelude," are a regular Exposition of the Motive, as in the Invention, and subject to the same rules (par. 40); but a cadence is not made, as a rule, until the *c. f.* (the first line of the chorale) has entered and has been conducted to its end.

The first tone of each line of the *c. f.* must be some *chord-interval*, but may be either consonance or dissonance (7th, 9th, etc.). The final tone of each line may be Root, 3rd or 5th of the chosen triad, but the latter must be fundamental (Root in Bass).

The *c. f.* should not be modified, excepting by an occasional, *strictly unessential,* passing-note ; or by some other equally harmless change.

Care must be taken not to proceed into a new chord or key so soon after the final tone of each *c. f.* line, as to leave the latter (after its cessation) *an implied dissonance ;* that is, the final tone should, for at least a full beat after its conclusion, appear (in the hearer's recollection) to harmonize with the thematic voices, and fade away in their subsequent conduct.

e. The end of each " Line " is, practically, the termination of a Section of the Invention, — though a definite cadence is not obligatory. Each succeeding Section begins with an " Interlude," devoted to continued thematic development in the figural voices while the *c. f.* voice pauses ; very similar in character and conduct to the " Prelude," but more free. The length of these Interludes is optional ; usually a measure or two, often more, — the *c. f.* reëntering, each time, when convenient. Review par. 99.

f. The very last tone of the *c. f.* (the final tone of the last line) should be a Root, if possible. The voice which has the *c. f.* — the Soprano, in this instance — may, after prolonging the final tone a few beats, join in the thematic elaboration, usually beginning its participation *with an announcement of the Motive.* This extension, the " Postlude," may be of any reasonable length.

101. In executing the task, the thematic (or figural) parts and the *c. f.* (when the latter is present) may be carried along abreast of each other, with constant regard to the announcements of the Motive ; or the M. alone may be inserted, beforehand, in one part and then another, where it promises to agree well with the *c. f.* — somewhat after the manner of leading parts (par. 64, which review).

At all events, the Motive should appear very frequently, if not incessantly, in some part or other ; and therefore great freedom may (must) be exercised in rendering the M. adjustable, by altering the quantity of its interval-progressions (rarely, however, by changing its rhythm, excepting for possible Augmentations, complete or partial).

Contrary motion, shifted rhythm, and stretto Imitations are to be freely employed.

The Pedal-bass should be conducted, in general, more quietly than the manual parts. It may, occasionally, be independent (par. 93). Progressions in alternate opposite direction, with or without skips, are peculiarly adapted to pedal-technique :

For general illustration of the process (No. 16 of the above Table of Chorales; Motive in large notes):

GOETSCHIUS.

M. extended.

etc.

*1) The contrary motion of the M. is very freely used.

*2) The *c. f.* enters as chord-seventh. See beginning of second Line, also. This is effective.

*3) Fragments of the Motive.

*4) The Line ends as chord-root.

*5) Observe that the abandoned *c. f.* tone (*f*) is understood as harmonic tone through the following half-measure; par. 100*d*, last clause.

See also Ex. 131, and analyze, thoroughly, the following:

4-voice elaborations. Bach, Organ Comp., Vol. VII, No. 42 (first four measures introductory, but thematic). Vol. VII, No. 48, Verse I (no Pedal; *c. f.* slightly embellished; an "introductory" motive, and a small figural motive; after entrance of *c. f.* the Tenor part discontinues). Vol. VI, No. 24 (several small motives; Pedal consists chiefly of canonic Imitations of the *c. f.* in Soprano).

3-voice elaborations. Bach, Vol. VI, No. 4 (quite free; mostly fragments of motive). Vol. VII, No. 46 (*c. f.* embellished; two motives; quasi 3-Part Song-form).

5-voice elaboration. Bach, Vol. VI, No. 12*a* (*c. f.* slightly embellished; quasi two motives, from chorale).—**Brahms,** *Choral-Vorspiele,* op. 122, No. 3; *c. f.* in Sopr., embellished.

EXERCISE 29.

A. Two examples of the Invention with chorale (minor and major, respectively), according to the above directions. *Cantus firmus* in the Soprano; 4-voice; the Motive at least one or two measures long; fairly strict manipulation.

B. One example for 3 voices, preferably for manual (without Pedal-bass).

C. One example for 5 voices. Review par. 81. Pedal-bass low.

CANTUS FIRMUS IN BASS.

102. When used as lowermost part, the *c. f.* is written for the Pedals, of course. The final tone of each line must be a chord-root. Especial care must be taken to avoid implied dissonance for a beat or more after the cessation of each final tone (review par. 100*d*, last clause). All other details correspond precisely to those given above (pars. 100, 101).

For general illustration (chorale 22 of the Table):

*1) The Motive is derived from the first Line of the chorale (par. 100*b*).

*2) The *c. f.* enters with a harsh dissonance; but its relation to the preceding bass tone (organ-point *e*), and its location as lowermost tone, render it permissible and extremely effective.

*3) From here on, the contrapuntal parts are purposely omitted, so as to exhibit more clearly the manner and places in which the M. is inserted. See par. 101, first clause.

Analyze, thoroughly, the following:

Bach, Organ Comp., Vol. VII, No. 35, *Stanza II* (meas. 11 to end); M. small,— series of 5 or 6 diatonic tones; 4-voice.

Bach, Vol. VII, No. 51; 3 Motives, — M. 1 during Part I, meas. 1–12; M. 2 from meas. 13–19, thereafter in alternation with M. 1, to meas. 31; M. 3 from meas. 32 to 36, thereafter in alternation with M. 1 to end; 4-voice. Vol. VII, No. 36; very elaborate, quasi Fantasia (par. 109); 4-voice; 2 motives in close alternation; a new, 3rd, M. is added for the last Line.

CANTUS FIRMUS IN TENOR.

103. The general details agree exactly with those given for the Soprano.

a. The *c. f.* may be written in the Tenor part in the usual manner; but it is desirable, and customary, so to arrange the parts that the chorale melody may be made prominent by being played upon a separate (louder) manual of the organ. In this case it stands alone on the middle staff, and, *during its presence*, the two thematic voices above it (Soprano and Alto) must be so written that they are playable together *with one hand* (i.e., within the compass of an octave). During the Prelude and the Interludes, this restraint is, of course, removed.

b. Or, the *c. f.* may be assigned to the Pedals (written in Bass register), and played with a 4-foot stop, so as to *sound an octave higher,* — i.e., in Tenor register. The middle staff then belongs to the Bass proper, and care must be taken to keep it below the *c. f.* (Tenor), as a rule; and, being played with the hand, it may be more free and lively than an ordinary Pedal-bass.

See **Bach,** Organ Comp., Vol. VI, No. 12*b*; 4-voice; *c. f.* written in Tenor part, somewhat embellished; M. in Soprano, meas. 1–4, derived from *c. f.*

Vol. VII, No. 56; 4-voice; *c. f.* written in Pedal (in Tenor register); M. in Bass, ½ measure (free).

Vol. VII, No. 63; 3-voice; *c. f.* in Pedal, as Tenor; M. in upper part, ½ measure (free).

Vol. VII, No. 59; 4-voice; 2-Part Song-form, M. for each Part, derived from *c. f.*; Bass chiefly independent, but based on a fragment of M. 1; *c. f.* in Pedal, an 8ve below Tenor register.

Vol. VII, No. 38; 3-voice; *c. f.* in Pedal, slightly embellished; each voice its independent M.

Mozart, "Magic Flute," *Finale* of 2d Act, *Adagio*, ₵-time, *c* minor (scene with "2 men in armor"); 4-voice, *c. f.* doubled in 8ves; small motive, one measure, and thematic Figure of 3 notes.

Cantus Firmus in Alto.

104. This is rare, especially in 4-voice counterpoint. Rules the same as for Soprano.

See **Bach,** Vol. VI, No. 5; 3-voice, no Pedal; 2 Motives (Soprano, meas. 3 and meas. 5) in close alternation and occasional conjunction.

Vol. VI, No. 16; 3-voice, no Pedal; 2-Part Form, and 2 Motives, derived from *c. f.*

Vol. VII, No. 48, *Stanza II;* 3-voice, no Pedal; small figural M.

Cantus Firmus in Alternate Voices.

105. Successive Lines of the chorale may be assigned to different voices; or, if definite 2- or 3-Part Form, different voices may assume the successive Parts. Or, at *any* point where it appears desirable or convenient, a change of voice may be made, — never, however, *during* a Line of the chorale.

On the termination of its share of the *c. f.*, the voice in question may (as at the end, during the Postlude — see par. 100*f*) immediately join the contrapuntal parts, usually, here again, with an announcement of the Motive.

The voice to which the *c. f.* is *next* to be given must rest during the whole (or a good portion) of that Interlude.

The choice of voice for the *c. f.* is wholly optional; but some attention is due to *technical* considerations; and the voices should be so written that, if possible, the *c. f.* may be played upon a separate manual, — when not in the Pedal-bass (comp. par. 103*a*).

See **Bach,** Vol. VI, No. 6; 3-voice; some of the Lines are repeated; the rests before the *c. f.* are very brief; Pedal independent.

Vol. VI, No. 29, Division I (¾ time); 3-voice; 2 Motives in conjunction (Double counterpoint).

Raff, Pianoforte Suite, op. 71, " Preludio " (*c. f.* original).

EXERCISE 30.

A. An example with *c. f.* in Bass; 4-voice; one Motive; strict manipulation.

B. *C. f.* in Tenor, written on middle staff; 4-voice.

C. *C. f.* in Tenor, written in Pedal; 4-voice.

D. *C. f.* in Alternate voices; one Motive; 4-voice.

E. *C. f.* in Alto; 3-voice; one Motive.

F. *C. f.* optional; 4-voice; two Motives, one for each Part of chorale.

G. 5-voice; two Motives.

Second Variety: Chorale as Invention–Group.

106. This variety differs from the preceding only in that a *new Motive* is devised and used *for each Line of the chorale in succession.* Consequently, each Line appears to constitute a complete brief Invention by itself, usually with a fairly decided cadence; and the whole is a group of Inventions.

As a rule (though not necessarily), the Motives are each time derived from the corresponding (following) Line of the chorale. They will, therefore, be independent; but they should all agree with each other pretty closely in character, especially as concerns their rhythmic formation. The *first* Motive may be reverted to, incidentally, at any moment. All rules as before.

See **Bach,** Organ Comp., Vol. VI, No. 14; 4-voice; *c. f.* in Soprano; new M. for each Line, in almost regular alternation with the contrary motion, and in stretto (comp. par. 73*a*).

Vol. VI, No. 23; 4-voice; *c. f.* in Soprano.

Vol. VI, No. 1; 4-voice; *c. f.* in Soprano; Motives from chorale, but distributed irregularly.

Vol. VII, No. 43; 4-voice; *c. f.* in Soprano; M. for each Line, but only as Prelude — not *with* the *c. f.*

Vol. VII, No. 58; 4-voice; *c. f.* in Soprano, slightly embellished; M. in regular and contrary motion, — par. 73*a*.

Vol. VII, No. 48, *Stanza III;* 4-voice; *c. f.* in Bass; four Motives, invented free — *not* derived from chorale lines; M. 4 "per moto contrario."

Vol. VI, No. 32; 4-voice, manuals; *c. f.* in Soprano; M. for each of first 3 Lines, invented without reference to chorale; last Line in alternating voices, Double counterpoint.

EXERCISE 31.

Two or three examples (minor and major) of the above variety.

Third Variety: Chorale as Aria.

107. This species of manipulation differs considerably from the specifically polyphonic elaborations of the chorale-accompaniment, inasmuch as it affects, chiefly, the chorale-melody itself, while the accompanying voices may be simply of a general imitatory character, or nearly (or quite) homophonic. Review, thoroughly, par. 94, especially *b.*

The main object is, so to embellish the *c. f.* tones with auxiliary notes (passing-, neighboring-notes, etc., in florid rhythmic form) that the original stern chorale-melody is completely transformed into a graceful (though dignified and impressive) *lyric* melody or "Aria." This dissolution of the *c. f.* must be so effected, however, as to preserve the original rhythmic disposition of the tones, i.e., the distinction of accented and unaccented tones, as closely as possible, — so that the ornate product, reduced to its tonal elements (at accented points), would correspond nearly to the original chorale. Hence, while the embellishment may include many additional tones (perhaps distant from the given ones), and may tend to shift certain of the given tones past their primary place at the beginning of their respective beats, it is rarely justifiable to evade the tone altogether, or to shift it entirely *beyond its beat,* into the next; and it is still more rare to anticipate a given tone, by shifting it *back* into the preceding beat. At the same time, it will be found possible to exercise considerable freedom, totally eradicating all resemblance to the chorale, and still preserve the fundamental melodic design of the original.

The chorale-Aria is almost always placed in the Soprano; the lower accompanying parts may be purely homophonic, — slightly figurated, — or imitatory, without being thematic; or, more rarely, they may adopt and manipulate a Motive, as in the 1st Variety. The Pedal-bass is frequently independent, and of a quiet rhythmic character.

For illustration of the treatment of the chorale:

Further:

GOETSCHIUS.

The following examples belong properly to the Small Species of chorale Figuration, and supplement those given in par. 94*a* : —

Bach, Organ Comp., Vol. V, No. 10; 4-voice; accompaniment thematic.

Vol. V, No. 26; ditto. — Vol. V, No. 45; 4-voice; accompaniment, general imitatory character; Pedal independent.

Vol. V, No. 51 (the very last of **Bach's** compositions); 4-voice; thematic accompaniment.

For examples of the Large Species, see —

Bach, Organ Comp., Vol. VII, No. 49; 4-voice; *c. f.* in Soprano, profusely embellished; Pedal independent; inner parts imitatory, but not strictly thematic.

Vol. VII, No. 45; 4-voice, *c.f.* in Soprano, copiously embellished, and *extended* — each Line similarly — in its course; Pedal independent (running auxiliary part); inner voices free.

Vol. VI, No. 9; 4-voice; *c. f.* in Soprano; inner parts thematic; 3 Motives (meas. 1 in Tenor, meas. 2 in Alto, end of meas. 2 in both parts) in close alternation and conjunction; Pedal uses first M. frequently.

Vol. VI, No. 8; 4-voice; *c. f.* in Tenor, richly embellished and *expanded;* Pedal independent; thematic upper parts quite elaborate.

FOURTH VARIETY: RITORNELLE WITH CHORALE.

108. In this variety the Motive (or, more properly, *Theme*) is much longer than in the foregoing; generally a complete 8-measure Period, or extended Period, or even Double-period. It is frequently a sort of running voice, in nearly or quite uniform rhythm; but sometimes a lyric melody of striking, impressive character. It may be invented entirely free, or (as is more common) may be derived from a Line or two of the *c. f.*, as an elaborate embellishment and radical modification of the latter.

This Theme appears as an introduction (or Prelude), usually with complete perfect cadence; *recurs*, generally at its full length, as an

Interlude (once or twice, according to the length of the chorale), and again as a Postlude, — hence the term " *Ritornelle.*" During the chorale lines it is present *in fragments only.*

See **Bach,** Organ Comp., Vol. VI, No. 2; 3-voice; *c. f.* in Soprano; Pedal independent.   Vol. VI, No. 17; 4-voice; *c. f.* in Bass; long Theme, in Tenor; upper two parts constantly imitatory.   Vol. VI, No. 3; 2-voice, no Pedal; *c. f.* in Soprano; M. from *c. f.,* treated with great freedom.   Vol. VII, No. 44; 3-voice; *c. f.* in Pedal, as Tenor; quasi running parts, independent rhythms. — **Brahms,** *Choral-Vorspiele,* op. 122, No. 4; *c. f.* in Sopr.; 4-voice; Ped. indep. — No. 7; *c. f.* in Sopr. and Bass alternately; 3 to 6-voice. — No. 10; *c. f.* in Ped. as Tenor; 4-voice.

Fifth Variety : Chorale–Fantasia.

109. The *c. f.* may consist of a *portion, or portions,* of the original chorale, instead of the whole; possibly of one or two characteristic lines only; or even of certain distinctive members of the lines (naturally the very beginning, or ending, of the chorale). These may appear in optional succession and frequency, generally in different parts, and in different keys and registers.

The accompanying voices may be conducted with great freedom; they are generally imitatory, but not necessarily thematic; and are likely to contain many, more or less disguised, allusions to the chorale.

The form is optional, but is most likely to be sectional, or "group," design.   A certain progressive structural idea should be embodied, as general outline, and one or more effective climaxes introduced. Review, carefully, par. 85.

See **Bach,** Organ Comp., Vol. VI. No. 22; 3-voice; *c. f.* embellished (at times) in alternate voices; accompaniment not thematic; treatment distinctly " Fantasia "-like.

Vol. VI, No. 7 ; 3-voice; Pedal independent; upper parts imitatory and generally thematic; form sectional, and very clear, with many confirmations; first two lines of chorale in Pedal, at the end.

Vol. VI, No. 15; 2- to 4-voice.

Vol. VI, No. 27 ; 3-voice; quasi chorale-Invention (par. 110) ; chorale in Pedal, during final Sections.

Vol. V, No. 34; 4-voice; built upon fragments of chorale; definite Sectional form; Pedal quasi "basso ostinato" (i.e., consisting in repetitions of the same Figure, generally upon the same scale-steps).

Vol. VII, No. 36 (already cited; quasi long Invention with chorale, but of free " Fantasia " character).

EXERCISE 32.

A. One or two examples of the Chorale as Aria.

B. One or two examples of the Ritornelle with Chorale.

C. One or two examples of the Chorale-Fantasia.

SIXTH VARIETY: CHORALE–INVENTION, OR PRELUDE.

110. See par. 83*c.* In this variety the chorale, as *c. f.*, *does not appear.* The whole is an Invention (as chorale-Prelude) of the usual character, based upon a Motive, or Motives, *derived from the first Line of the chorale* (or from some other characteristic Line).

> See **Bach,** Organ Comp., Vol. VII, No. 40*A*, and No. 40*B* ; 4-voice; 3 Sections.
> Vol. VI, No. 27 (already cited, quasi " Fantasia ").
> Vol. V, page 70, Partita III (also Partita V, same Motive, different treatment; 3-voice).
> Vol. V, page 73 (4-voice, chromatic).
> Vol. V, page 83 (4-voice).
> Vol. V, page 84 (4 to 5-voice, Pedal independent).

CHORALE VARIATIONS.

111. A number of different elaborations of the same chorale, in the various methods shown above, may be associated as a set of Variations. The manner in which the Varieties of manipulation are chosen, and the number of variations collected, are subject to no rule ; but decided contrast (especially in reference to rhythm and measure) must be obtained ; and the interest should be progressively increased, by choosing the more elaborate and effective species for the final numbers.

> See **Bach,** Organ Comp., Vol. V, pages 60–67 ; 68–75 ; 76–91. **Mendelssohn,** Organ Sonata, op. 65, No. 6, movements one to four (up to the Fugue). **Brahms,** Motet, op. 74, No. 2 ; chorale in first verse, with contrapuntal accomp. ; the following 3 verses (II, III, and IV) are elaborations with the *c. f.* (more or less embel.) in different voices.

EXERCISE 33.

A. One or two examples of the Chorale-Invention.

B. One or more sets of Chorale-Variations.

———

In conclusion, attention is directed to a scholarly collection of " 200 Choral-Vorspiele " by CARL PIUTTI, in which the principal varieties of manipulation are represented.

DIVISION FOUR.

THE FUGUE.

INTRODUCTORY.

112. The Fugue differs from the Invention chiefly in being a more *strict and serious* contrapuntal form. Review par. 37. While the Invention is subject only to the *general* conditions of contrapuntal treatment, the Fugue, on the other hand, involves certain *special* conditions and limitations.

These special qualities, which distinguish the Fugue, are as follows:

(1) The Subject or Theme of a Fugue is usually more extended, and has a more definite form, than the " Motive ";

(2) The Subject is first announced alone, in a Fugue, unattended by auxiliary tones;

(3) During the first Section, or *Exposition*, the Subject is (as a rule) announced alternately in the Tonic and Dominant keys, i.e., it is imitated alternately in the 5th and 8ve; and

(4) There is, throughout, less freedom of detail, and greater seriousness of character and manipulation.

THE FUGUE–SUBJECT.

113. The thematic germ of a Fugue is called " Subject " or " Theme."

The former term is used in a specific sense; the term "Theme" as a general designation of the thematic basis.

a. It is, with rare exceptions, definite in form, being either a complete Phrase or (more rarely) Period, and closing as a rule with a distinctly *cadential* effect. Its length is optional, — from one large measure (**Bach,** Well-temp. Clav., Vol. I, Fugue 17) up to 6, 8, or even more measures (**Bach,** Well-temp. Clav., Vol. II, Fugue 15; Organ Comp., Peters compl. ed., Vol. III, Fugues Nos. 3 and 8).

b. Generally it begins either upon the 1st, 3rd, or 5th scale-step of the key; but in any case the Tonic note should appear *near* (*if not at*) *the beginning*. It may begin upon an accented beat, or upon the preceding unaccented beat; but by far the best and most common practice is to begin the Subject *with a brief rest, i.e., immediately after an accent* (Ex. 134).

It ends, frequently, upon the 3rd scale-step, or upon the Tonic (more rarely upon the Dominant), of the principal key; or upon the Tonic or 3rd step of the *Dominant key.* Other cadences are possible, but very rare. The final tone falls usually upon an accented beat, and produces a decided cadential impression; but there are exceptions to this rule, and it is sometimes difficult to determine precisely where the Subject terminates (see **Bach,** Well-temp. Clav., Vol. I, Fugue 9,— doubtful whether the Subject ends on 3rd beat of second measure, or on 1st beat of third measure). The Subject may contain *transient* modulations, in its course, but can scarcely end in any other than the *principal,* or the *Dominant,* key; possibly in the Relative major, from minor.

c. As Subject of a Fugue, and as complete melodic sentence, it should be distinctly *individualized.* Its melodic and rhythmic contents must be serious, but characteristic, and pregnant (susceptible of manifold polyphonic manipulation); and its delineation must be distinct and moderately striking, — to the exclusion of vagueness, of a too lyric melodic form, but also of eccentricity. *Sequences* are seldom absent, in good Subjects; the harmonic basis is clear, natural, and forcible; and there is usually at least one salient rhythmic feature (an effective tie, syncopation, or contrasting figure). The compass of effective Subjects seldom runs beyond an octave. Review par. 38*a.*

EXERCISE 34.

A. Inspect, minutely, every Fugue-Subject in both volumes of **Bach's** Well-tempered Clavichord, with reference to each detail given above.

B. Write a large number of original Subjects.

THE CONSTRUCTION OF THE " RESPONSE."

114. As stated above, the Subject or Theme is to appear, during the first Section (the **Exposition**) of a Fugue, first in the principal key, then in the Dominant key, and so on, alternately in the Tonic and Dominant registers, as far as the number of voices dictates.

The first announcement (tonic) is called the *Subject* proper; the second announcement (dominant) is called the *Response* or *Answer.*

115. In order to place it in the Dominant key, the Subject must be imitated in the perfect 5th above (or perfect 4th below). Hence, the fundamental rule for the construction of the Response is:

To imitate each tone of the Subject in the **perfect fifth.**

This gives what is known as the " real " Response or Answer.   For example :

*1)   The adjustment is perfect, and no circumstance exists which would neces-
sitate an exception to the fundamental rule.

116.   But this strict imitation often gives rise to awkward or abrupt
modulation, and a lack of adjustment at the extremes (beginning or
end) of the Response.   The element invariably involved in such embarrassment is the *Dominant.*   Hence, the first general exception to
the fundamental rule is :

That the Dominant element, wherever peculiarly conspicuous in
the Subject, is to be imitated in the **perfect fourth,** instead of 5th.

a.   This applies (1) to the Dominant *tone* at the very beginning ; or
(2) near the beginning (as 2d, 3rd, or 4th tone of the Subject, especially
when connected with the Tonic note) ; (3) to all tones *inseparably connected* with this initial Dominant (as embellishment, repetitions, and the
like) ; (4) to a strong Dominant *chord*-impression at, or very near, the
beginning ; (5) to the cadence in the Dominant *key* (at the end of
the Subject) ; and (6) to all tones that pertain inseparably to this final
Dominant.   All such tones should be imitated in the perfect 4th.

This is called the " tonal " Response.

117.   *a.*   The Dominant note at the beginning.   For illustration :

*1)   The Dominant note at the very beginning would, if answered in the perfect
5th, transfer the Response abruptly, and bodily, into the Dominant key (*c* minor).

Thus:

etc.

The first tone, *g*, would not adjust well with the cadence tone of the Subject (*ab*). In a word, this initial *g* is the Second-dominant (Dominant of the Dominant) in the key of *f* minor thus far pursued; and while this comparatively remote tone, or any other, can be reached *in time*, it is certain to sound abrupt at the very beginning of the Response. Therefore the above Subject is imitated as follows, the first (Dominant) tone in the *4th*, and the remainder, as usual, in the 5th:

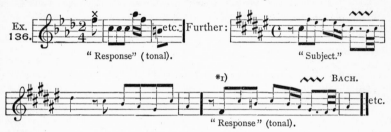

By this means the Response is *retained for an instant in the original key*, until perfect adjustment, at the beginning, is secured. It is called the "tonal" Response because of this (at least temporary) adherence to the *tonality* of the Fugue; the *Tonic* elements being answered by the *Dominant*, and the *Dominant* elements (where salient) by the *Tonic* (imitation in the 4th).

*1) All large notes indicate the imitation in the 4th; the small notes that in the 5th.

b. The Dominant note *near* the beginning:

This always applies to the Dominant as *second* note of the Subject, *when it follows the Tonic*; and, in case the initial Tonic note is embellished, it may be the 3rd or 4th tone of the Subject. Thus:

*1) The initial Tonic (*f*) is simply embellished; therefore the Dominant (as 4th tone, *c*) is near enough to the beginning to be the second essential tone.

*2) The second tone of the subject (*e*) is here imitated in the *diminished* 5th (*b♭*). Similar substitutions of the diminished or augmented 5th (and 4th) for the perfect 5th (and 4th) are quite common, and are due to the very same principle that gives rise to the general exception under discussion (par. 116). See Note to Ex. 136. Here the *b♭* confirms the principal key, *F* major. — See also Ex. 146, No. 3.

*3) Same as Note *2).

c. Repetitions or embellishments of the Dominant, at or near the beginning :

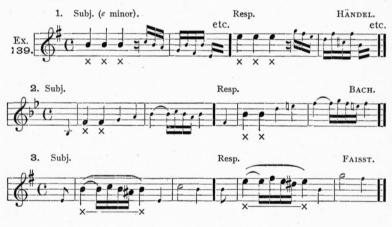

Or, adding to this last Theme (Ex. 139–3) various embellishments of the initial Tonic (as in Ex. 138), the results would be :

*1) In every case (excepting No. 4) this *g* is imitated in the *augmented* 5th (*d* ♯), because of the principal key. Comp. Ex. 138, Note *2).

*2) No. 4 is a regular (real) Response. The tone *a* in the Subject changes the whole situation. Partly because the *a* does not pertain to the initial Tonic, and partly for reasons given in par. 118, the Dominant *b* must be answered in the 5th. See further Ex. 145, No. 6.

d. A cluster of tones at (or *very near*) the beginning, that constitute a very obvious Dominant *chord :*

See also Ex. 144, No. 3.

e. As declared in par. 116*a* (3), all tones that pertain *inseparably* to the Dominant at or near the beginning of the Subject, share with it in the exception to the rule. To this class belong the repetitions and embellishments illustrated in Ex. 139; also a diatonic *run* from the initial Tonic *down* to the Dominant; thus :

Possibly also the *nearly* continuous run from Tonic *up* to Dominant :

This comes under the head of Ex. 140; but there is a subtle distinction between it and Ex. 140, No. 4 (which it closely resembles), that is left to the student's analysis.

f. Finally, the Dominant *key*, at the *end* of the Subject, when introduced by a palpable modulation, is subject to the exception.   Thus:

*1) An important question in connection with the final Dominant key is, *how far back from the end* the imitation in the 4th is to extend.   It is best solved according to the principle of par. 117*e*; — all tones that are *inseparable* from the final Dominant, as belonging obviously to the total impression of the "Dominant key," are imitated in the 4th.   In the above case the tonal imitation begins at the very point where the modulation was made, in the Subject; and, further, at the rest which marks a semicadence.

*2) Here **Bach** appears to regard the *a* (3rd measure of Subject) as inseparable from the following modulatory movement into the Dominant key, and therefore begins the imitation in the 4th at that point.

g. The puzzling questions can, in many instances, be determined only by carefully *testing the effect*, and preserving a good, smooth, modulatory and melodic result. The trouble consists, as stated, simply in deciding which tones are inseparably connected with the Dominant; and this may depend upon the melodic structure, the modulation, rhythm, or other circumstances bearing upon the *characteristic formation of the Subject as a whole.* Therefore, the ultimate decision is, here and elsewhere, very often indeed a matter of common-sense judgment, or individual taste.

118. Partly in keeping with this last idea, and partly for general reasons, a third rule must be observed, which constitutes in a sense an exception to the rule of tonal imitation (par. 116), and therefore reverts partially to the fundamental rule, namely:

Under no circumstances shall any *characteristic feature* of the Theme be violated.

Consequently, neither the real nor the tonal imitation can be insisted upon at any point where they threaten any tone or figure of the Subject that is significant or characteristic. For illustration:

*1) These tones are all harmonically inseparable from the Dominant modulation; and the preceding interval (falling 7th) is so characteristic that it, too, is included in the tonal imitation.

*2) This *g* is a conspicuous Dominant note, near the beginning; but it is answered in the 5th, because of the sequential formation of the Theme.

*3) **Bach** evidently regarded this *d* (Dominant near the beginning) as an essential harmonic factor of his Theme, and imitates it in the 5th to preserve the triad-effect of the first figure.

*4) A remote key, but unavoidable because of the definite chromatic character of the Subject.

*5) Dominant as first tone, — imitated in the 5th, with its repetitions, apparently because of the structure of the whole Theme.   Comp. Ex. 149, Note *2).

*6) To **Bach** this was a tone-group inseparable from the Dominant (*b*), and therefore the whole figure reappears in the 4th.

*7) Augmented 4th; see Ex. 138, Note *2).

*8) This peculiar leap of an Augmented 4th is an inviolable trait of the Theme, and therefore it renders the foregoing tones likewise inseparable from the final Dominant key, — back to the second tone of the Subject.

119. The single Dominant note at the *end* of a Subject is not to be imitated in the 4th (tonal), unless it is strongly suggestive of the Dominant *key*, or Dominant *chord:*

*1) This final Dominant note is more strongly indicative of the Dominant *chord* than those of the preceding examples, because it occurs at the bar, where a *change* of harmony (from the foregoing I) is expected. Therefore, it is imitated in the 4th, — although the 5th (*d*) would have been entirely defensible.

*2) At the points marked N. B. the necessity of using *diminished* (instead of perfect) 5ths, in order to obtain a sensible and natural total modulatory result, is strikingly illustrated. Comp. Ex. 138, Note *2).

*3) This case is similar to No. 3, being an accent, and therefore suggesting a change of harmony (from I to V). Besides, the whole Theme is so brief, and so nearly all Tonic, that the final Dominant seems near enough to the beginning to demand tonal treatment (par. 117*b*).

120. *a.* When the Theme begins with the Dominant note, and *also ends in the Dominant key*, it may be possible, and necessary, to imitate the initial Dominant in the 5th. Thus:

*1) As the Dominant key has already been reached, there is no danger of imperfect adjustment, and therefore the "real" imitation is entirely feasible.

b. Further, when the Dominant effect prevails decidedly through the whole or a great part of the Theme, it may be necessary to imitate it *in the 4th throughout.* Thus :

In both of these cases all that is not actually Dominant appears to be *inseparable* from the prevailing Dominant effect.

MISCELLANEOUS.

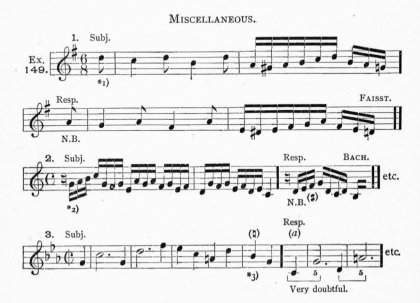

Possible, and not improbable.

Probably the best Response.

4. Subj. Resp. MOZART.

*4)

5. Subj. Resp. BACH.

*5)

6. Subj.

*6)

Resp. BACH.

N.B.

7. Subj.

*7)

Resp. WEINLIG.

N.B.

8. Subj.

*8)

Resp. MOZART.

N.B.

*1) This initial Dominant is answered in the 5th (contrary to par. 116a), because of the characteristic formation of the Theme. Comp. par. 118.

*2) The initial Dominant is here simply one of a series of unimportant passing-notes leading into the Tonic, and is therefore answered in the 5th. Further, **Bach** chooses *f*♮ for the 3rd tone of the Response (instead of the expected *f*♯), in order to preserve for an instant the impression of the original key.

*3) In case Response (*c*) were to be chosen, this would be *b*♮ in preference to *b♭*.   Otherwise, the latter is more probable.

*4) The final tone is imitated in the *augmented* 4th, to preserve closer relation to the original key,— probably because the Subject is brief.   Compare Ex. 138, Note *2).

*5) Same as Note *4).

*6) The striking modulation into the Dominant key, so near the beginning, must be answered in the 4th, — similar to par. 117*d*.

*7) The prominent Leading-tone, when absolutely indicative of the Dominant chord (as here), and not merely an embellishing note of the Tonic (as in Ex. 138, No. 1, 2nd tone), is subject to tonal imitation, with all that is inseparable from it. Comp. par. 117*d*.

*8) Like Note *7).

EXERCISE 35.

A. Analyze all the Responses in the Well-temp. Clavichord of **Bach**.

B. Write the Responses to all the original Subjects invented in Exercise 34.

And invent a number of new Themes (and Answers), with reference to the above traits.

CHAPTER XII.

THE FOUR–VOICE FUGUE. — THE EXPOSITION.

121. The Exposition or first Section of a Fugue contains as many announcements of the Theme (Subject and Response alternately — par. 114) as there are parts employed.   In the 4-voice Fugue the order is, therefore (when *regular*), Subject, Response, Subject, Response.

a. The first Response may begin simultaneously with the final tone of the Subject (**Bach**, Well-temp. Clav., Vol. I, Fugue 8).   Or immediately *after* the Subject ends (Vol. I, Fugue 6).   Or still a little later, so that one or more tones must be added to the Subject, as *intervening figure* (Vol. I, Fugue 1, one intervening tone ; Vol. I, Fugue 2, ditto ; Vol. I, Fugue 12, two intermediate tones ; Fugue 11, three tones ; Fugue 3, four tones ; Fugue 7, seven tones, — more than this number could scarcely be justified).   Or, more rarely, the Response may enter *before* the cadence tone of the Subject, as brief stretto (Vol. I, Fugue 9 ; the

Response overlaps the Subject one beat, possibly three, — the length
of Subject is somewhat uncertain).

b. In the third of these possible cases, where *intermediate tones* are
used, the latter must be carefully chosen, in keeping with the conduct
of the Subject, and with a view to their subsequent employment as
thematic basis of the *episodic* passages (as in Vol. I, Fugue 7).

122. The **first counterpoint** — that which follows the Subject in the
same part, as contrapuntal associate of the Response — is sometimes
called the " Counter-subject "; as this term is misleading (in the Single
Fugue), it will be spoken of here simply as the " Counterpoint."
Comp. par. 34.

It is a very important factor in the Fugue (or may become so), and
especial pains must, therefore, be taken with its formation. It may be
derived from the figures of the Subject itself:

*1) Both of these figures of the Counterpoint are derived from those of the
Subject, in *contrary motion.* See also **Bach,** Well-temp. Cl., Vol. II, Fugue 5.

Or the Counterpoint may be more or less independent of the Theme,
its conduct being governed by the general conditions of good contrapuntal association.

Or it may assume a *characteristic* rhythmic or melodic form, in intentional opposition to the current of the Response, or as a wholly individual factor of the entire Fugue.   Thus:

*1) The Counterpoint is admirably individualized by the line of sequences. See further, **Bach,** Well-temp. Cl., Vol. I, Fugue 18, similar; Vol. I, Fugue 2 — rhythmic contrast with the Theme; Vol. I, Fugue 12 ; Vol. II, Fugues 10, 11, 16, 20 (rhythmic), 22 (chromatic).

In any case, but especially in the last mentioned, the first Counterpoint is more than likely to reappear from time to time in connection with later announcements of the Theme, as part of the thematic material of the composition ; and this possible use must be kept in mind, and must emphasize the thoughtfulness and *strictness of technique* with which the Counterpoint is to be devised. It is well to make several experiments, in various styles, and choose the most promising version.

EXERCISE 36.

A. Examine the formation of the first Counterpoint in every Fugue of the Well-temp. Clavichord.

B. Write, upon one or two staves at option, each of the Subjects of the preceding Exercise, in the most convenient register, *followed by the Response* in the next higher or next lower part, and add the Counterpoint (as in Exs. 150, 151). Each Subject is to be manipulated twice, — with the Response respectively above and below.

123. These and the succeeding announcements of the Theme, during the regular Exposition, are determined by the following formula :

(1) *Subject,* — in either one of the four parts ;

(2) *Response,* — invariably in the next higher or next lower part;

(3) *Subject,* — in the **parallel part** to that in which the Subject first appeared, an octave higher or lower than the former announcement;

(4) *Response,* — in the remaining part, i.e., the parallel to the part in which the first Response appeared, and an octave higher or lower than the latter.

In other words, the Subjects appear in parallel parts, and the Responses, likewise, in the other parallel pair of parts.

N. B. Parallel parts are those which are separated by one part, namely, Soprano and Tenor, Bass and Alto.

See **Bach,** Well-temp. Cl., Vol. I, Fugue 5 : Bass, Tenor, Alto, Soprano.

Bach, Well-temp. Cl., Vol. I, Fugue 17 : Tenor, Bass, Soprano, Alto.

Bach, Well-temp. Cl., Vol. I, Fugue 18 : Tenor, Alto, Soprano, Bass.

Bach, Well-temp. Cl., Vol. I, Fugue 20 : Alto, Soprano, Bass, Tenor.

Beginning with Soprano, the order would be : Soprano, Alto, Tenor, Bass.

124. In some, comparatively rare, instances the Exposition is *irregular,* for some valid reason, and in one of the following respects :

(1) The order of the parts ;

See **Bach,** Well-temp. Cl., Vol. I, No. 1, — the order is, Alto, Soprano, *Tenor, Bass,* instead of Alto, Soprano, Bass, Tenor ; i.e., the 3rd announcement is not in the parallel of the first part.

(2) The alternation of Subject and Response ;

See, again, Fugue 1, Vol. I ; the order is Subject, Response, Response, Subject (the second announcement of the Subject is in the parallel of the first part, but occurs too late — as fourth voice). See also Vol. I, Fugue 12 ; Subject, Response, Subject, Subject, in Tenor, Alto, *Bass, Soprano.* — Vol. I, Fugue 14 ; Vol. II, Fugue 17.

(3) The number of announcements, which may be more (very rarely less) than the total number of parts.

The " extra " announcement is rare in the 4-voice Fugue, though common in the 3-voice. See **Bach,** Well-temp. Cl., Vol. II, Fugue 17 ; the Exposition is irregular, as already seen ; and a 5th announcement (" Subject ") is added in Bass, meas. 13–15. Vol. II, Fugue 23, extra announcement (Bass), in meas. 19–22. **Bach,** Org. Comp. (Peters compl. ed.), Vol. II, Fugue 3, extra announcement, somewhat abbreviated, in Bass, meas. 45–49. Vol. IV, Fugue 2.

125. *a.* After the first Response (second announcement of the Theme), an episodic interlude of one or more measures is generally inserted, partly by way of variety, but chiefly as a means of modulating back into the original key, and preparing for the next announcement of the Subject. The episode must, of course, be *strictly in keeping* with what precedes, and is usually derived directly from it. Review par. 41*b.* For illustration, Ex. 150 continues thus :

Ex. 152.

See further, **Bach,** Well-temp. Cl., Vol. I, Fugue 14, meas. 7 (derived from end of meas. 2); Fugue 17, meas. 3-4 (sequences in Bass, followed by modified form of the Counterpoint); Vol. II, **Fugue 5, meas. 4;** Fugue 7, meas. 13; Fugue 22, meas. 9-10.

In Vol. I, Fugue 18, there is *no* episode before the second announcement of the Subject; and the same in Vol. I, Fugue 23, and Vol. II, Fugue 9.

In Vol. I, Fugue 5, the episode is made of new material, but rhythmically related to what precedes.

Vol. I, Fugue 20, meas. 7, new figure (scale-line); Vol. I, Fugue 22, meas. 6-9, new, but closely related to the foregoing; rhythm curiously shifted (a figure of 6 beats in a 4-beat measure).

Vol. II, Fugue 8, meas. 5-6; **new, but partly derived** from Subject.

b. As a rule, there is **no** further episodic interlude (in the 4-voice Fugue) before the last (4th) announcement of the Theme, — the last Response. But when the latter is finished, an episode, more or less lengthy, is almost obligatory, as a means of establishing the key in which, at this juncture, the Exposition is expected to close. It is during this final episodic passage that an extra (5th) announcement of the Theme (as " Subject," probably) may occur. See par. 124 (3).

126. The Exposition ends, as a rule, with a perfect cadence in the Dominant key (from a *major* beginning), or in the Relative key (from a *minor* beginning). Other keys, especially the original key itself, are possible, however, and not infrequently chosen. The perfect cadence is often (perhaps most commonly) made fairly strong, by the emphatic succession V–I in Bass, Tonic in Soprano, on an accented beat. But sometimes it is much lighter; and occasionally it is so transient and indefinite that the actual close of the Exposition can be defined in a general way only, or not at all. In no case, however, no matter how strong the harmonic form of the cadence may be, is any decided check of the rhythmic movement permissible. Review par. 40*h.*

See **Bach,** Well-temp. Cl., Vol. I, Fugue 23 ; the Exposition ends in meas. 9, firmly, on the I of the Dominant key; there are no episodes at all.

Vol. I, Fugue 5, meas. 6, cadence in Dominant key, fairly firm ; no second episode.

Vol. I, Fugue 16, meas. 12, firm perfect cadence in Relative key ; second episode, meas. 8-12, designed like the first one.

Vol. I, Fugue 17, meas. 7 (2nd beat), or meas. 10 — probably the latter, but very indefinite in either case.

Vol. I, Fugue 18, meas. 11, cadence in Dominant key from *minor* beginning.

Vol. I, Fugue 20, meas. 14, ditto; by altering the chord-3rd (*g*) to *g♯*, the I of the Dominant key is changed, in a characteristically abrupt manner, into the V of the original key.

Vol. II, Fugue 5, meas. 10; light Dominant cadence.

Vol. II, Fugue 7, meas. 30; strong Dominant cadence.

Vol. II, Fugue 8, probably meas. 11; very vague.

Vol. II, Fugue 9, meas. 9; Dominant cadence, 3rd in Soprano.

Further, Vol. I, Fugue 1; Exposition irregular; ends in meas. 7, with light *Tonic* cadence.

Vol. I, Fugue 14; Exposition irregular; ends in meas. 20, with firm Dominant cadence (from minor beginning).

THE FUGHETTA.

127. The Fughetta is a small Fugue, containing no more than one Section (the Exposition, possibly extended by one or two extra announcements of the Theme) ; or perhaps two Sections, — the Exposition and one additional Section. In the *first* of these cases, the Exposition must terminate with a strong perfect cadence in the original key.

Bach, Air with 30 Var. (Clav.), Var. 10; two " Parts " or Sections.

Bach, Organ Comp. (Peters ed.), Vol. V, No. 7; No. 18 (irregular Exposition, two Sections).

Schumann, "Fughettas" for pianoforte, op. 126; No. 2 (two Sections, very vague cadence; begins with "Response"); No. 3 (three Sections, cadences vague); No. 4, ditto; No. 5, ditto (new, characteristic counterpoint in Sec. III); No. 7 (three Sections, cadences fairly clear, stretti in Sec. III). These are all scarcely more than elaborate Inventions.

EXERCISE 37.

A. Write several examples of the Exposition of the 4-voice Fugue, using some of the Subjects of the preceding Exercises. Employ major and minor Subjects alternately, and different rhythmic styles and *tempi*.

B. Write two or three examples of the complete 4-voice Fughetta of *one* Section; i.e., an Exposition closing with perfect cadence in the original key.

THE SECTIONAL FORM.

128. The Exposition (first Section) is an essential and characteristic factor of this form of composition, appearing in every genuine Fugue, no matter what its subsequent development (its design as a whole) may be.

That which follows the Exposition, however, is not (as a rule) subject to any further specific conditions, — excepting such as may be involved in some "special design" of the Fugue as a whole (to be considered further on). The constraint of special rules is relaxed ; in the second Section, and other following ones, it does not matter how often the Theme appears, in which parts, nor on which scale-steps. The subsequent conduct of the Fugue may be as free as that of the Invention, always excepting that a certain dignity and general seriousness of style should be maintained. After the Exposition the writer is free to realize more definite structural purposes; to carry out more extensive modulatory designs; to develop the thematic resources of the subject, both as a whole, *and in its component figures;* and to pursue some broad (quasi dramatic) design, leading in successive stages to effective climaxes, at, or near, the end.

129. The most convenient and common design for the Fugue is the simple *Sectional form;* for this provides the most natural means for the simple progressive development of the resources of the Theme. Review par. 39.

The number of sections is optional (from 3 to 6 or 8). Their cadences, and the modulatory design of the whole, correspond to the directions given for the Invention. ·

130. *a.* The second Section may begin with an announcement of the Theme, in any part, and in any next-related key, preferably the one in which the Exposition closed.

See **Bach,** Well-temp. Cl., Vol. I, Fugue 16 (meas. 12); Fugue 18 (meas. 11).

And, as already stated, this section, and all which follow, may contain as few or as many successive announcements as appears convenient or desirable, — as a rule, however, not in the same part twice in *immediate* succession.

b. Or the Section may begin with a carefully planned *Episode.* This seems to be the best and most common practice.

See **Bach,** Well-temp. Cl., Vol. I, Fugue 5 (meas. 6, — episode derived from Theme).
Vol. I, Fugue 23 (meas. 9–11; derived, with quaint rhythmic modification, from Theme, and containing frequent allusions to the first figure of the Counterpoint, — descending scale).
Bach, Org. Comp. (Peters ed.), Vol. II, Fugue 1 (meas. 19–28, derived from Theme).
Vol. II, Fugue 2 (meas. 17–26).

c. Such an episode is likely to acquire a certain independent importance in the Fugue, and to *reappear,* in the same section or in later ones, — not literally, but in the same general thematic form; in differ-

ent keys, naturally, and in various inversions.   This is the case with
the episodic passages in general.

See **Bach,** Well-temp. Cl., Vol. 1, Fugue 17; the episode in meas. 11 (with
sequence in following measure) reappears in meas. 14, 15, and 19, 20, each time in a
different key, and with inverted parts.   Also Vol. I, Fugue 14; similar episodes in
meas. 7, 18, and 28.

These recurrences of the episodic material not only institute well-
defined variety (as opposed to the thematic announcements), but contribute to the *unity* and definite *form* of the whole.   In some instances,
especially in the broader organ fugues of **Bach,** the episodes assume an
importance fully equal, if not superior, to that of the thematic portions,
and lend (by their frequency, extent, and characteristic treatment) a
very effective physiognomy to both form and contents.

See, for example, **Bach,** Org. Comp. (Peters ed.), Vol. III, Fugue 3; the episodes are constructed, throughout, in very similar fashion upon an auxiliary motive
(derived from a figure of the Counterpoint); they appear in meas. 15–17, 25–28,
36–42, 50–56, 64–66 (new episode), 67–70, 78–80, 88–100, 108–114, etc., etc.   Also
Vol. II, Fugue 4; *episodes after nearly every announcement of the Theme:* meas. 7–9,
12–14, 18–21, 28, 32–36, 39–43, 47–50, 54, 57–65, 68–79 (similar to preceding one),
82–93 (ditto), 97–100 (like 47–50), 106–109 (like 32–36).

131.   Each succeeding Section of the Fugue may (perhaps should)
contain some new traits, — most naturally, new " Counterpoints " to the
Theme.   And each Section should be more interesting and effective
than those which preceded.   Therefore it is customary to introduce the
contrary motion of the Theme, in later Sections; and, near the end,
good *stretto*-imitations are desirable.   *Review, very thoroughly, par. 33*
(Ex. 83).

Analyze, very minutely, the following Fugues from the Well-temp. Cl. of **Bach :**

Vol. I, Fugue 23; Section II begins in meas. 9, with episode, followed by one
announcement of Theme (Tenor); Sec. III begins in meas. 13, with same episode,
followed by Theme in Alto; Sec. IV begins in meas. 18, with Theme in contrary
motion (Soprano), followed by same in Alto, then original motion in Bass and in
Tenor; Sec. V begins in meas. 26, with former episode, followed by Theme in Alto,
and then in Soprano.

Vol. I, Fugue 16; Sec. II begins in meas. 12, with impressive solo-announce-
ment of Theme, — further, Theme in Bass, Soprano, then Bass and (2 beats later)
Alto *in stretto ;* the Alto Theme extends partly over into Sec. III, which begins in
meas. 18, and contains Theme in Bass, Soprano, and Alto; this section closes, peculiarly, with a firm perfect cadence in the *principal key ;* Sec. IV is exclusively episodic, and seems to be a Retransition, leading back to the beginning, — intimating
(in connection with other traits) that this Fugue is designed in the 3-Part Song-form
(par. 136); Sec. V begins in meas. 28, with a stretto of the Theme in Alto, Tenor,

and Bass (the latter only fragmentary), followed, after an episode, by Theme in Alto (meas. 31), and. finally, in Tenor.

In Vol. II, Fugue 5, the stretto-design is more elaborate. *Analyze minutely.* There are eight sufficiently definite sections; in Sec. V (meas. 27) a 2-voice stretto appears; in Sec. VI (meas. 33) a 3-voice stretto; and in Sec. VIII (meas. 44) a 4-voice stretto.

In Vol. II, Fugue 8, there is a *double-announcement* of the Theme in simultaneous original and contrary motion, in Soprano and Tenor, in the Codetta (last four measures).

In Vol. I, Fugue 5, there is a definite and characteristic arrangement of episodic passages; Sec. III begins (in meas. 9) with an almost homophonic episode, derived, by Augmentation, from the Theme, and continued during two measures; it recurs at the beginning of Sec. IV (meas. 17) inverted, and extended to three measures; and again in meas. 21 in the original form.

See further, **Bach,** Org. Comp. (Peters ed.), Vol. II, Fugue I; Sec. II begins in meas. 19, with an episode, followed by Theme in Tenor; Sec. III begins in meas. 35 with Theme and characteristic (new) Counterpoint; Sec. IV, in meas. 55 with new episode; Sec. V, in meas. 85 with remainder of Theme announced in preceding measure (Tenor). These sections are considerably longer than in the Fugues of the Well-temp. Clavichord.

Also Vol. IV, Fugue 2; the Exposition contains an extra (5th) announcement, in meas. 28; Sec. 2 begins in meas. 34 (cadence light) with an episode; then Theme in Alto, episode, Theme in Tenor, episode, Theme in Soprano, episode, Theme in Bass; Sec. III begins in meas. 71, with a long episode (to meas. 83); Sec. IV, in meas. 105, with remainder of Theme in Alto, and closes in meas. 132; from there to end, Coda. The first Counterpoint is retained *approximately*, throughout (par 132). The episodes alternate almost regularly with the thematic announcements.

132. As intimated above, it is quite common to *retain the first Counterpoint*, and to use it more or less constantly with later announcements of the Theme. This retention of the " Counterpoint " is not, however, to be too persistent in the " Single " Fugue, — such *constant* recurrence of a contrapuntal associate being a distinctive condition of the " Double-fugue," as will be seen.

It may be retained during the Exposition only; perhaps recurring from time to time in later sections ; or it may be abandoned after the first Response, and recur later; it may be used entire, or in part; and may be modified to any extent.

See **Bach,** Well-temp. Cl., Vol. I, Fugue 14; Subject in Tenor, Response in Alto ; during the latter a characteristic Counterpoint is carried by the Tenor; it recurs in Alto (meas. 8–10) against Theme in Bass, extended at the beginning by an anticipation of the first figure; it recurs again in Bass (meas. 15–17) against Theme in Soprano, with the same introductory extension; and again in Alto (meas. 25–27), in Soprano (meas. 29–31), and, somewhat modified, in Alto (meas. 37–39). This retention of the Counterpoint is *almost* as persistent as in the Double-fugue.

Vol. I, Fugue 23; the Counterpoint lies first in the Tenor (meas. 3-4, — beginning with the characteristic descending scale, out of which, by the way, all the *episodes* are largely constructed) ; it recurs in Alto (meas. 5-6), and in Soprano (meas. 7-8), — that is, it is retained during the Exposition. But it does not occur again (save as occasional fragmentary allusion) until near the end (in Alto, meas. 31-32), against the Theme in Soprano.

Vol. II, Fugue 8; the Counterpoint is characteristic, consisting of 4 sequential figures (Ex. 151) ; it recurs at each following announcement of the Theme, in Tenor (meas. 7-8), Bass (meas. 9-10), Soprano (meas. 15-16). Then it is once absent, reappearing next in Bass (meas. 19-20), and in Tenor (meas. 21-22). It then disappears altogether.

In Vol. II, Fugue 9, the Counterpoint runs thus :

Ex. 153.

It occurs in Bass (meas. 3), recurs in Tenor (meas. 4-5), and Alto (meas. 6). It reappears *episodically* (without the Theme) in Tenor (meas. 8). In meas. 11-12 it appears, somewhat modified, in Tenor ; and immediately afterward in Soprano, curiously modified thus,

Ex. 154.

Augmentation.

in which form it is at once carried through the four parts, episodically, as stretto after a half-measure (Soprano, Alto, Bass, Tenor). It reappears in its original form in Soprano (meas. 36), Alto (37), and Tenor (38), — the last time extended sequentially.

Vol. II, Fugue 22 ; the Counterpoint is largely chromatic, occurring first in Alto (meas. 5-8), then *again* in Alto (meas. 11-14), then in Bass (meas. 17-20). When the Theme appears, later, in contrary motion, the Counterpoint, *also in contrary motion*, again accompanies it : Alto, meas. 42-44 ; Tenor, meas. 46-48 ; Alto again, 52-54 ; and a fragment in Soprano, meas. 59-60.

Vol. II, Fugue 23 ; a very striking Counterpoint is retained throughout the Exposition only ; Bass, meas. 5-8 ; Tenor, meas. 10-13 ; Alto, meas. 14-17 ; Soprano, meas. 19-21. It is absent during the remainder of the Fugue (which, as a whole, will be cited again as a " Double-fugue ").

EXERCISE 38.

A. Analyze, very minutely :

Bach, Well-temp. Cl., Vol. I, Fugue 18.

Bach, Well-temp. Cl., Vol. II, Fugues 5, 8.

Bach, Org. Comp. (Peters ed.), Vol. II, Fugue 1 ; Fugue 3 (seven sections ; Counterpoint retained *nearly* throughout, — absent in Sec. V and part of Sec. VI ; one stretto in Sec. VI).

Bach, Org. Comp., Vol. III, Fugue 5 (various Counterpoints ; many episodes).

Bach, Clavichord works, Peters ed. 212, No. 4 (p. 66).

B. Write a number of complete 4-voice Fugues (at least two) in Sectional form. Both major and minor. Different species of measure, and different character *and tempo*, to be adopted for each example.

ADDITIONAL MISCELLANEOUS DIRECTIONS.

133. Review, thoroughly, par. 41*a* and par. 61*a*. As repeatedly shown, and confirmed by the analysis of the authoritative contrapuntal works of **Bach** and other great polyphonic writers, the original source of all multi-voice music is the **chord ;** and the prime impulse of all associated voice-movements is, obviously, the natural law of chord-succession (par. 18). For a certain period, the choice of tones and the melodic movements will be, and must be, dictated by the rules of chord-progression ; the voices or parts cling, for a time, to the *harmony* for their support, as children (so to speak) are led by their older and stronger associates. But the time finally arrives when (in the growing experience and skill of the student) the " voices " outgrow this guardian-ship of fundamental harmonic law, and exercise greater independence in their movements ; and, in fact, the exercise of independent melodic will may become so imperative as to reverse the conditions, so that the parts dictate the chord-successions. In other words, as the student's command of melodic conduct increases until he can trace the course of three or more simultaneous melodic parts unerringly, so that *each part by itself is a perfect melody,* moments will arrive when these individual voice-movements will determine the succession of harmonic nodes, called " chords " ; when, instead of the parts moving obediently towards the several harmonic points fixed by each succeeding chord (in the pre-defined order of natural chord-progression), the parts themselves assume the lead, and dictate what the chord-successions shall be. For if *each part* describes a faultless melodic line, and the parts *harmonize,* the result will be acceptable and legitimate, whether it conforms to the common law of chord-sequence or not.

For **example,** the chord-successions in the following examples cannot be satis-factorily defined in accordance with the common rules of chord-progression ; and yet the result of the three or more associated melodies is good.

$E\flat VA\flat???\ E\flat IV I \qquad\qquad g\ \overset{7\sharp}{IV}\ \overset{7}{II} \qquad ? \qquad I$

*1) " Passing-chord "; this effect is very common in **Wagner.**

*2) Sequence in the Alto-part. The harmonies are simple and regular, but the passing- and neighboring-notes create totally unexpected chord-effects.

When this result is achieved, the product belongs to the highest grade of polyphonic thought. But it is scarcely conceivable that this lofty phase of polyphonic effort can be often reached or long sustained ; even in the works of **Bach** and **Brahms,** unmistakable evidences of emancipation from natural harmonic law are rare ; in those of **Beethoven** and other great homophonic masters, naturally still more so. And in the more modern writings of **Wagner, Rich. Strauss,** and others, where such evidences are again more frequent, one cannot always quite escape an uncomfortable sensation of harmonic bewilderment. The growing vigor and independence of melodic conduct may incite to occasional successful rebellion (so to speak), but the student will *never wholly outgrow* the necessary and wholesome habits of harmonic action contracted during early studies. The habits formed during the discipline of deriving all melodic movements from the sub-current of natural harmonic sequence, will, in polyphonic texture of **greatest power and stability,** never cease to assert themselves.

Hence, the present student will apply this most eminent resource of polyphonic development chiefly as a means of defining the *choice* between many possible chord-structures which await each coming beat; and far more rarely, with much caution, as a legitimate device for obtaining unexpected harmonic clusters, and evolving greater freedom and opulence of harmonic movement. Review, further, pars. 59 and 60; and, particularly, pars. 61 *c*, *d*, and *e*. Also par. 75.

134. *a*. The voice-movements should be *conjunct*, in largely preponderant measure. Skips, of course, can not and should not be avoided altogether; but they must be made with caution, and may require careful testing. They are *always* good when occurring within any unchanged chord, or when the first of the two tones is common to the following chord. It is best to avoid leaping to any sharply dissonant, or inharmonic, tone.

Transient harsh effects, even extreme, cannot be precluded; they are as essential in effective polyphony as are the pure consonances; but the manner of their *approach and departure* must be very guarded, — *abrupt* dissonances are usually objectionable.

b. Review, *thoroughly*, par. 64. It is absolutely necessary that one of the four parts should assume the lead, for a more or less extended period, — until another of their number becomes in turn the "leader." This function devolves, naturally, upon the part which has the Theme, though not to the exclusion of some concurrent part, *especially Soprano or Bass*, — one of which is very likely indeed to contribute most noticeably, in this way, to the tracing of the Form.

A good illustration of this vital condition is seen in **Bach,** Well-temp. Cl., Vol. I, Fugue 22, meas. 6–12 in Soprano. See also Vol. II, Fugue 18, meas. 85–93 in Bass. Vol. II, Fugue 9, last 6 measures in Soprano.

Mendelssohn, Organ Fugue, op. 37, No. 1, — the "leading" character of the Soprano, especially, is obvious in many places; see meas. 18–19, 20–22, 41–45. Without such definite, and, if need be, *lengthy* melodic lines, a Fugue can hardly escape monotony, diffuseness, and vague, ineffective form.

c. For this very reason, sequences are of the utmost importance. Review par. 41*c*.

d. Review par. 63*b* and *c;* par. 75*e*. It is well to avoid long rests during the Exposition, until the four parts have all appeared with the Theme. Short rests are always good (**Bach,** Well-temp. Cl., Vol. I, Fugue 23, meas. 5–6); especially in the Theme itself (Vol. II, Fugue

22), or in the first Counterpoint (Vol. I, Fugue 12). **And longer rests are not only permissible, but desirable, in the later course of the Fugue.** It is positively unwise to keep all four parts constantly present and moving.

e. In the Exposition avoid any circumstance that tends to obscure the successive announcements of the *beginning* of the Theme.

Observe how effective the entrances of the parts are in Vol. II, Fugue 9 and Fugue 8. In Vol. II, Fugue 7, the last note in meas. 6 interferes somewhat with the Response in the next. Observe, further, the entrances in **Mendelssohn**, op. 35, Fugue 1, especially in meas. 6.

f. The character of the Subject influences its Exposition to a certain extent. A heavy Theme is somewhat likely to appear first in Bass or Tenor (i.e., low). A Theme that ends higher than it begins must appear first in a *high* voice, to avoid interference with its next imitation, and vice versa.

The *tempo* of the Subject must be taken into account also; it influences the number of parts, the number of rests, the degree of liveliness (or of stateliness) in the rhythm of the first Counterpoint, and, in fact, of the entire Fugue; and, somewhat, the number, extent, and quality of *dissonances*. Attention is again directed, particularly, to par. 33.

Continue the work of thorough analysis with the following sectional 4-voice Fugues:

Bach, Organ Comp. (Peters compl. ed.), Vol. III, Fugue 10; 3 sections; brief and simple, but effective; many episodes.

Vol. IV, Fugue 5; 3 sections; 5 announcements in Exposition, ending with vague cadence (meas. 20); Pedal in last section only.

Vol. IV, Fugue 9; for manual organ; 4 sections and free Coda; Counterpoint retained approximately throughout; many episodes.

Vol. VIII, Fugue 10; manual organ; very regular, " Subject " and " Response " throughout; cadences vague.

Vol. II, Fugue 10; three different *thematic* counterpoints, besides several incidental characteristic ones; thus:

Cpt. *a.*

Ex. 156.

Theme.

Char. Cpt. *b*.

Theme.

and: BACH.

Theme.

Char. Cpt. *c*.

Bach, Clavichord Works: Peters ed. 212, No. 6 (*a* minor). Peters ed. 216, No. 8 (p. 48); many stretti. Peters ed. 216, No. 9 (p. 52); contrary motion in middle sections, and later in alternation with the original motion.

Mendelssohn, Organ Comp., op. 37, Fugue 1; fine example of both detailed and continuous structural design; intimation of 3-Part Song-form (par. 136).

Op. 37, Fugue 2; cadences vague.

Sonata, op. 65, No. 4, last movement; Fugue with homophonic Introduction and Coda; 3 sections, cadences vague.

Sonata, op. 65, No. 5, 5th movement; Fugue; 3 Sections, cadences vague.

Mendelssohn, Pianoforte Comp., op. 35, No. 2, Fugue.

Bach, "Art of Fugue" Fugue 1; probably sectional, though the cadences are very vague,—more like one long, unbroken Section; fairly frequent episodes, based upon a brief episodic (auxiliary) motive, and corroborative of each other. Analyze this and the following *very thoroughly and minutely.*

Fugue 2; an Exposition, and one other long Section (cadences, if any, very vague); an auxiliary motive (meas. 8–9, Bass) and several episodic motives are utilized.

Fugue 4; five Sections, fairly definite cadences; many long episodes, based on an auxiliary figure (of two notes, meas. 14–15 in Soprano, 23–26 in Bass), and an episodic motive (of 4 tones, descending scale, meas. 18–19 in Bass); a characteristic trait of the Counterpoint (repeated measure) is also occasionally used.

Händel, Clav. Suites, No. III, second movement.

Händel, Clav. Suites, No. VIII, second movement (partly 3-voice).

Schumann, Pianoforte Fugues, op. 72; Fugue 1, five Sections and Coda; augmentation of Theme (abbreviated) in Sec. V.—Fugue 3, Romantic style, four Sections and Coda; in Sec. II an auxiliary M. appears twice (with small auxiliary figure), and reappears similarly in Sec. III; in Sec. IV there is a new and characteristic Counterpoint.

EXERCISE 39.

Write a large number of 4-voice Fugues, in sectional form; major and minor alternately; different species of measure, different style and tempo for each example.

THE SONG–FORMS.

135. The Two-Part Song-form. The chief difference between this and the sectional design is the distinctly marked cadence (usually perfect) in or near the middle of the Fugue.

The First Part is likely to consist of the Exposition, and one additional section; the latter may be brief and largely episodic, or it may be longer and more independent; but in either case it leads into a well-prepared and *fairly emphatic cadence* in the Dominant key (possibly the Relative major, in a minor Fugue, or some other next-related key).

Part II is often individualized to some extent; most commonly by adopting the contrary motion of the Theme (for a time), or by means of a new and characteristic Counterpoint. At the same time, Part II may (perhaps should) exhibit more or less distinct parallelism with its First Part, — especially in its episodes; and, as usual, the last few measures may corroborate the ending of Part I. A Codetta or Coda may be added. Review par. 45.

See **Bach,** Well-temp. Cl., Vol. I, Fugue 14; Part I (the Exposition, and 3 episodic measures) closes in meas. 20, with a strong Dominant cadence. Part II begins with Theme in Alto in contrary motion; then Theme in original motion in Soprano with disguised beginning (meas. 25), leading to cadence in meas. 28, — thus dividing the Second Part into two sections. In meas. 35–36 the episode of meas. 19 reappears, followed by Theme in Soprano. The contrary motion occurs again in Bass, meas. 32–34.

Vol. I, Fugue 17; Part I ends in meas. 16; a very faint intimation of a Third Part occurs in meas. 27.

Vol. II, Fugue 2; Part I is 3-voice texture throughout; it closes in meas. 14 with a positive perfect cadence in the Dominant key. Part II is characterized by two announcements of the Theme in Augmentation, and, further, by the addition of a 4th voice. The last 5½ measures are a Coda.

Vol. II, Fugue 7; Part I closes in meas. 30; Part II largely episodic.

Mendelssohn, Organ Fugue, op. 37, No. 3; quasi sectional,— suggestion of a separation into two Parts in meas. 32; the last 25 measures are Coda.

Organ Sonata, op. 65, No. 2, last movement; Part II characterized by a more animated counterpoint (partly thematic); few episodes until near the end.

136. The Three-Part Song-form. Part I the same as in the 2-Part Song-form. Part II is here again generally characterized in some manner; and is led into a more or less distinct semicadence upon the

Dominant of the original key, usually confirmed by an emphatic (some-times quite extended) organ-point.

Part III must be, as usual, a well-marked " Return to the begin-ning "; but it does not need to contain any more than the first few measures (two or three) of Part I, — enough to establish key and for-mal design ; its subsequent contents are likely to be entirely independ-ent, and should be more elaborate and interesting than any preceding Section ; hence, stretto-imitations are peculiarly appropriate, and more brilliant (even partly homophonic) episodes are legitimate and desirable. A Coda or Codetta is frequently added.   Review pars. 49, 50 ; also 33.

See **Bach,** Well-temp. Cl., Vol. I, Fugue 16; already cited among the sectional forms; there is a strong indication of a " Return to the beginning " in meas. 28.

Vol. I, Fugue 23; ditto; intimation of Third Part n meas. 6 from the end.

Schumann, op. 72, Fugue 4; in Part II (*più vivo*) two different *modified forms of the Theme appear :*

EXERCISE 40.

A number of 4-voice Fugues in the 2-Part and 3-Part Song-forms.

THE FUGUE WITH SPECIAL DESIGN.

137. No good Fugue is barren of some structural design, as the foregoing paragraphs show.   But it is possible to pursue some *special* plan in the manipulation of this polyphonic form, evolved more particu-larly out of the resources of its Theme, and therefore peculiarly iden-tified with the processes of Thematic Development.

The *formal* plan is usually that of the sectional Fugue ; and the " special design " consists in assigning to each Section in succession some specific method of thematic treatment, resulting in a *systematic presentation* of such possibilities of manipulation and combination as are latent within the Theme (e.g., effective *stretti*, contrary motion, etc.). These possibilities, or resources, are usually *determined beforehand by most thorough examination and experiment with the Theme ;* and it is more than likely that these resources may be systematically multiplied by judicious revision and alteration of the Subject, — possibly created outright in draughting the Theme.

Review Chap. IV ; especially pars. 29, 33, 36.

Analyze, most thoroughly, the following :

Bach, Well-temp. Cl., Vol. I, Fugue 20; the "design" is strikingly manifest; Sec. I is a regular Exposition, to meas. 14 ; Sec. II is an equally complete Exposition of the Theme in *contrary motion*, to meas. 27 ; Sec. III is the exposition of a *stretto* in the 8ve after two beats (Soprano and Tenor) carried through all the parts, up to meas. 48 ; Sec. IV is a similar exposition of the same stretto *in contrary motion* (Alto and Tenor) through all the parts, somewhat abbreviated in the last measures, 62–64 ; Sec. V is the condensed exposition of a *new stretto*, after two beats in the 5th, first in original motion (meas. 64–65, Bass and Tenor), then in contrary motion (Soprano and Alto) ; Sec. VI, meas. 73, contains miscellaneous stretti, to the cadence in meas. 83 ; the rest is Coda.

Vol. II, Fugue 22, is similar; Sec. I is a regular Exposition up to meas. 25 ; Sec. II is the Exposition of a remarkable *stretto*, after one beat in the 7th (meas. 27, Tenor and Alto) ; Sec. III, meas. 42, is an Exposition of the Theme in *contrary motion ;* Sec. IV, meas. 67, the same stretto as before, but in *contrary motion* (Alto and Soprano). Thus far, to meas. 77, the Fugue consists of two similar double-sections, one in regular and the other in contrary motion. Sec. V, meas. 80, is the Exposition of a new stretto, after one beat, in *regular and contrary* motion (Soprano and Tenor). Near the end, as climax (meas. 96), there is an extraordinary double-stretto, regular and contrary motion, each Theme doubled in the 3rd (the first one part of the way in the 6th).

Vol. II, Fugue 9 ; "Gregorian" Theme; Sec. I, Exposition; Sec. II, meas. 9, stretto in 4th after two beats (Alto, Tenor, Bass, Soprano) ; Sec. III, meas. 16, new stretto, in 5th after one measure (Alto, Soprano, Bass, Tenor) ; Sec. IV, meas. 23, new stretto, in 5th after one beat, with *modified form of the Theme* (Soprano, Alto, Bass, Tenor) ; Sec. V, end of meas. 26, Exposition of the *Diminution* (Soprano, Alto, Tenor, Bass) ; Sec. VI, meas. 30, contains original Theme, and its Diminution, in regular and contrary motion, — faintly suggestive of Sec. I ; Sec. VII, meas. 35, is substantially the recurrence of Sec. II ; from meas. 38 to end is in the nature of a Coda.

Vol. I, Fugue I ; the special design is not as obvious as in the above examples, but the persistent stretto-treatment of the Theme after the Exposition (meas. 7–24), especially the 4-voice stretto in meas. 16–18 (Soprano, Alto, Tenor, Bass), seems to be more than merely accidental.

Bach, "Art of Fugue," Fugue 3 ; appears to begin with "Response," instead of "Subject," — (a peculiarity of irregular Exposition — par. 124 — seen also in **Bach,** Org. Comp., Vol. III, Fugue 4, and Vol. IV, Fugues 1 and 4).

The "Subject" (meas. 5) runs thus:

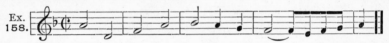

There are four Sections, separated by very vague cadences, but distinguished by their thematic contents; Sec. I is the usual Exposition; Sec. II (meas. 23) presents the Theme in the following form:

Sec. III (meas. 39) returns to the original form; Sec. IV (meas. 55) uses the following form twice,

and also the original form. The first counterpoint (partly chromatic) is retained nearly throughout.

Bach, " Art of Fugue," Fugue 12 ; 4-voice; Special Design in 2-Part Song-form; Part I is a regular Exposition, with a thematic Counterpoint (par. 163) retained; Part II is an exposition of the Subject in still more richly embellished form than those illustrated in Ex. 158. The following Fugue (No. 12*b*) is the exact Contrary motion and Inversion of the preceding ; compare them minutely.

Mendelssohn, op. 7, No. 5 ; very elaborate sectional form; about nine Sections (including the Exposition) and a brief Coda ; Sec. III, contrary motion ; Sec. IV, Augmentation; Sec. V, Diminution ; Sec. VI, episodic, animated tempo and rhythm; Sec. IX, stretti.

EXERCISE 41.

Two or more Fugues with Special Design.

CHAPTER XIII.

The Fugue with Less or More Than Four Parts. — The Three–Voice Fugue.

138. **The Exposition.** The three parts are called lower, inner, and upper, without reference to voice-compass, though they are likely to represent adjacent registers. The regular Exposition contains Subject,

Response, and Subject (comp. par. 123), the *last Subject always either an octave higher or lower than the first Subject.*

The enlargement of the Exposition to *four* announcements is, however, quite common in the 3-voice Fugue; the last announcement is again "Response," usually an 8ve lower or higher than the first Response.

See **Bach,** Well-temp. Cl., Vol. I, Fugue 19; the 4th announcement is made noticeable by the peculiar leap in Bass (meas. 5–6).

Vol. I, Fugue 8 (meas. 12).   Vol. II, Fugue 11 (meas. 21).   Vol. II, Fugue 19 (meas. 7).

139. The Theme of a 3-voice Fugue is likely to be of a more spirited rhythmic character, and possibly wider compass, than that of the 4-voice Fugue; otherwise there is no essential difference. The structural designs and all details of treatment are the same.

140. Sectional form. Review pars. 128 to 132, and analyze the following, most thoroughly :

Bach, Well-temp. Cl., Vol. I, Fugue 9; Exposition to meas. 5; Sec. II to meas. 17; episode in meas. 13-15, recurring in meas. 23–24; in meas. 19 there is an intimation of a return to the beginning (quasi 3-Part Song-form). Vol. I, Fugue 11, four Sections.

Vol. II, Fugue I. — Fugue 6 (contrary motion and stretti employed in later course). — Fugue 10 (episode in meas. 18–20, corroborated in meas. 47–49; characteristic Counterpoint recurs occasionally). — Fugue 11 (quasi 2-Part Song-form; Exposition to meas. 29; many episodes). — Fugue 12. Fugue 15. Fugue 19.

Bach, Clavichord Comp., Peters ed. 212, No. 2 (p. 59). Peters ed. 213, No. 1, 2nd movement; elaborate episodes. Peters ed. 213, No. 2, 2nd movement (p. 21); broad sectional form; elaborate episodes, largely similar. Peters ed. 214, No. 2 (p. 12); many fairly strong cadences, Sections small; compare minutely with the "Variante," p. 48. Peters ed. 215, p. 23. 216, p. 50 (No. 8, fifth movement). 216, No. 10 (p. 57); many cadences, Sections brief.

Bach, *Musikalisches Opfer,* No. 1 (*Ricercata,* — same as *Fuga*).

Rubinstein, Fugue op. 53, No. 2 (contrary motion and stretti ingeniously used).

Schumann, op. 126, No. 1 (2 Sections, cadences vague); No. 6, 4 Sections.

Jadassohn, Pfte. Fugues and Preludes, op. 56; Fugue No. 6; also Nos. 2 and 3; the latter contain effective stretti and the Contrary motion, — cited again, among the Concert-fugues (par. 148).

141. Two-Part Song-form. Review par. 135, and analyze the following :

Bach, Well-temp. Cl., Vol. I, Fugue 6; Part I closes in meas. 21 (almost exactly in the middle of the Fugue) with a strong perfect cadence in the Dominant

key; Part II uses the contrary motion freely, and later, from meas. 31 on, corroborates Part I closely; the last 5 measures of each Part correspond exactly (except in
key).

The Fugue as Gigue form (par. 51), with contrary motion as basis of Part II, is
illustrated in **Bach,** Org. Comp., Vol. I, " Pastorale," last movement.

142. Among the many devices adopted for the characterization of
the Second Part (the most common being the contrary motion of the
Theme, pars. 48*b*, 51), there is one that is peculiarly effective in the
Fugue, namely, the introduction of a *new and striking Counterpoint*,
retained more or less constantly throughout the Part, as new *thematic*
member.   This process was touched upon in Ex. 156, which see.   For
illustration see —

Bach, Well-temp. Cl., Vol. I, Fugue 13; Part I (Exposition and episodic extension) closes in meas. 11; the new " thematic counterpoint " appears in meas. 12–13
in Bass, and twice later; it grows out of the foregoing episodic figure (meas. 7).

Vol. II, Fugue 21; Part I to meas. 32; the thematic counterpoint is in Soprano,
meas. 33–36, and reappears often; the two Parts close alike.

Vol. II, Fugue 24; the form is sectional (no decisive cadence to mark ? First
Part); the thematic counterpoint first occurs in meas. 29–32, in Bass

Händel, Clav. Suite, No. 4, 1st movement; 4-voice.
This design is the type of the Double-fugue, *Third* Species (par. 178, class 1)

143. The Three-Part Song-form.   Review par. 136, and see —

Schumann, op. 72, Fugue 2; light cadence at end of Part I (Exposition); the
first figure of the Counterpoint is used constantly; the contrary motion of the Theme
appears in later course of Part II; Part III contains only fragments of Theme, — a
end in Augmentation.

The Second Part is strongly characterized by an *animated rhythmic counterpoint* in **Bach,** Well-temp. Cl., Vol. I, Fugue 19; Part I ends in meas. 20; an
interlude of 3 measures follows, leading into Part II (meas. 23); the animated
counterpoint is not exactly " thematic " (that is, it has no definite and permanent
thematic form), but is based upon a set of similar figures; Part III, meas. 42, falls
back into the original quiet rhythm, which again yields to the animated form during
the Coda (meas. 49).   This form corresponds to par. 70.   Comp. also par. 142.

The **5-Part Song-form** (two digressions, Parts II and IV, and two returns to
the beginning, Parts III and V) is illustrated in —

Rubinstein, Pfte. Fugue, op. 53, No. 5; effective use of Diminution and stretti.

144. The Special Design.   Review par. 137, and see —

Bach, Well-temp. Cl., Vol. I, Fugue 8; the Exposition ends in meas. 19; Sec
II contains stretti, and a curious *partial* Augmentation (Alto, meas. 24–27); Sec. III
meas. 30, is an Exposition of the contrary motion; Sec. IV, meas. 44, closely resem
bles Sec. II (in contrary motion); Sec. V, meas. 52–61, contains triple stretti in regu-

lar and contrary motion, and one regular (single) announcement of the Theme ; Sec. VI, meas. 61–83, is an Exposition of the *Augmentation* (Bass, Alto, Soprano) ; the rest is an extremely beautiful Codetta. Vol. I, Fugue 15 ; Sec. I, Exposition, to meas. 20 ; followed by an Exposition of the contrary motion ; and later, various stretti ; analyze thoroughly. The episodic sections in this Fugue are very distinct, and corroborative of each other.

THE 2–VOICE FUGUE.

145. The Fugue with two parts only is naturally rare, because such slender means are inadequate to the dignity and richness that distinguish this polyphonic form.

The Theme must be of a lively rhythmic character, and ample compass. Episodes are frequent and somewhat free (brilliant) ; and the occasional addition of an auxiliary part, or parts, is permissible, — almost necessary. See —

Bach, Well-temp. Cl., Vol. I, Fugue 10 ; very clearly defined 2-Part Song-form ; Part I closes (with a unique passage in intentional octaves) in meas. 20, in the Subdominant key ; Part II, which follows immediately, is an *exact reproduction* of the First Part, but with inverted voices, and, on the first beat of meas. 29, a shift to the next higher step, in order to cadence upon the original keynote, *e*, instead of *d* (as would be the case if the preceding *Subdominant* modulation were pursued). Compare meas. 29 with meas. 10. Part II ends, with the same octave-passage, in meas. 39 ; the rest is Codetta (Theme in Soprano, pried asunder by an interposed measure, with imitation of first half in Bass).

Rheinberger, op. 5, No. 3.

Bach, Duetto II (Peters ed. 208, No. 4), 3-Part form. Also Duetto III (with exceptional auxiliary part at beginning — par. 112, 2) ; 3-Part form.

THE 5–VOICE FUGUE.

146. The extra, 5th, part is either a second Soprano, second Tenor, or second Bass (rarely an additional Alto) ; and the compass as a whole is somewhat expanded, either by adding to the height of the usual Soprano, or the depth of the Bass, or both.

Review par. 123. The Exposition consists of Subject, Response, Subject, Response, Subject. The " Subjects " must be *an octave apart ;* the " Responses " likewise. Parallel parts (those which are to announce the " Subject "), be it recalled, are separated by one (or three) parts.

Five-voice Fugues are seldom effective for the pianoforte, but entirely so for organ. In any case, however, it is desirable to use rests frequently ; especially protracted rests which reduce the texture occasionally to 4-voice, or even 3-voice.　Review, carefully, par. 134*d* and par. 75*e*.

The Subject is usually brief, stately, and narrow in range.

The very positive difficulties attending the addition of a 5th part may be minimized : (1) by preserving a perfectly distinct consciousness of the **chord-basis,** and the harmonic progressions in general; (2) by sustaining at least one of the parts upon some lengthy tone, important in the chord (as root), or in the key (Tonic, Dominant), — that is, by refraining from leading all the parts abreast, in active rhythm; (3) by using many parallel 3rds and 6ths and reciprocal figures, illustrated in Exs. 113 and 114 (which see); and (4) by judicious use of brief rests.

For general illustration :

a I———F I V————d V^9———I—

a V^7——I B♭ V^7 I=F IV————?———I—

*1) Observe the profusion of parallel 3rds.   *2) Parallel 3rds and 6ths.   *3) The two basses run in 6ths constantly.   Observe the thematic character of the first (highest) bass part; the very definite melodic conduct of *both outer parts;* and the chord-analysis.   *4) From here on, 4-voice texture.   *5) A neighboring-chord.   *6) The Motive (in 8th-notes).   *7) C♮ substituted for the expected *c♯* (par. 19*c*). *8) Probably the Dominant of *F;* see par. 133, Ex. 155.

Analyze, very minutely, the harmony, thematic texture, and form of the following:

Bach, Well-temp. Cl., Vol. I, Fugue 22; *Two-Part Song-form;* Part II, beginning in meas. 25, contains three well-defined Sections; in the last Section there is a double announcement of the Theme in 3rds (in the two Sopranos), and a five-fold stretto (beginning in meas. 9 from the end).

Bach, Org. Comp., Vol. II, Fugue 5; a fine example; 5 Sections; many different effective "Counterpoints"; after the Exposition the rhythm is more animated; Secs. III and V are largely 3- and 4-voice texture.

Vol. II, Fugue 7; *Special design;* the Theme is brief, and almost constantly present (i.e., few episodes); the texture is 4-voice up to Sec. VI, when the Pedal enters with *Augmentation* of Theme (to the end); Sec. II, meas. 8, begins with a striking sequential Counterpoint in the Soprano (see par. 134*b*); Sec. IV is an Exposition of the contrary motion; Sec. V contains stretti in regular and contrary motion.

Vol. II, Fugue 6; *Two-Part Song-form ;* 6 announcements in the Exposition; in Part II there is a new thematic Counterpoint (see par. 142), utilized first in abbreviated form, as a long 3-voice episode (meas. 59–86).

Vol. III, Fugue 4; begins with "Response"; 7 Sections and Coda; many effective episodes, somewhat homophonic in character.

Vol. IV, Fugue 1, also begins with " Response "; it is 4-voice texture, with occasional brief intimations of a 5th part.

Jadassohn, Pfte. Fugues, op. 56; Fugue No. 9; sectional.

Fugue with Six and More Parts.

147. It is very uncommon to employ more than five parts in the Fugue, or any other strictly polyphonic form, not only because of the technical difficulty, but chiefly that of rendering the form intelligible. As the parts are multiplied, the style becomes more and more harmonic, and all voice-individuality is lost.   The most effective device consists in so using protracted rests that, for the most part, no more than 5 of the voices appear at one time together.   In any case, the extent will rarely exceed that of a Fughetta.

See **Bach,** *Musikalisches Opfer*, No. 2, Ricercata (i.e., Fugue) for 6 parts.

An example of 6-voice writing may be found in **Bach,** Org. Comp., Vol. VI, No. 13 (Fugue-group, par. 157).

Further, **Bach,** " B-minor Mass," No. 20 (Second Division, *Pleni sunt coeli*); vocal fugue, par. 152 ; properly speaking, only a Fughetta.

Bach, 8-voice motets (vocal, — Peters ed. 28), No. 2, *Allegro non tanto ;* 8-voice double quartet; first announcement of Theme in 1st Soprano, accompanied; followed by 8 Imitations in the other parts.

Motet No. 4, letter C to D ; 8-voice Exposition.   Also the following *Vivace.*

EXERCISE 42.

A. Four or more examples of the 3-voice Fugue, respectively in sectional form (par. 140), 2-Part Song-form (pars. 141 *and 142*), 3-Part Song-form (par. 143), and with Special Design (par. 144).   Employ different species of measure and different tempo for each, and alternate major and minor modes.

B. An example of the 2-voice Fugue.

C. Two examples of the 5-voice Fugue, for organ.

D. A Fughetta (one Section) with 6 parts, for organ.

CHAPTER XIV.

MISCELLANEOUS VARIETIES OF THE FUGUE–FORM. — THE CONCERT–FUGUE.

148. It is entirely feasible, and permissible, so to elaborate the Fugue-form that, without violating any of its essential conditions or materially modifying the dignity of its character, it may exhibit those qualities of brilliancy, passion, and freedom which better adapt it for public concert use, or, in a word, enhance its effectiveness and external beauty. Such a version bears about the same relation to the more genuine, serious Fugue that the Prelude bears to the Invention. Review par. 83.

The consequent relaxation of fugue law, and general freedom of treatment, will affect: (1) The *Theme* itself, which may be more characteristic; (2) the *tempo*, which is usually more lively; (3) the *number of parts*, — very frequently limited to three fundamental parts, but freely augmented by the occasional addition of auxiliary lines or whole "bunches" of auxiliary tones (incidental chords); (4) the *episodes*, which are both more frequent and more extensive, and often nearly or quite homophonic and "figural" in character; (5) the *form*, which is perhaps most likely to be definite 2- or 3-Part Song-form, with firm cadences, — often embracing purely homophonic (or at most "imitatory") transitional passages, or complete contrasting sections; (6) the *dramatic design*, embracing more pronounced dynamic and rhythmic contrasts, and the steadily progressive development of one or more brilliant climaxes.

The strictest fidelity to the Theme is, however, indispensable; not necessarily to the *whole Theme*, nor *constantly*, but to its pregnant or salient figures. This (the original Theme, entire, and in fragments), the contrary motion, possibly Augmentation, stretti, and an effective variety of "Counterpoints," constitute the thematic material of the Concert-fugue; to which are to be added striking episodes (as usual, largely corroborative of each other), and all the factors which contribute to an impressive dramatic design, as a whole, and brilliancy of detail.

The most of these traits are forcibly exhibited in **Mendelssohn**, Pfte. Fugue in *e* minor (with Prelude), op. 35, No. 1; 4-voice; definite 3-Part Song-form; after Part I the tempo and rhythm are gradually and persistently accelerated; Part II contains the contrary motion of the Theme (further transformed by substituting *staccato* for the original *legato*), and leads to a splendid climax in Part III, which, after a powerful bass *cadenza*, culminates in a distinct Coda consisting of an original chorale with running bass; the latter gradually subsides to the original tempo and rhythm, and is followed by a second brief Coda with the Theme in major, treated more homophonically.   Analyze, further:

Mendelssohn, Pfte. Fugue, op. 35, No. 3; 3- to 4-voice; distinct 3-Part Song-form, contrary motion throughout Part II; in Part III, regular and contrary motion in stretto.

Op. 35, No. 5; 3- to 4-voice; sectional, quasi 3-Part Form.

Op. 35, No. 6; 4-voice; sectional, quasi 3-Part Song-form.

Op. 7, No. 3; 4-voice; large 2-Part Song-form.

Fugue in *e* minor (with Prelude, no opus-number); 4-voice; sectional, quasi 3-Part Form.

Bach, Organ Comp. (Peters compl. ed.), Vol. II, Fugue 2; 4-voice; stretti in last Section; many and lengthy episodes, — the Theme appears (after the Exposition) in periodic *single* announcements, isolated between effective episodes (mostly of consistent thematic origin, but brilliant and free).

Vol. II, Fugue 4; similar to the above; quasi 3-Part Song-form.

Vol. II, Fugue 8; 4-voice; sectional; similar to above.

Vol. III, Fugue 8; 4-voice; sectional; characteristic Counterpoints; first Counterpoint retained, approximately, until last Section.   Many episodes.

Vol. IV, Fugue 3; 4-voice; 10 Sections; many episodes, similar in substance; first Counterpoint retained, approximately, throughout.

Vol. IV, Fugue 4; 4-voice; about 4 Sections, cadences vague; appears to begin with "Response"; many effective episodes, lengthy, and free, but related to the Theme and to each other.

Bach, Clavichord Comp., Peters ed. 211, No. 2; 3-voice.

Bach, "Chromatic" fugue for Clavichord (with Prelude); 3-voice; sectional.

Rubinstein, Pfte. Fugues and Preludes, op. 53, Fugue 3; 4-voice; definite 3-Part Song-form.

Brahms, op. 24 ("Händel" – Variations for Pfte.), *Finale.*

Raff, Pfte. Suite, op. 71, *Finale;* 3-voice.

Other miscellaneous examples of the Fugue of more or less free structure, or in (and influenced by) homophonic surroundings, may be found as follows:

Beethoven, Pfte. Sonata, op. 110, *Finale.*   Pfte. Variation, op. 35, *Finale.*

Saint-Saëns, Pfte. Études, op. 52, No. 5; 4-voice.

Paderewski, op. 11, Variations and Fugue (*Finale*); 3-voice.

Nicodé, op. 18, Variations and Fugue (*Finale*); 4-voice.

MacDowell, op. 10, No. 5, 4-voice Fugue; independent Coda.

MacDowell, op. 13, Prelude and Fugue; 4-voice.

Guilmant, Organ Comp., op. 25, No. 3 (4- to 5-voice). — Op. 40, No. 1 (4-voice). — Op. 49, No. 6 (4-voice). — Op. 44, No. 2 (4-voice). — Op. 69, No. 4. — Op. 72. — Organ Sonata, Op. 50, *Finale.* — Op. 86, Movement III (quasi Double; counterpoint retained).

Arthur Foote, op. 15, No. 1, Prelude and Fugue; 3-voice.

J. K. Paine, op. 41, No. 3, *Fuga giocosa ;* 3-voice.

Aless. Longo, op. 9, Fantasia e Fuga (*stile libero*).

Clementi, *Gradus ad Parnassum,* Part III of the revised edition by Max Vogrich (Schirmer); No. 89 (orig. ed. No. 13); 4-voice. — No. 90 (orig. ed. 18); 3-voice; brief Introduction. — No. 91 (orig. ed. 25); 4-voice; brief Introduction. — No. 92 (orig. ed. 45), 4-voice; with Prelude. — No. 93 (orig. ed. 43). — No. 94 (orig. ed. 40). — No. 95 (orig. ed. 69). — Nos. 99 and 100 (orig. ed. 56, 57), Prelude and Fugue.

J. Rheinberger, op. 78, No. 2 ; 3-voice; 3-Part Song-form; in Part II a brief auxiliary chromatic Motive is thematically treated (alone, *per moto contrario,* par. 158), and reappears in Part III, at times in conjunction with the Theme. Many more fine examples of the Fugue may be found in the Organ Sonatas of RHEINBERGER (and of other writers also).

Raff, Suite, op. 72, *Finale ;* 3-voice; 3-Part Song-form; contrary motion freely used; also stretti and Augmentation ; in Part III a new Counterpoint appears, which assumes considerable importance in subsequent episodes, and in the Coda.

Jadassohn, Preludes and Fugues for pianoforte, op. 56, Fugue 1 ; 4-voice; 2-Part form; stretto in 2nd Part. — Fugue 2 ; 3-voice; sectional; stretti and contrary motion. — Fugue 3 ; 3-voice; ditto. — Fugue 4 ; 4-voice; sectional ; various effective Counterpoints, in successively accelerated rhythms. — Fugue 5 ; 4-voice; 2-Part form; much parallel movement in thirds and sixths. Some of these Fugues, and particularly those which follow, are quite strict in design and treatment : Fugue 6 ; 3-voice; sectional. — Fugue 7 ; 4-voice; sectional ; stretti. — Fugue 8 ; 4-voice; sectional; animated Counterpoint in last Section. — Fugue 9 ; 5-voice; sectional.

Reinecke, op. 157, No. 4 ; Fugue ; 4-voice; sectional form; Augm. in last Section.

An exceedingly interesting work, well worthy of most thorough scrutiny and analysis, is : Prelude, Chorale, and Fugue for Pianoforte, in *b* minor, by **César Franck** (ed. Litolff, 1578). The three numbers are coherent, and to some extent thematically inter-related ; the chorale is original, and bears no relation to the traditional German church-melody ; it occurs, rather episodically, during the Fugue, and even in brief (fragmentary) connection with the Theme (not as shown in par. 154) ; the Fugue is ostensibly 4-voice, but very free; an animated thematic Counterpoint appears in a later Section.

Émile Bernard, Prelude and Fugue in *g* minor, op. 14 ; 3-voice; 3-Part form.

149. The Concert-fugue seldom, if ever, appears as an isolated composition, but either as a movement of a larger work, or at least in company with an Introduction or *Prelude.*

The latter, as stated in par. 83*a*, may be connected thematically with the Fugue, or may be a totally separate piece, independent of the Fugue in every respect, *excepting in key*, which should be the same. Review par. 82*a*, thoroughly; and examine, again, the Preludes of Bach, Mendelssohn (op. 35, 37), and Rubinstein (op. 53).

EXERCISE 43.

Several examples of the Concert-fugue of various types, major and minor alternately. They may be written for Pianoforte (for two, *or for four hands*), or Organ.

N. B. Each Fugue must be preceded by an effective *Prelude*, polyphonic, semi-polyphonic, or homophonic, at option.

THE FUGUE FOR OTHER INSTRUMENTS.

150. For String-quartet. The four instruments used are first and second Violin, Viola, and Violoncello. Their notation and *average* compass are as follows :

The Viola is written in a C-clef (the so-called Alto C-clef), and the student, if not yet familiar with it, should embrace this opportunity of learning it *thoroughly*. In performing this task, the student should adopt the following system : The C-clef should be learned *by itself, and not by comparison with, or reference to, the G- or F-clefs*. That is, the name of each line or space must be independently mastered. The clef-sign (𝄡) indicates the letter c^1 (the "middle" c of the pianoforte). Thus :

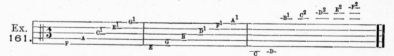

After learning this perfectly, write familiar melodies or Themes in the new clef. Then read or play the Viola part alone of the String-quartets of **Haydn, Mozart,** and **Beethoven.** Then play, at the pianoforte, the String-trios of Beethoven, and afterwards the above-named quartets, slowly, and with less reference to the rhythm than to melody and general harmony. This being accomplished, the student may write a few fairly simple 4-part harmonizations of the chorales given in Exercise 26, upon the four staves of the String-quartet.

There is no essential difference between the Fugue for string-quartet and that for pianoforte, as regards the form and structural treatment. But the *technique* differs materially, because of the superior freedom and independence of the string-parts; hence, the parts may diverge, or cross, more freely. In a word, the constraint of keyboard technique is wholly removed.

For examples, see **Haydn,** String-quartets (Peters ed. 1026*a*), No. 6, *D* major, *Finale* — one-flat signature; 4-voice Fugue, Exposition only.

Mozart, String-quartets (Peters ed. 1037*a*), No. 1, *G* major, *Finale ;* Exposition of one Theme at beginning, and of another 30 or 40 measures later.

Beethoven, String-quartets, op. 18, No. 4, *Andante ;* a partial Exposition in first 19 measures. — Op. 59, No. 3, *Finale ;* Exposition (irreg.) in first 40 measures or so. — Op. 131, whole of first movement. — Op. 95, second movement, meas. 34–64, and again later ; Counterpoint retained. — **Brahms,** String-quintet, op. 88, portions of *Finale.*

151. The Fugue for **Pianoforte and one or more Solo instruments** (Violin, 'Cello, etc.) will derive its character and treatment from the technical nature of the instruments employed ; but will be, in any case, more free and more effective than the pianoforte Fugue.

For examples, see **Brahms,** Sonata for pianoforte and 'cello, op. 38, *Finale*, first 53 measures, — and again further on.

Tschaikowsky, Trio op. 50 (*a* minor), 2nd movement, Var. VIII.

Bach, Sonatas for Clavichord and Violin, No. 1, 2nd movement. — No. 3, 2nd movement. — No. 4, 2nd movement. — No. 5, 2nd movement. — No. 6, 4th movement (*Adagio*). All very free ; more like elaborate Inventions than Fugues.

The Vocal Fugue.

152. The constraint of technical treatment is most imperative in the Fugue for vocal parts. The compass of each voice must be respected, constantly and rigorously ; awkward intervals, rhythms, or any other circumstances which impair the melodiousness and " singableness " of the several parts, must be scrupulously avoided; and good balance of effect (excluding wide spaces, though not an occasional crossing of the parts) must be preserved.

The form should be fairly definite (strict) and intelligible. Episodes are necessary, but they must be of a more sober character than in the instrumental Fugue, and must be held well within the general thematic atmosphere of the Subject. Particular attention should be directed *t~* the *uppermost* voice, which is mainly responsible for the clear and effective melodic form of the whole.

The Theme should always be a striking setting of some brief, pregnant text-sentence, — melodious, but *rhythmically characteristic*, — and it accompanies the same words throughout. The voices not occupied with the Theme, however, are generally written *without regard to the text*,— the latter being subsequently adjusted to the finished tones, with strict regard to grammatical sense and order, and to the correct prosodic disposition of accented and unaccented syllables and words.

Rests are indispensable; short ones for breathing, and occasional protracted silence (especially before an announcement of the Theme) for variety and contrast.

153. If, as is almost invariably the case, the Vocal fugue is to be *accompanied,* the instrument chosen (pianoforte or organ) may either be limited (1) to an exact duplication of the parts, *unisono ;* or (2) may double either outer part, especially the Bass, in octaves, perhaps adding an occasional full chord to support the vocal parts where their effect is somewhat meagre ; or (3) the accompaniment may add materially to the bulk, or to the rhythmic movement (or both), of the vocal parts,—even to the extent of introducing independent imitations and announcements of the Theme. Further, the accompaniment may provide a brief instrumental Introduction, occasional Interludes, and a Postlude, if necessary or desirable.

See **Bach,** " B-minor Mass," No. 6 ; *Gratias agimus,* 4-voice ; Accompaniment simple. *Compare No. 24.* — No. 3, *Kyrie,* 4-voice.— No. 1, *Kyrie,* 5-voice ; thematic instrumental Prelude and Interlude ; large 2-Part Form. — No. 13, *Patrem omnipotentem,* 4-voice ; partly harmonic Accompaniment, otherwise elaborate.— No. 12, *Credo in unum Deum ;* 5-voice ; *Running Bass in Accompaniment.*

Mendelssohn, "St. Paul," No. 29, *Is this He ?* — simple Fugue, with homophonic Interlude, derived from the Counterpoint to Theme. — No. 43, *See what love;* irregular Exposition. — No. 15, *Behold now total darkness;* Running Accompaniment, chiefly Soprano.

Haydn, "The Creation," No. 11, *For He both heav'n and earth ;* Accompaniment elaborated.— No. 29, *We praise Thee now ;* Running Accompaniment (figural).

Händel, "Messiah," No. 26, *He trusteth in God.*— No. 6, *And He shall purify ;* free, somewhat irregular ; homophonic episodes. — No. 37, *And their words ;* Exposition irreg. (Response, Response, Subject, Subject). — No. 52, *Amen ;* an Exposition, Interlude, and long episodic passages, with fragments of Theme.

Händel, "Judas Maccabaeus," No. 26, 2nd Part, *Where warlike Judas ;* Exposition irreg. (4 " Subject "-announcements).

Mozart, "Requiem," No. 8, *Quam olim ;* independent Accompaniment, quasi harmonic.

Cherubini, "Missa solemnis " (in *D*), *Kyrie eleison* (*Allegro moderato*) ; Accompaniment partly harmonic, partly running rhythm, and partly single duplication. — *Dona nobis pacem ;* observe different forms of accompaniment.

Mendelssohn, "Elijah," No. 1, *The harvest now is over ;* effective Imitation (echo) of last member of Theme ; brief harmonic episode. — No. 22, *Though thousands languish ;* Accompaniment partly harmonic. — No. 29, *Shouldst thou, walking in grief.* — Final chorus, *Lord, our Creator.*

Händel, "Israel in Egypt," No. 4, *They loathed to drink.* — No. 10, *He brought them out with silver and gold.* — No. 16, *And believed the Lord ;* homophonic episodes. — No. 18, *I will sing,* and *For He hath triumphed ;* two Themes in fairly regular alternation, — *not together* (comp. par. 52). — No. 26, *Thou sentest forth Thy wrath.* — No. 13, *He led them through the deep* (Double-chorus, 4- to 8-voice texture) ; characteristic Counterpoint, *thematic* (quasi " Double "). — Etc.

Brahms, "German Requiem," No. III, final tempo (*Der Gerechten Seelen — The souls of the righteous*) ; the entire Fugue rests upon a persistent Tonic organ-point. — No. VI, final tempo (*Herr, Du bist würdig — Thou art worthy*) ; powerful thematic episodes ; variety of Counterpoints. **Brahms,** Motet, op. 29, No. II ; 2nd movement and *Finale.*

Horatio W. Parker, " Hora Novissima," No. 4, *Pars mea, Rex meus.* — No. 10, *Urbs Syon unica* (unaccompanied). — No. 11, quartet, *Urbs Syon inclyta ;* Subject of unusual length, 11 measures (cited again in par. 189). — **H. W. Parker,** " St. Christopher," Act III, Scene 2, *Quoniam Tu solus sanctus* (Contrary motion ; Augmentation).

Beethoven, " Mass in C," op. 86, *Cum sancto spiritu ;* simple Exposition ; Interlude, chiefly harmonic ; new Exposition with chromatic Counterpoint. — *Et vitam venturi ;* instrumental Interludes, and vocal *Soli.* — *Osanna in excelsis.*

Beethoven, " Mass in D," op. 123, *In gloria Dei patris, Amen ;* elaborate ; Counterpoint retained through the Exposition ; partly double-quartet. — *Osanna in excelsis* (both versions).

Verdi, " Falstaff," Finale, *Tutto nel mondo è burla ;* large chorus, but practically 4-voice ; Counterpoint retained during first section, and used later episodically ; frequent contrary motion.

EXERCISE 44.

A. Two Fugues (each with brief Introduction, or Prelude) for String-quartet, — major and minor ; different measure and tempo for each.

B. A Fugue, with Prelude, for Pianoforte and Violin.

C. Two or more Fugues for mixed quartet (or chorus), with organ or pianoforte accompaniment. The text may be taken from any of the above examples, or from any part of the Bible.

FUGUE IN CONNECTION WITH CHORALE.

154. Fugue with Chorale. This form corresponds in design exactly to the Invention with Chorale, but differs from the latter in that greater degree of seriousness and strictness which distinguishes the Fugue in general from the Invention. All the specific directions are given in paragraphs 99 to 105, *which must be thoroughly reviewed.*

The introductory measures (par. 100*d*) are usually a regular Exposition (par. 121, etc.), during the later course of which the chorale melody appears, in the part *left vacant* for the purpose. Thereafter the form is that of the ordinary sectional Fugue, into the texture of which the chorale Lines are successively interwoven, apparently as incidental addition, — though naturally they influence (or even dictate) the pro-gressive development.

The Subject is almost invariably evolved out of the first Line of the chorale, with more or less freedom.

Analyze minutely: **Bach,** Organ Comp. (Peters compl. ed.), Vol. VI, No. 30; 3-voice; *Cantus firmus* in Bass; long Theme, independent of the chorale, with two very quaint modifications. — Vol. VII, No. 39*a;* 4-voice; *c. f.* in Soprano; Theme derived from first two Lines of chorale; a stretto-Imitation, with which the Fugue begins (after two beats, in the 5th), recurs frequently; other stretti, and contrary motion, also appear. This is an extremely interesting and instructive example. Compare it carefully with the next, Vol. VII, No. 39*b,* which it closely resembles in all essential respects; 4-voice; *c. f.* in Tenor.

Guilmant, Organ Sonata, Op. 80, Finale.

Mendelssohn, "St. Paul," No. 36, *But our God;* 5-voice; chorale in 2nd Soprano; two Themes, in fairly regular alternate Sections, both *independent* of the chorale.

155. Chorale as Fugue-group. This is the parallel form of the cho-rale as Invention-group, explained in par. 106, which review thoroughly.

Out of each successive Line of the chorale a Subject is evolved; each Subject in turn is carried strictly through the parts, as Exposition, in which the chorale finally participates, as usual. Thus the whole constitutes a group or chain of Fugues (or Fugue-Expositions, — *Fughettas*), corresponding to the number of Lines in the chorale.

See **Bach,** Organ Comp., Vol. VI, No. 21; 4-voice; *c. f.* in Soprano, each time as last announcement of the Theme. — Vol. VI, No. 28; 4-voice; *c. f.* in Soprano, as Augmentation of Theme. — Vol. VII, No. 37; 4-voice; *c. f.* in Soprano, some-what embellished, and each time as last announcement of the Theme; a new (10th) Motive for the Coda, in animated rhythm. — Vol. VII, No. 50; 4-voice; the last announcement of Theme each time in Bass, as *Cantus firmus.* — Vol. VII, No. 55; 4-voice; the Pedal is added as *duplication of the Bass* at end of each Exposition, to emphasize the *c. f.* — Vol. VI, No. 13; 6-voice; *c. f.* in 1st Bass, as Augmentation of the Theme; several thematic Counterpoints. — **Brahms,** *Chorale-Vorspiele,* op. 122, No. 1. — **Brahms,** Motet, op. 29, No. 1; 5-voice; *c. f.* in 1st Bass.

156. The Chorale-Fugue. Somewhat allied to the Chorale-Invention, par. 110, which review. The Subject, or Subjects, are derived from the first, or later, Lines of the chorale, and manipulated in the usual manner. *But the chorale-melody, as such, is absent.*

See **Bach,** Org. Comp., Vol. VI, No. 33; 4-voice; many stretti; two auxiliary, or episodic, Motives. — Vol. VI, No. 11; 3-voice; thematic Counterpoint in later Sections. — Vol. VI, No. 20; 4-voice; special design. — Vol. VII, No. 41; 4- to 5-voice; secondary Motive, derived from Counterpoint. — Vol. VII, No. 60; 4-voice; *basso ostinato* in Pedal (*transposed* recurrences); thematic Counterpoints.

A smaller variety, **the Chorale-Fughetta,** is illustrated in the following:

Bach, Org. Comp., Vol. V, No. 20; 3-voice. — Vol. V, No. 43, 3-voice. — Vol. VII, No. 61 ; 3-voice. — Vol. VII, No. 40*c ;* 4-voice; Exposition in stretto. — Vol. VII, No. 54; 3-voice; the Subject, and two secondary Motives, are derived from three Lines of the chorale; Line 4 is intimated by the descending scale, constantly present in the Counterpoints.

THE GROUP- (OR MOTET-) FUGUE.

157. The Fugue-group is similar to the form described in par. 155, but is usually broader in design, and by no means necessarily identified with the chorale. Different Subjects — usually, though not necessarily, of similar character (and perhaps related in contents) — are successively, sometimes alternately, manipulated as separate *complete* Fugues (or Fughettas), more or less extensively and independently.

See **Bach,** Org. Comp., Vol. III, Fugue 6; 4-voice; large 3-Part form; the first Subject is the basis of Part I; a totally different Subject (chromatic) is manipulated in Part II, as separate Fugue, so to speak; in Part III the first Subject is resumed; this Part is a nearly exact recurrence of the first *Section* of Part I, abbreviated at the beginning, and extended at the end. — Vol. III, Fugue 7 ; 4-voice; the first Division is a Double-fugue (to be analyzed later); the second Division is a brief Interlude (free, similar to the Prelude to the whole number); the third Division is based upon a *rhythmically modified Augmentation of the first measure of the preceding Fugue-subject;* animated rhythmic Counterpoints in later course. — Vol. III, Fugue 9; 4-voice; interjoined with the Praeludium (meas. 1–39); Division I is a Double-fugue (see later), to meas. 62; Division II has a different Theme, though somewhat related to the preceding; an independent Coda, similar to the Introduction, is added. — Vol. VI, No. 10; Chorale-fugue (chorale itself *absent*), in group-form; 3-voice; three sections; two different Subjects alternating (returning to first). — Vol. VI, No. 34; ditto ; 4-voice; 5 Themes (or Motives, — quasi Invention-group).

Bach, "B-minor Mass," No. 19, last Division (*Vivace e allegro*), *Et expecto* and *Amen ;* 4 Themes.

Mendelssohn, " St Paul," No. 23, *For all the Gentiles,* and *Now are made manifest ;* 5-voice; large 3-Part form, quasi Song with Trio. — No. 20, *The Lord He is good,* and *For His word ;* successive Expositions, and then close alternate treatment (*not* " Double-fugue"). — Final chorus, *Bless thou the Lord,* and *All ye His angels ;* 4-voice; two Subjects.

EXERCISE 45.

A. One or two examples of the Fugue with Chorale (par. 154).

B. One or two examples of the Chorale as Fugue-group (par. 155).

C. An example of the Chorale-Fugue (par. 156).

D. One or two examples of the Fugue-group (par. 157). To each of the latter a Prelude, or free Introduction, is to be prefixed.

IRREGULAR FUGUE—SPECIES

158. The Fugue in Contrary motion (per moto contrario). In this species the first and third Imitations of the Theme are made in *Contrary motion*, so that the 4-voice Exposition consists of the alternate "regular" and "contrary" motion (the latter standing each time for the usual "Response"). This arrangement may extend through the entire Fugue; or it may be confined wholly (or nearly) to the Exposition; and, further, the alternation may be more or less irregular (for instance, in the Exposition, or later, the regular motion twice, followed by the contrary motion twice; etc.).

The relation of the contrary motion to the original form of the Theme is generally that defined in par. 29*a*, particularly Ex. 72, which review. See also Exs. 73 and 74. The Theme in contrary motion may be announced in the original key, or, as usual, in the Dominant key (by simple transposition to the upper 5th or lower 4th).

Analyze, thoroughly, **Bach,** "The Art of Fugue," Fugue No. 5. The Exposition runs as follows:

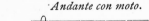

Six measures later (in meas. 17) the Exposition closes, with a vague cadence. The Fugue has a Special Design, extending through 5 Sections; Sec. II (meas. 17–33) is very similar to the preceding one; Sec. III (meas. 33–46) is based upon a stretto in contrary motion; Sec. IV (meas. 47–65) upon a stretto in parallel motion, after one and one-half measures; Sec. V (to meas. 86) upon a parallel stretto, after one measure. The Coda (last 5 measures) is based upon a *simultaneous* (or double) announcement, in regular and contrary motion. — "Art of Fugue," Fugue No. 13; 3-voice; *per moto contrario*, absolutely regular alternation; frequent episodes, all similar; cadences vague. The following number (13*b*) is the exact contrary motion, and partial Inversion, of the preceding. — "Art of Fugue," two Fugues for 2 pianofortes; both 4-voice, and *per moto contrario ;* the Fugues are different manipulations of the same Subject. Compare them minutely.

Brahms, Fugue in *ab* minor for Organ, first 27 measures; 4-voice; Counterpoint retained, in regular and contrary motion.

Händel, "Israel in Egypt," No. 11, *Egypt was glad,* first 30 measures; 4-voice; the Dominant (*b* in *e* minor) is answered by the Tonic (*e*), in the first " Response "; the two following announcements are both in the original motion; later the alternation is more regular.

Mendelssohn, "Elijah," No. 16, *The flames consume ;* Exposition in contrary motion.

Beethoven, String-quartet, op. 127, *Scherzando vivace ;* Exposition in contrary motion ("fugato," — i.e, in fugal style, imitatory, but not exactly a Fugue).

Bach, Org. Comp., Vol. VII, No. 39*c ;* Fugue *per moto contrario,* with Chorale; 5-voice; *Cantus firmus* in Bass; stretto-imitations throughout.

159. The Fugue in Augmentation, or in Diminution. In this species, which is very similar to the above, the Augmentation, or Diminution, of the Subject is substituted for the contrary motion; or, in rare instances, is combined with the latter.

See **Bach,** "Art of Fugue," Fugue No. 6; this is a 4-voice Fugue in "Diminution and Contrary motion"; probably 3 Sections and Coda; the Exposition begins thus :

"Art of Fugue," Fugue No. 7; 4-voice Fugue in "Augmentation and Contrary motion"; contains also a series of Double-augmentations, and fragments of the Diminution (end of 7th measure, in Soprano); cadences very vague; the form is either simply one broad section, constituting the Exposition of the Double-augmentation, through the four parts (Bass, Tenor, Alto, Soprano, alternately in contrary and regular motion); or it contains four Sections, with one announcement of the Double-augmentation in each.

Händel, "Messiah," No. 33, *Let all the angels;* Fugue in Augmentation.

160. The Fantasia-fugue. This somewhat contradictory term may be justified in the case of those Fugues which begin seriously, and contain a more or less legitimate Exposition, but thereafter degenerate into a free, fantastic series of sections or sentences (passages), based upon *fragments* only of the Theme, possibly in distorted forms.

A beautiful and entirely defensible illustration occurs in **Bach,** Well-temp. Cl., Vol. II, Fugue 3; it is 3-voice, sectional form; the Exposition is in stretto, and Contrary motion (Subject in Bass, 1½ measure), ending in meas. 7; in Sec. II (meas. 7–11) the 2nd half of the Theme is reconstructed; Sec. III (meas. 11–14) is episodic; Sec. IV (meas. 14–17) reverts to the original form of the Theme; the last Section (meas. 17 to the end) does not contain the original Theme entire, but is one long episode, or Fantasia (18 measures), in which intimations of the Diminution, Augmentation, and a unique mixture of other thematic fragments occur. — See also **Bach,** Clav. Comp., Peters ed. 216, No. 6, "Capriccio"; the purpose is evidently that of a Fugue, but the extensive episodic passages (quasi homophonic figuration), and the general treatment, make the title "capriccio" more appropriate.

Kindred forms are (1) the **Recitative-fugue:**

See **Mendelssohn,** Pfte. Sonata, op. 6, *Adagio* movement; no definite measure; 4- to 5-voice; large 2-Part form, with a homophonic (lyric) section as Interlude, and Postlude, in ¾ time.

and (2) the **Harmonic fugue,** i.e., a fugal thematic design, but of marked *harmonic* character, or with distinctly harmonic auxiliary parts.

See **Schumann,** op. 32, No. 4, "Fughetta." — **Bach,** Clav. Comp., Peters ed. **211,** No. 3.

EXERCISE 46.

One example each of the Fugue in Contrary motion (par. 158), and the Fugue in Augmentation, — or in Diminution, at option, — (par. 159).

***

CHAPTER XV.

THE DOUBLE–FUGUE.

161. The Double-fugue is one in which **two Subjects** appear, and are manipulated, **simultaneously.**

It is not to be confounded with the forms cited in par. 52, par. 106, par. 155, and par. 157, in which two (or more) Themes are treated *successively*, each by itself for the time being; but takes its name from the fact that its thematic basis is a *Double-theme* — thematic duet.

It is not necessary that the two Subjects should always be together, for, as will be seen, either (or each) may be announced alone, or even have a separate Exposition; but, in order to achieve the idea and purpose of the Double-fugue, the Themes must appear *in conjunction*, distinctly, and during a reasonably extended section of the whole.

162. The Double-fugue has its inception in that variety of the single Fugue in which, as shown in par. 132, the first Counterpoint is *retained*, more or less persistently, throughout a part, or the whole, of the Fugue; for such companionship between the Subject and its Counterpoint approaches the effect of an intentional *double* thematic basis. Review par. 132, and context, thoroughly. But there still remains a characteristic difference between such examples of retained Counterpoints and the *genuine* Double-fugue.

163. An important intermediate grade, sufficiently independent to merit separate treatment, is

THE FUGUE WITH THEMATIC COUNTERPOINT.

An ordinary contrapuntal associate of the Theme, such as is found in the majority of simple Fugues, could not be called " thematic," even if "retained" and introduced occasionally in subsequent announcements, for the reason that it provides no especial thematic feature, does

not enrich the thematic resources, and takes no active part in the development of the design.

In order to be *thematic*, the Counterpoint must be to a certain
extent characteristic, must contain rhythmic and melodic features which
distinguish it somewhat from the Theme; must recur often enough and
emphatically enough to become a recognizable (though not obtrusive)
line in the physiognomy of the Fugue; must influence the development,
and enter actively (though not vitally, or perhaps even essentially) into
the thematic texture as a whole.   All this the "Counterpoint" may be,
without becoming a genuine Secondary *Theme*, or subject to any special
conditions with regard to time, place, frequency, or accuracy of recurrence.

To this class belongs, properly speaking, the example already cited in par. 132:
Bach, Well-temp. Cl., Vol. II, Fugue 9; see Ex. 153.   Also Vol. I, Fugue 14;
possibly also Vol. II, Fugue 22.

More genuine examples of the Fugue with Thematic Counterpoint are the
following, — to be carefully analyzed:

Bach, Well-temp. Cl., Vol. II, Fugue 17; 4-voice; sectional form; Subject and
Counterpoint as follows:

Lento.

The Thematic Counterpoint is absent during 3 or 4 announcements of the Theme,
and is often freely modified.

Further, **Bach**, Org. Comp., Vol. IV, Fugue 7; 4-voice; 4 sections; Counterpoint
retained throughout, but modified freely. — Vol. IV, No. 10, "Canzona" (equivalent
to Fugue), *Division I;* 4-voice; 2 sections; few episodes; Thematic Counterpoint
retained, but modified.

Bach, Clavichord Comp., Peters ed. 212, No. 3; 3- to 4-voice. — In the same
volume (212), No. 5, the same principle is somewhat extended, inasmuch as *two
different* Thematic Counterpoints appear, in different rhythms; this approaches the
idea of par. 179.

Further, **Bach**, Well-temp. Clav., Vol. I, Fugue 2; 3-voice; sectional form;
Subject and Counterpoint as follows:

Subject._____

Response._____

Thematic Counterpoint._____

In order to perceive the melodic beauty and thematic validity of this Thematic Counterpoint, it should be played or sung *alone*. It accompanies the Theme everywhere, with but one exception (in the Codetta, last 2½ measures), and participates in all the episodes. For these reasons the Fugue barely escapes being "Double"; it would be unquestionably so were the Counterpoint more nearly *coördinate, in character and importance*, with the Theme proper.

To the same class, closely approximating the Double-fugue, belong Fugue 3 and Fugue 7 of Vol. I (Well-temp. Clav.); and Fugue 13 of Vol. II. — Also Partita No. 6 (Clav.), "Gigue"; large 2-Part form; Contrary motion in Part II; Thematic Counterpoint retained, but considerably changed in Second Part.

164. During the Exposition the Thematic Counterpoint appears, at each succeeding announcement of the Theme, in the part which *last* contained the latter; i.e., the Counterpoint follows the Theme, each time, in the same part (whether interrupted by episodes or not). *After* the Exposition, however, the location of the Counterpoint, like that of the Theme, is optional; and it may be occasionally omitted, or more or less modified.

EXERCISE 47.

One or two examples of the Fugue (3- or 4-voice) with Thematic Counterpoint.

THE GENUINE DOUBLE–FUGUE.

165. In the authentic Double-fugue, the two Subjects are strictly coördinate. The secondary Theme (sometimes so called merely by way of distinction), or Counter-theme, is not a "thematic counterpoint," but an *essential part of the thematic material*, subject to precisely the same specific limitations as the principal Theme.

Rule 1. Each Subject must be a perfectly good melody, in and by itself. Hence, each must be tested *alone*, in order to verify its individual validity as thematic sentence.

Rule 2. Each Subject must be well individualized ; must differ from its fellow (chiefly as regards its *rhythmic* formation) sufficiently to contrast perceptibly in character, though not obtrusively. They should not begin exactly together, nor need they end upon the same beat.

Rule 3. The two Subjects must constitute peculiarly faultless counterpoint, — not by any means to the exclusion of characteristic dissonances, but without any awkward irregularities. They should not cross each other ; and, as a rule, should not run much beyond an octave or tenth apart, in their original associated form, when designed for a Fugue with 4 or more parts.

Compare these rules with the primary definition of polyphony on page 1, of which they are simply a singularly severe and just exposition.

Rule 4. After the Double-subject has been completed, it must be tested in *inverted form,* i.e., the parts so exchanged that the upper becomes the lower. Also, though less urgently, in their joint *Contrary motion.*

This is necessary, not only because it is impossible to avoid Inversion, in the development of the Double-subject, but because the art of the Double-fugue consists in a great measure in these, and many similar, changes in the relations of the two Themes to each other. Review pars. 55 to 58, *especially par. 57 ;* and refer, briefly, to Artificial Double-counterpoint, par. 169, etc.

Examples of Double-subjects :

*1) The Themes are marked thus, *A* and *B ;* generally in the order in which they appear, — *A* being the first. — *2) A fine example. Play each Th. alone.

See further, **Bach,** Well-temp. Clav., Vol. I, Fugue 12, meas. 4–6; Theme *B* begins with $b\natural$ in the 3rd beat of the 4th measure. — Vol. II, Fugue 16, meas. 5–9; Theme *B* begins one 16th-note after *A.* — Fugue 18, meas. 97–101 ; Theme *B* begins on the 3rd 8th-note. — Fugue 20, meas. 3–5 ; Theme *B* commences with the 32nd-notes. — Fugue 23, meas. 27–30.

166. Double-fugues are divided into three classes or Species, according to the degree of importance assumed by *Theme B*.

The First Species of Double–Fugue.

167. In this Species, the two Subjects are **announced together** at the beginning of the Fugue.

a. They may appear in any two of the parts to be employed, but are almost certain to be in *neighboring* parts (either the upper, inner, or lower pair). During the Exposition, for instance in 4 parts, the rules of par. 123 (which review) apply to each Theme independently of the other; i.e., *each one takes its way through the four voices in the usual order.* For instance (assuming them to start in the inner pair of voices):

Soprano,	A . . B . .		B . . A . .	B . . A . .
Alto,	A . . B		A . . . . B . .	A . . B . . . .
Tenor,	B . . . . A . .	or :	B . . A	or : B . . A . . . .
Bass,	A . . B . .		B . . A . .	A . . B . .

If announced in *parallel* parts, a collision is possible, but always easily to be avoided. Thus:

Soprano,	A . . . . . B		A . . . .
Alto,	A . . . . B . .	but of course not thus :	AB . .
Tenor,	B . . . . . A		B . . . .
Bass,	B . . . . A . .		

These principles can also be readily applied to the Fugue for 3 or 5 voices.

b. After the Exposition these regulations are relaxed, as usual; the two Themes may appear in any pair of parts, in optional frequency; and, possibly, one or the other of the Themes may *occasionally* appear alone, though this should occur very rarely, as it militates against the specific conditions of this species of the Double-fugue. Review par. 128. Either Subject may, as usual, be slightly modified or abbreviated, as occasion or necessity arises, but not to the extent permitted with a mere " Thematic Counterpoint."

The formal designs, and all other structural details, correspond exactly to those given in Chapters XII, XIII, and XIV.

Analyze, very minutely, the following examples of the First Species :

Bach, Org. Comp., Vol. II, No. 6, *Praeludium ;* the whole is a brilliant example of the Concert-species (par. 148), in 3-Part Song-form ; Section I is a largely homophonic introduction, exactly reproduced at the end as Sec. V, or Third Part ; the Double-fugue begins with Sec. II (meas. 25) and extends through Secs. II, III (Part II) and IV ; it is 4-voice, and slightly irregular, as regards the order of voices, in the Exposition.

Vol. III, No. 9, *Fuga,* first Division ; 4-voice ; 2 Sections (meas. 39–63 of whole piece).

Vol. IV, No. 8, *Fuga ;* 4-voice ; 4 Sections and Coda ; lengthy episodes ; Theme B enters two measures later than Theme A ; Exposition somewhat imperfect.

Vol. IV, No. 10, " Canzona," *Division II* ($\frac{3}{2}$ time) ; the First Division has already been cited as Fugue with Thematic Counterpoint ; this Second Division is a Double-fugue, based upon the same Themes, rhythmically and melodically modified ; form sectional, cadences vague ; 4-voice.

Bach, Clav. Duetto, No. I (Peters ed. 208, No. 4).

Bach, Clav. Toccata in *d* minor (Peters ed. 210, No. 4) ; Third Division, *Presto ;* 3-voice, sectional, very free ; the first 2 measures in lower part are *introductory* auxiliary tones, derived from Theme A, and frequently recurring ; Theme B begins in meas. 3 ; another auxiliary Motive appears later. — Same Toccata, *Finale;* 3-voice ; also very free ; the first 11 measures are introductory.

Bach, Org. Comp., Vol. VI, No. 18 ; 3-voice ; *per moto contrario ;* Choralefugue. — Vol. V, No. 23 ; 3-voice ; Double-fughetta.

Händel, Clav. Suite No. 6, 3rd movement.

Beethoven, op. 120, Var. 32 ; 4-voice ; in final sections a new thematic Counterpoint, in animated rhythm, is introduced.

Rubinstein, op. 53, No. 6 ; 4-voice ; 3-Part form ; Concert-species.

Clementi, Gradus ad Parnassum, Schirmer ed., No. 97 (orig. ed. No. 54), Fugue, with Prelude ; 4-voice ; contains *Retrograde* Imitations (par. 29b). Also No. 98 (orig. ed. No. 74) ; 4-voice.

Haydn, "Creation," No. 27b, *Glory to His name,* and *He sole on high exalted reigns.* Also No. 33, *Jehovah's praise for ever,* and *Amen;* Theme B fragmentary, and not constant.

N. B. In some of these examples Theme B might, probably, be more justly regarded as a Thematic Counterpoint only.

Händel, "Israel in Egypt," No. 9, *He smote all the first-born.*

Cherubini, " Missa solemnis," *Cum sancto spiritu.* Also *Amen* of the *Credo.*

Mozart, " Requiem," No. 1, *Kyrie ;* reproduced as *Finale,* with different text.

EXERCISE 48.

A. Invent a large number of Double-subjects, in various styles, tempi, keys, and modes.

B. Write two 2-voice Inventions, with Double-subject, 1st Species. Models for this work will be found in **Bach,** 2-voice Inventions, Nos. 5, 6, 9, 11, 12, and 15; and Well-temp. Clav., Vol. I, Prelude 3; Vol. II, Prelude 20; analyze thoroughly.

C. Two Double-fughettas (one or two Sections), major and minor respectively; 4-voice and 3-voice.

D. Two complete Double-fugues, 1st Species, 3-, 4-, or 5-voice; for Pianoforte, Organ, String-quartet, or Vocal parts.

THE SECOND SPECIES OF DOUBLE–FUGUE.

168. In the Second Species, Theme B enters as *first contrapuntal associate, in connection with the second announcement of Theme A* (i.e., with the first "Response"). It therefore corresponds, in this respect, to the Fugue with Thematic Counterpoint; but all the conditions detailed in par. 165 must be strictly observed.

The order of voices during the Exposition is simpler than in the First Species, because Theme B naturally (and almost invariably) follows Theme A in the same voice,— precisely as shown in Exs. 164, 165, excepting that the contrapuntal associate is a genuine Counter-theme, and not merely a thematic counterpoint. But, as Theme A thus appears once alone, the Exposition is generally extended by one extra announcement, in order that Theme B may appear in every part; i.e., in the 4-voice Fugue the Exposition usually embraces five announcements of Theme A, the 5th time in the voice which began the Fugue.

See **Bach,** Well-temp. Clav., Vol. I, Fugue 12; Theme A is announced in Tenor, then in Alto (meas. 4), Bass (meas. 7 — this is irregular — par. 124), Soprano (meas. 13), and *again in Tenor* (meas. 19); Theme B follows, each time, in the same voice; the Exposition closes in meas. 22. Exactly the same in Vol. II, Fugue 16, in every particular, excepting that the order of parts is regular; the Exposition closes in meas. 24. — In Vol. II of the Org. Comp., Fugue 9, the Exposition is *not* thus extended.

The distinction between the 1st and 2nd Species is limited, thus, to the Exposition alone. The subsequent development is identical. Analyze, very carefully, the following; observe, here again, the degree and quality of freedom of detail exercised, and endeavor to recognize the factors that must be regarded as vital and inviolable:

Bach, Well-temp. Clav., Vol. I, Fugue 12; 4-voice, sectional; the 6 tones immediately following the cadence of Theme A (meas. 4, beats 1 and 2) are *intermediate —* see par. 121*b;* they constitute the staple of all the episodic passages, which are of frequent and very regular occurrence throughout this Fugue; Theme A appears *alone* in meas. 40–43. — Vol. II, Fugue 20; 3-voice, sectional.

Bach, Org. Comp., Vol. II, Fugue 9; 4-voice; definite 3-Part Song-form, Part III an exact reproduction of Part I, modified only at beginning; Concert-species;

many brilliant episodes, in animated rhythm. — Vol. III, Fugue 7, first Division; 4-voice, sectional.

Bach, Clav. Comp. (Peters ed. 211, No. 1), Fugue, with Toccata; 4-voice, sectional, regular and simple; Contrary motion frequent.

Duetto No. IV (Peters ed. 208, No. 4); 2-voice, sectional. — Toccata in *J* minor (Peters ed. 210, No. 2), Division IV, $\frac{6}{8}$ time; 4-voice, sectional. — Partita No. VI, "Toccata"; 3 Divisions, embracing the Double-fugue (3-voice, sectional) between a thematically related Prelude and Postlude. — (Same Partita, "Gigue"; already analyzed, as Fugue with Thematic Counterpoint).

Händel, Clav. Suite No. II, *Finale.*

Bach, Org. Comp., Vol. VII, No. 47; Fugue with Chorale; 4-voice; *cantus firmus* in Bass. — Vol. V, No. 39; chorale-fughetta, 3-voice.

Händel, "Messiah," No. 23, *And with His stripes.* — "Samson," No. 9, Part II, *Was ever the most High.*

Bach, "B-minor Mass," No. 4, *Et in terra pax.*

EXERCISE 49.

A number of Double-fugues, 2nd Species; 3-, 4-, or 5-voice; different character and tempo; instrumental or vocal. Some of the Double-subjects of Exercise 48*A* may be utilized.

ARTIFICIAL DOUBLE–COUNTERPOINT.

169. The term "artificial" is adopted (in its most serious sense) in distinction to "natural," with reference to those varieties of Double-counterpoint in which the harmonious result is not a matter of course, but must be assured by *calculation.* Review par. 55.

As stated in pars. 55*b* and 56, when the Double-counterpoint is obtained by inversion in the 8ve, no change of interval-relations takes place, and an equally harmonious agreement results, naturally. But no such natural guarantee exists when any other interval of inversion is used. Therefore, Double-counterpoint in the 8ve, without any other modification, is the only Natural kind, *while Double-counterpoint in any other interval, or with any other modification of either part, belongs to the Artificial kind,* and is to be determined only by calculation or experiment.

170. Double-counterpoint in the Twelfth. Double-counterpoint is obtained by transferring one part towards *and past* the other; and the species is defined by the interval of inversion involved. For example, if the lower part remains, and the upper part is shifted downward a 12th (an 8ve and a 5th, or perhaps two 8ves and a 5th) the result is **Double-counterpoint in the 12th.** For illustration:

(*a*) The Original Counterpoint.

(*b*) Inversion in the 12th (affecting Th. A).

*1) Theme A is shifted up, past its fellow, a 12th; Theme B remains where it was.

*2) Such modifications as this (*f* changed to *f♯* by the accidental) are often absolutely necessary, and are to be freely employed, with discretion, in favor of better modulatory agreement. Their use is entirely legitimate, inasmuch as the two forms (the Original and the Invention) never appear together. The change, however, may only affect the accidental, — *never the letter.*

An apparently new result is obtained by moving the *other Theme down*, past its fellow, a 12th. But this, or any other movement of both parts together, equivalent to the 12th, represents simply a transposition of the Inverted form. Thus:

(*a*) Inversion in 12th (affecting Th. B).

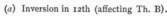

(*b*) Inversion in the 12th (affecting both Themes).

171. The invention of a Double-subject (or any two-voice sentence) which may thus submit to Inversion in the 12th — or any other interval excepting the 8ve — is so largely a matter of incessant experiment, tone for tone, that scarcely any valid rules can be given. At the same time, there is a certain device for each separate species of Double-counterpoint, which systematizes and simplifies the formation to some extent.

The device for Double-counterpoint in the 12th consists in the frequent use of *the interval of a 3rd (or 10th)* in the Original form; for this interval, when inverted in the 12th, *results again in a 3rd;* for example:

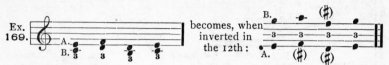

This point, and others, are illustrated in the following:

3. *Andante.*

*1) That is to say, the same *tones* (letters) as before. The change of register makes no difference, as long as the parts *pass* each other, in the stipulated interval.

*2) From the orchestral Variations upon a Theme by **Haydn,** op. 56, Var. IV. *See also the next 20 measures, which are followed by a similar exact Inversion in the 12th.*

See also **Bach,** "The Art of Fugue," Fugue 9   Original counterpoint in meas. 35–43 (Soprano and Tenor) ; Inversion in the 12th in meas. 45–53 (Tenor and Alto).

Same work, Canon IV; Original counterpoint in meas. 9–35; Imitation in 12th in meas. 42–68 (the upper part is shifted down a 12th, while the lower part retains the same tones, shifted up two octaves); a long and instructive example, to be carefully analyzed.

172. Double-counterpoint in the 11th. Frequent use of the interval of a 6th will, as a rule, yield a good Inversion in the 11th (the 6th becoming again a 6th). For example:

This species, Double-counterpoint in the 11th, is the companion (the counter-part) of that in the 12th; and, because of the harmonic similarity between the 6th and the 3rd, is scarcely distinguishable from it. One is, technically speaking, simply the 8ve-inversion of the other. For illustration: invert the parts in Ex. 167*a* (in the octave), and also invert Ex. 167*b* in the same manner; upon comparing the *two results* with each other they will be found to constitute Double-counterpoint in the 11th.

173. *a*. Double-counterpoint in the 10th. The best device for Double-counterpoint in the 10th consists in *doubling one of the Themes in the 3rd*, and counterpointing the other Theme against this double line. In order to yield counterpoint in the 10th, the duplication must fall *between* the principal lines as a so-called *inner 3rd;* i.e., it must be the lower third of the upper voice, or the upper third of the lower. Thus:

Ex. 172.

*1) The large notes constitute the Original counterpoint; the inner part (small notes) is a duplication of the upper Theme in the *lower or inner 3rd*, in order to provide for Double-counterpoint in the 10th *by inverting the parts*, thus:

Ex. 173.

b. Although Double-counterpoint always implies *Inversion of the parts* (as stated in par. 55), it must be understood that the *principle* is the same whether the Inversion actually takes place or not; and therefore Ex. 172 is as certainly Double-counterpoint, with its duplication of one part in the 3rd, as Ex. 173, or any other of the inverted forms.

c. Such a duplication in the 3rd is less difficult and hazardous than might be suspected, and will quite frequently be found practicable with little or no change, in any ordinary counterpoint. The only necessary condition or limitation is, that the parts shall move in **contrary directions** (at those points where both are moving). This may be verified in Ex. 172. It is applied, with precisely equal certainty, to the other part (Theme B) of the above example, by **Bach** himself. Thus:

Ex. 174.

N. B. Each lower part *alone* must be valid with the upper.

d. Further, exactly the same result is obtained by duplicating either part in the *outer 6th* (instead of *inner 3rd*, as in Exs. 172 and 174). Thus:

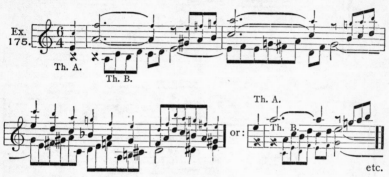

Ex. 175.
Th. A.
Th. B.
Th. A.
Th. B.
or:
etc.

N. B. Play each duplicated part *alone* with the other. And write out the Inverted forms of each example, complete, as in Ex. 173.

174. Double-cpt. in the 13th (or 6th). This is the companion-species of that in the 10th, and is obtained by duplicating either Theme in the *outer 3rd* (comp. par. 173*a*), or *inner 6th* (par. 173*d*). For example:

Ex. 176.
Th. A.
Th. B.

Th. B (as before).

Inverted in the 13th: etc.

Th. A (13th lower).

N. B. Play each upper part *alone* with the other. Write out the example also with duplication of the *lower* part in the *outer* (i.e., *lower*) *3rd*. Write out each example in its Inverted form, complete.

175. It is sometimes possible to apply the device of duplication in the 3rd (or 6th) to *both parts at once*. Thus:

*1) Slightly changed from the Original (**Bach,** Well-temp. Clav., Vol. II, Fugue 16, meas. 59–63). Comp. with meas. 9–13; and see, also, meas. 45–49; 51–55; 69–73.

The complication of Double-cpt. " Species " involved in such two-fold duplications can be defined only by reference to the Original form (here shown in large notes): it is exceedingly confusing, — and no doubt wholly unnecessary.

A long and instructive example of Double-counterpoint in the 10th may be found in **Bach,** " Art of Fugue," Canon III; meas. 5–39 are inverted in the 10th in meas. 44–78; the lower part one 8ve higher, and the upper a 10th lower, than before.

Bach, 3-voice Inv. No. 8, meas. 17–18; upper part duplicated in the inner 6th. — Well-temp. Cl., Vol. II, Fugue 22, meas. 6–3 from the end (double duplications, partly in 6ths, and partly in 3rds). — **Bach,** Org. Comp., Vol. VI, No. 18, meas. 22–23; Theme A in Bass, Theme B doubled in 3rds, slightly embellished, in upper parts.

176. Double-cpt. in the 9th, and its companion, **in the 7th.** For these extremely difficult and rare species there is no other guide than the rigid application of the two general principles of (1) *stepwise progression* and (2) *contrary direction.* For example:

(*b*) Inversion.

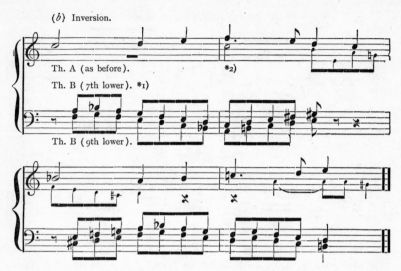

Th. A (as before).   *2)

Th. B (7th lower). *1)

Th. B (9th lower).

*1) Theme B is written out in both species of Double-cpt. at once, in this instance, because they produce, together, a somewhat fuller and more plausible harmonic result than either would alone. This, however, is not (or should not be) necessary.

*2) The addition of another part, as here, is often of the utmost consequence in defining more fully the harmonic intention.

A double-subject, devised thus strictly in contrary directions, and with exclusive stepwise progressions, will generally prove available for *every* species of Double-cpt. That is the case with Ex. 178, as the student may (and should) verify.

Other Varieties of Artificial Double–Counterpoint.

177. These are **purely experimental,** and cannot be obtained by any method of calculation. They consist in multiplying the relations of the two Themes to each other by applying the ordinary modifications (Contrary motion, Shifted rhythm, Augmentation, or Diminution) to *either Theme alone*, while the other retains its original form. For illustration, Ex. 167 chances to admit of transformation as follows:

1.   Th. B, as before.

Ex.
179.

Th. A, in Contrary Motion.

2.   Th. B, in Shifted rhythm.

Th. A, as in Orig. cpt.

And Ex. 170, No. 2, reappears later thus:

Th. A, as before.   BACH.

3.

Th. B, Shifted rhythm.

*1) See Ex. 178, Note *2).

See further, **Bach,** 2-voice Invention, No. 11 ; Original cpt. in meas. 1–2, Theme A in upper, Theme B in lower part; inverted in meas. 3–5, Theme A as before, but in lower part, Theme B in upper part *in Contrary motion and Shifted rhythm.* — **B .ch,** Well-temp. Cl., Vol. II, Fugue 23; comp. meas. 60–63 with meas. 27–30 (Theme B in Shifted rhythm).

EXERCISE 50.

A. A number of Double-subjects in Double-cpt. in the 12th (par. 171). Each example is also to be written out in the *8ve-Inversion,* and in *complete* Contrary motion (i.e., *both Themes together* in Contrary motion). See par. 165, Rule 4.

B. Double-subjects in Double-cpt. in the 11th (par. 172). Each to be subjected to the same Inversions as at *A.*

C. The same in Double-cpt. in the 10th (par. 173*a-c*).

D. The same in Double-cpt. in the 13th (par. 174).

E. The same in Double-cpt. in the 9th, — and in the 7th.

F. The Double-subjects invented in Exercise 48*A* are to be subjected to very thorough experimental tests, with reference to the duplication of either, or both, of the Themes in the inner, or outer, 3rd.

G. All of the above Double-subjects (including Exercise 48*A*) are to be exhaustively examined with reference to the experimental species of Artificial Double-cpt., illustrated in par. 177.

THE THIRD SPECIES OF DOUBLE–FUGUE.

178. In this species, which may be regarded as the most genuine and distinctive of the Double-fugue, the entire Exposition (first section) is devoted to Theme A alone. And, in the broader Song-forms, this

Exposition may be extended a section or more, so as to complete the measure of a full First Part.

The following sections or Parts may then be designed in either of two ways:

(1) Theme B may simply join Theme A, so that they appear in conjunction the rest of the way; or (2) Theme B may also be first manipulated *alone*, for one section or Part, and the conjunction of the two Subjects follow in the final Sections, or Third Part.

In the latter case, where each Subject is manipulated alone before they appear together, care must be taken to avoid contrapuntal associates that *resemble the other Theme* too closely, especially with regard to their rhythmic formation; otherwise the subsequent conjunction of the Themes will not be striking enough, and the product may be monotonous.

An incipient type of the first class is shown in par. 142, which review. The first class is illustrated in the following (to be thoroughly analyzed):

Bach, "The Art of Fugue," Fugue 9; 4-voice; 3 Sections, cadences vague; Theme A alone to meas. 34; A and B together from meas. 35 to the end. Contains Double-cpt. in the 12th. — Same work, Fugue 14; 4-voice; Theme A alone to meas. 21; A and B together from meas. 22 to the end; in Section III (meas. 34) there is a regular Exposition of an auxiliary Motive, derived from the first Counterpoint (meas. 6–7); in Sec. V (meas. 67) another brief auxiliary Figure appears. Contains Double-cpt. in the 10th and 12th.

The second class is illustrated in the following:

Bach, Well-temp. Cl., Vol. II, Fugue 18; 3-voice; 3-Part Song-form; Theme A alone to meas. 60; Theme B alone from meas. 61 to 96; A and B together from meas. 97 to end. The first counterpoint differs but little from Theme B, but the latter is nevertheless characteristic enough.

Vol. II, Fugue 4; 3-voice; Theme A alone to meas. 19; in meas. 20–21 Theme B is introduced tentatively, once (in upper part), and in modified form; meas. 24–29 Theme A again alone, Exposition of Contrary motion; in meas. 30 Theme B is again "attempted" (lower part) in still another modified form; meas. 35–39 Theme B, in correct form, has a regular Exposition alone; A and B together from meas. 48 to end. Artificial Double-cpt. freely applied.

Bach, "The Art of Fugue," Fugue 10; this is practically the same as Fugue 14 (analyzed above), with which it must be *very carefully compared;* it differs from No. 14 in containing an *additional first Section* (meas. 1–22), *devoted to the Exposition of Theme B;* i.e., it begins with the "secondary Subject"; thereafter it corresponds very closely to No. 14. Hence it contains: Theme B alone in Sec. I, Theme A alone in Sec. II, both together the rest of the way. The Subjects are well contrasted.

Bach, Org. Comp., Vol. IV, No. 6; 4-voice; 3-Part Song-form; Theme A in Part I, Theme B in Part II, both together in Part III; the last 14 measures are an independent Postlude, quasi free Fantasia. The Pedal announces both Themes almost invariably in simplified rhythmic form; frequent perfect cadences in course of the Sections; few episodes until near the end. Themes well contrasted.

Bach, Well-temp. Cl., Vol. I, Prelude 7; 3 rhythmically contrasted Divisions; texture more free than in the genuine Double-fugue.

Mendelssohn, Pfte. Comp., op. 35, Fugue 4; 4-voice; 3-Part Song-form; Theme A in Part I, to meas. 46; Theme B alone to meas. 96, often in modified form; A and B together, with some freedom of treatment, from meas. 97 to end. Themes rhythmically contrasted.

Analyze, further, the following *miscellaneous* examples (irrespective of class):

Bach, Partita (Clav.) No. 5, "Gigue"; large 2-Part form, Gigue-species.

Bach, Clav. Comp., *Toccata* in *c* minor (Peters ed. 210, No. 3); Divs. I and II are introductory; Div. III, lengthy Exposition of Theme A (3-voice, Concert-species); a brief interlude follows, and then Div. IV, with Themes A and B together. — *Fantasia e Fuga* in *a* minor (Peters ed. 208, No. 2); excellent example; 4-voice; 3-Part Song-form.

Mozart, String-quartet (Peters ed. 1037*a*), No. 1, *G* major, *Finale;* Double-fugue in homophonic surroundings (as Sonata-movement). Regular Exposition of two different Subjects, one at the beginning, and the other 30 or 40 measures later; both together in final Division (the "Recapitulation").

Raff, Pfte. Suite, op. 69, *Finale.*

Saint-Saëns, Pfte. Études, op. 52, No. 3, Fugue with Prelude; only a very concise Exposition of Theme B, and no more than brief fragmentary conjunction with Theme A, in last Section.

Rubinstein, Pfte. Fugues and Preludes, op. 53. Fugue 1, 3-voice. — Fugue 4, 4-voice; 5-Part Song-form;* contains Contrary motion, and Augmentations.

Händel, Clav. Suite IV, first movement; 4-voice.

Vocal: **Händel,** "Israel in Egypt," No. 11, *Egypt was glad* (Fugue in Contrary motion). — The same, No. 21, *And I will exalt Him,* and *I will exalt Him.*

Mendelssohn, "St. Paul," No. 22; *Sing His glory,* and *Amen.*

Bach, "B-minor Mass," No. 19, *Confiteor,* and *In remissionem ;* near the end a *Cantus firmus* is interwoven, first in canonic imitation, and then single, in Augmentation.

Irregular (4th) Species of Double–Fugue.

179. An irregular variety of the Double-fugue, which might be designated as the 4th Species, consists of one principal Theme, with two or more *contrasting thematic Counterpoints,* one or the other (or all) of which may assume the importance of a genuine secondary Theme.

---

* *Homophonic Forms,* Chap. XVI.

The thematic Counterpoints (or Counter-themes) are likely to appear in successive sections, or Parts, of the usual forms.

Analyze, thoroughly, **Bach,** Well-temp. Cl., Vol. II, Fugue 23; 4-voice; the first 27 measures are an Exposition of the principal Subject, with a characteristic thematic counterpoint, appearing first in meas. 5–8 (Bass); after meas. 27 it is permanently abandoned. In Part II (meas. 27–74) a second thematic counterpoint, or, rather, a genuine Counter-theme, appears, first in Soprano; in meas. 60–62 it is shifted backward a half-measure (par. 177); and Double-cpt. in the 12th abounds throughout. At the beginning of Part III (meas. 75) Theme A occurs once alone.

This example resembles those of par. 142 (which see), but is more nearly a genuine Double-fugue.

See further, **Bach,** Org. Comp., Vol. III, Fugue 1; 5-voice; 3 distinct Divisions, —somewhat like the Fugue-Group (par. 157); Div. I, $\frac{4}{4}$ time, Exposition of principal Theme; Div. II, $\frac{6}{4}$ time, contains an Exposition of the First Counter-theme alone, in *slightly modified form,* and the conjunction of this with the principal Theme (rhythmically modified on account of the change in measure); Div. III, $\frac{12}{8}$ time, consists in a similar Exposition of the Second Counter-theme alone, and its conjunction with the principal Theme, again with modified notation. Analyze minutely, and compare with the next-following Fugue.

Vol. III, Fugue 2; 4-voice; 3-Part Song-form; the First Counter-theme is associated with the principal Theme in Sections I and II (to meas. 70) as a Double-fugue of the 2nd Species; the Second Counter-theme has an independent Exposition in meas. 70–128, as Part II; Part III begins with one conjunction of the *First* Counter-theme with the principal Theme, but consists thereafter of the association of the latter with the *Second* Counter-theme. Neither of these examples must be confounded with the Triple-fugue (par. 180), for nowhere are *all three* Subjects combined.

Bach, Clav. Comp. (Peters ed. 212, No. 5); 4-voice; two different thematic Counterpoints, in different rhythms, and slightly modified,—i.e., not genuine Counter-themes.

Raff, Pfte. Suite, op. 91, first movement; elaborate Introduction, as Fantasia; first announcement of Fugue-subject interwoven with last vanishing chords of the Introduction; two different thematic Counterpoints, in accelerated rhythms.

Beethoven, "Mass in D," op. 123, *Et vitam venturi ;* two different Counter-themes.

EXERCISE 51.

A. A number of Double-fugues, 3rd Species, 3, 4, or 5 parts, for pianoforte, organ, string-quartet, or vocal parts. Any Double-subject of former Exercises may be used, preferably those of Exercise 50, with a view to manipulation in both Natural and Artificial Double-cpt.

B. One or two Double-fugues of the 4th Species, according to par. 179.

CHAPTER XVI.

The Triple–Fugue.

180. The Triple-fugue is based upon three different coördinate Themes, which appear *together*, as a threefold Subject, during some portion of the composition.

All the rules of par. 165 apply strictly, and must be reviewed. The chief difficulty in devising a Triple-subject is, so to individualize *each one* of the three Themes that it constitutes by itself a wholly independent and characteristic melody, especially in its rhythmic formation; and that, furthermore, each one may serve equally well as Soprano, Bass, or inner part.   Compare par. 57.

Probably the best plan is to follow the principle of par. 61*b* (which review), i.e., to invent the Themes *successively;* first, Theme A, in stately rhythm (preponderantly ◯ and ◡ - notes); then to add Theme B to this in more animated rhythm (♩ - notes), and then Theme C to these, in still another form of more active rhythm.   This is, however, by no means imperative.

Illustrations of the Triple-subject:

*1) Themes A and B end here, while Theme C runs on a few beats. In the other illustrations it will be seen that the 3 Themes usually *close* exactly, or nearly, together. But observe that they do not *begin together*.

*2) From the String-quartet, op. 18, No. 4, second movement, meas. 64–68 from the Double-bar.

See also **Bach,** 3-voice Invention No. 9, meas. 3–4.

Bach, Well-temp. Cl., Vol. I, Prelude 19, first 2½ measures. — Vol. I, Fugue 4, meas. 51–54 (Tenor, Bass, Soprano). — Vol. I, Fugue 21, meas. 9–12.

181. The Inversion of a Triple-counterpoint yields a fivefold result (or 6 forms in all), thus:

Original cpt., { Theme A,
{ Theme B,   Inversions, { A,   B,   B,   C,   C
{ Theme C,   { C,   A,   C,   A,   B
                                            { B,   C,   A,   B,   A

a. As in Double-cpt., it is generally a foregone conclusion that the 8ve-inversions will all be possible (par. 56), though some embarrassment, with regard to *register*, may be encountered; and it may be necessary at times both to cross the parts and to allow them to diverge widely.

b. On account of the multiplied complications, only the Natural species (8ve-inversion) need claim attention. The Artificial species are exceedingly difficult to obtain, though sometimes one or another of the devices shown in par. 173 and par. 177 may be ferreted out by patient and exhaustive experiment.

Ex. 181.

*1) Each Theme starts with the *letter a 4th above* the original first tone, Theme A being transferred to a *lower*, B and C to a *higher* register. — *2) Each Theme in the 7th of the original counterpoint, excepting the first tone of Theme B. The counterpoint is therefore in each case Natural Species.

See **Beethoven**, Pfte. Sonata, op. 2, No. 3, *Finale*, meas. 55–62; very simple.

182. The Triple-fugue, like the Double, may also be divided into three Species.

In the **First Species,** all 3 Subjects are announced together at the outset, and the order of voices during the Exposition is to be defined strictly according to par. 167*a;* that is, *each* Theme passes from part to part in the established order (par. 123), independently of the others — common sense being employed to avoid collisions. For example (4-voice):

Sop., Th. A ...... C .. B   A .. C*1) .... B   A .. C .. B ..
Alto, Th. B .. A C   B .. A .. C ...   A .. C .. B
Ten., Th. C .. B .. A ...   or: B .. A .. C   or: B ...... A .. C   etc.
Bass,   C .. B .. A   C ..... B .. A   C .. B ..... A

*1) Theme C in Soprano following C in Bass. This is not passing to the "next higher or lower voice," it is true; but it is equivalent, because these are not *parallel* voices.

Irregular Expositions are not uncommon. See also par. 167*b*.

Analyze, thoroughly, **Bach,** Well-temp. Cl., Vol. I, Prelude 19; 3-voice; the first tone in Bass is auxiliary; the Triple-subject is $2\frac{1}{2}$ measures long; the design is 3-Part Song-form; Part I is a regular Exposition, to meas. 12; Part II (meas. 12–17) begins with the original counterpoint; Part III (end of meas. 17) contains two announcements.

Beethoven, String-quartet, op. 18, No. 4, second movement, measures 64 to 81 *from the Double-bar;* original counterpoint given in Ex. 180, No. 2; a complete Exposition, 4 announcements.

183. In the **Second Species,** Themes A and B begin together, and Theme C follows immediately (usually in one of the same voices).

See **Bach,** 3-voice Invention No. 9; Theme A in inner, B in lower part; the first Bass note is auxiliary; in meas. 3, Theme A appears in the upper, B in the inner, and C is added to these in the lower voice; the form is sectional; analyze thoroughly. — **Bach,** Org. Comp., Vol. I, "Passacaglia," *Finale;* 4-voice, sectional (quasi 3-Part form); Exposition to meas. 29, with brief cadence in meas. 21, contains 5 announcements, in order that each part may exhibit all three Themes; Theme C occasionally modified at its end. — In Vol. II, Fugue 4, there are many passages in Triple-cpt., and even some evidences of Triple-fugue design. — Vol. VIII, No. 12; 4-voice; sectional; somewhat irregular. — **Beethoven,** 3rd Symphony, *Adagio,* measures 10–29 from *second change of signature* (i.e., back to 3 flats); Theme A in half-notes, and B in quarters and eighths, together in Viola and 2nd Violin; followed immediately by Theme C, 16th-notes, in 2nd Violin; a complete Exposition, 5 announcements.

A sub-variety of the Second Species is illustrated in **Bach,** Well-temp. Cl., Vol. I, Fugue 21; the 3 Subjects enter *successively* (in closer analogy to the 2nd Species' of the Double-fugue); 3-voice; sectional; Theme C, meas. 9–12, in upper part, is very fragmentary, but thoroughly characteristic and persistently retained (with slight modifications).

Also **Brahms,** Fugue with Chorale (*O Traurigkeit*) for organ, in *a* minor; chorale in pedal-bass; Theme A derived from first Line of chorale; *per moto contrario* throughout (par. 158); orig. cpt. given in Ex. 180, No. 4.

184. In the **Third Species,** Theme A is manipulated *alone* during the whole Exposition, or Part I; thereafter, several different designs are possible and equally legitimate. For example, — among many possible arrangements, in successive Sections (or Parts):

Theme A alone.	B alone, or A and B together.	C alone, or A and C together. or B and C together.	A, B, and C together.

Analyze diligently **Bach,** Well-temp. Cl., Vol. I, Fugue 4; 5-voice, Two-Part form; Theme A alone in Part I (to meas. 35); Theme B begins with Part II, **in**

Soprano, as counterpoint to Theme A in Tenor; after one other announcement of A and B (meas. 44), Theme C joins them, in meas. 49, Tenor; the 3 Themes are then developed pretty steadily together to meas. 81–84, whereupon Theme B gradually withdraws entirely, leaving the rest of the Fugue to A and C; these, in meas. 94, begin a series of extremely powerful stretto-announcements together, extending nearly to the end. — Vol. II, Fugue 14; 3-voice, Two-Part form; Theme A alone in Part I (to meas. 20); Theme B then follows, in Bass, slightly modified at its end, and is manipulated alone, in somewhat abbreviated stretti, to meas. 28; at the end of meas. 28 Theme A appears (inner voice), Theme B following in Bass *two measures later;* in meas. 36 Theme C enters (inner voice, 16th-notes), and is developed *alone* to meas. 51; after one announcement of A alone (meas. 52–54, inner voice), the 3 Themes are combined (A at end of meas. 54 with disguised beginning, upper voice, — C in next measure, Bass, — B in meas. 56, inner voice), and remain together to the end.

Bach, "The Art of Fugue," Fugue 8; 3-voice, sectional; design as follows (Themes named A, B, and C, in the order of their appearance — C being the *principal Subject*): Sections I and II, Theme A alone; Sec. III (meas. 39) and IV, Themes A and B; Sec. V (meas. 94), Theme C; Sec. VI, (meas. 125), Themes A and B; Sec. VII (meas. 147), Themes A, B, and C. **Compare carefully with same work, Fugue 11.** The latter uses the same Themes as No. 8, but begins with the *principal Theme;* further, the Themes are all in the Contrary motion of the former. It is much longer and more elaborate, introducing a characteristic chromatic counterpoint (to one of the secondary Themes) which is retained and much used, — almost as 4th Theme (meas. 28–29), though all four do not appear anywhere *together*, thus escaping the design of a Quadruple-Fugue (par. 185). The design is as follows (Themes named as in No. 8): Sec. I, Theme C; Sec. II (meas. 27), Theme A, with thematic counterpoint "D"; Sec. III (meas. 71), Theme C in Contrary motion; Secs. IV (meas. 89) and V, Themes A and B (also two isolated announcements of C); Sec. VI (meas. 146), Themes A, B, and C to the end. — Same work, Fugue 15; the 3 Themes are strikingly contrasted in rhythm and character (the third one based upon the notes "*b-a-c-h* "). This Fugue was interrupted by the master's death, after the Exposition of the 3rd Theme, and before all three Subjects were united. — **Bach,** Org. Comp., Vol. VI, No. 31; chorale as Fugue-group (par. 155); 4-voice; *cantus firmus* in Bass; new Theme for each Line; Double-cpt. during first Line; Triple-cpt. in all following Lines. — **Thiele,** Fugue (with chromatic Fantasia) for organ; 4-voice; Theme A alone, then A and B together, and then all three. — **Brahms,** Fugue in *ab* minor for the organ; 4-voice; sectional; Thematic Counterpoint in first Sections; stretti, augmentation, diminution, and shifted rhythm in final section; *all per moto contrario.* A superb masterpiece, worthy of most diligent analysis.

QUADRUPLE AND QUINTUPLE COUNTERPOINT.

185. The invention and employment of a complex of more than three Subjects, for the Fugue-form, is so difficult and of so little practical effectiveness as to be naturally very rare; and even for technical discipline it is of but limited value.

Brief examples of good 4- or 5-voice counterpoint with well-contrasted, independent parts, may be introduced episodically in the course of a Fugue, and reproduced in inverted forms (in 8ve-cpt. only) with good results.

A brilliant specimen of Quintuple-cpt. may be found in **Mozart,** Symphony in *C* major (sometimes called the " Jupiter " symphony), *Finale.* The complex of 5 Subjects, which first appears in meas. 40 *from the end*, is as follows (in the orchestral String-quintet) :

This is followed by a complete Exposition, 5 announcements in all, up to meas. 22 from the end. But this is not all; the entire *Finale* is, in fact, a Quintuple-Fugue of the 3rd Species, molded in the form of the " Sonata-Allegro," and so designed that nearly all of the Subjects appear successively, and are manipulated, alone or together, in stretti, contrary motion, diminution, and even retrograde imitation, before their ultimate conjunction in the final Coda. Analyze thoroughly, *from the orchestral score.*

In conclusion, the student is recommended to analyze the 48 Fugues of **A. A. Klengel** (" Canons and Fugues in all the keys "; 2 vols., Breitkopf & Härtel ed.). This distinguished and interesting work, to which frequent reference will be made in the next Division, has been intentionally omitted in the preceding pages, in order to provide opportunity for an extended course of independent analysis. The Fugues are almost exclusively " Single "; Contrary motion, Stretti, Augmentation, and Diminution abound, and even Retrograde Imitation occurs in one instance (in the unique 2-voice Fugue, Vol. I, No. 16).

EXERCISE 52.

A. Invent a number of Triple-subjects, in various styles, and write out all five 8ve-inversions of each.

B. Two brief Triple-fugues, or Fughettas, one in the First, the other in the Second Species, major and minor.

C. Two or three complete Triple-fugues, Third Species.

D. A few experiments in Quadruple- and Quintuple-counterpoint, with Inversions (as explained in pars. 180–181).

DIVISION V.

THE CANON.

186. The Canon-forms differ from the foregoing classes of polyphonic composition in two respects : (1) The Imitation is entirely, or nearly, **strict** (par. 26) ; and (2) it is **continuous** ; that is, not limited, as in the Fugue, to the Subject alone, but extended to include all that follows in the same voice, to the end of the Section, or Part, or entire composition.

187. *a.* The part which begins, or leads the canonic progression, is called the Leader (*proposta*) ; the following or imitating part is called the Follower, or responding part (*risposta*).

b. The principal distinction between canonic species (among many) is defined, precisely like the stretto, according to the distance of the Follower from the Leader in *time,* and in melodic *interval;* for instance, " Canon in the 8ve (or 2nd, 3rd, etc.) after one measure (or two, or more)."

c. Another important distinction is made between the Unaccompanied (or Independent) and Accompanied Canon ; and further, between the Round and the Progressive Canon. Other traditional distinctions will either be defined in the following pages, or will be intentionally omitted because of their doubtful utility ; for the latter the curious student may consult Dr. **Baker's** " Dictionary of Musical Terms," or **Grove's** " Dictionary."

CHAPTER XVII.

THE ROUND, OR ROUND–CANON.

188. The simplest and most venerable application of the principle of Continuous Imitation is made in the so-called Round-canon. This is usually written for at least three, sometimes four, but seldom more, *vocal parts,* and is nearly always a Canon in *unison* (or *8ve*) *Imitation.*

The Leader begins with a distinctly lyric (melodious) Phrase, commonly 4 measures long, with a fairly definite semi-cadence; more rarely it is a 2-measure member, or a Period (8-measure, or irregular) with the usual two cadences. Thereupon the first Follower reproduces (or imitates) this leading phrase, while the Leader continues with a counterpoint, similar in character but *melodically well contrasted* (see par. 35*a*, and par. 165, Rules 1, 2, 3), if possible with a modulation, to avoid monotony. After the leading phrase is thus again finished, the second Follower enters and announces it, while the first Follower continues with the preceding " counterpoint," and the Leader adds a new contrapuntal phrase to these, again well-contrasted. At this juncture the original counterpoint (in a 3-voice Round) is complete, and represents a Triple-subject, exactly as in par. 180, but with *less rhythmic diversity,* and so contrived that the 3 parts (A, B, and C) *constitute a continuous melody* in phrase-group form, and *returning to the beginning* (whence the designation " Round ").

What follows, as the voices continue their rotatory Imitation, or following, of the Leader, is simply Inversion of the voices, and presents nothing new, — in the unison-canon not even the *effect of Inversion;* therefore the Imitation is generally extended only until the last Follower has finished the entire phrase-group, whereupon a free cadence, of any length, is added, to terminate the Canon.

If a low voice (Alto or Tenor) is used in company with two high ones, or if, in any way, the Triple-subject is so devised as to embrace different registers, the *8ve-Imitation* may also be employed; and in that case the effect of Inversion will be secured, subject to the usual tests (par. 181*a*).

For a 4-voice Round the process is the same, but the desirability of 8ve-Imitation, in company with the unison, is greater; hence, *parallel* voices are likely to be chosen (2 Sopranos and 2 Tenors, or Altos and

Basses). The text must be so chosen as to cover either the leading phrase only, or exactly the entire group of 3 (or 4) phrases.

For illustration (3-voice Round-canon):

*1) From here to Note *2) appears the union of the three voices, or the "Triple-subject" which constitutes *the body of the entire Canon.* — *2) Here the

Leader ends the canonic melody, and *returns to the beginning.* — *3) The 1st Follower continues with the third Period (that of the Leader at Note *1). — *4) The 2nd Follower continues with the 2nd Period (meas. 8). — *5) In the Original, the 3 voices continue thus together for 14 measures, or until the 2nd Follower has finished the canonic melody. The student is to *write out* these measures, and, if possible, have the whole Round sung.

It is evident that the single canonic melody — the upper staff alone up to Note *2) — is all that need be written in order to indicate the contents of the whole. The 3 singers may all read from this single staff, but *beginning successively*, at each new Period, and continuing as long as desired. Or, it is also possible to write out the Round in score, precisely as shown from Note *1) to *2). In that case each singer begins with the *lowermost* staff, passes successively to the next higher, and finally around to the lowermost again, and so on. This method is illustrated in the following:

Write out this Round in its *complete* form, beginning as in Ex. 183, and continuing until the 3rd Follower has completed the canonic melody. **Mozart** made no provision for a perfect cadence (Tonic); the Round is therefore "endless." Such provision could, however, easily be made by adding a free codetta of one (or more) measures, when, as here, the Canon is written in score. Or a stopping-place may be indicated, either for each part successively, or for all together, by the ⌢ sign.

These examples are both taken from the Breitkopf & Härtel ed. of **Mozart's** complete works (Serie 7, Nos. 41 to 61).

See further, from the same, No. 46; Round for 3 voices, unison; Follower begins after 10 measures (irreg. Period-form); ends with perfect cadence. — No. 47; 3-voice, unison, after 14 measures (Group of 3 phrases, extended); perfect cadence. — No. 52; Round for 4 voices, unison, after 6 measures; the Canon is "endless," but provision is made for a cadence. — No. 45; 4-voice, unison, after 8 measures; no cadence. — No. 55; 4-voice, unison, after 4 measures; "endless," but a stopping-place is marked. — No. 56; 4-voice, unison, after 3 long measures; no cadence. — No. 57; 4-voice, unison, after 6 measures; no cadence. — No. 59; 4-voice, unison, after 8 measures; no cadence. — No. 60; 4-voice, unison, after 4 measures; "endless," but cadence provided for. — No. 44, Round for 6 voices; all unison, after 4 measures; no cadence. — No. 48; 6-voice, first Follower in unison, the other four in *lower 8ve*; after 2 measures; no cadence. — **Brahms,** Round-canons, op. 113, No. 1; 4-voice, unison, after 4 measures; cadence provided for. — No. 2 ; 3-voice, unison, after 7 measures. — No. 3. — No. 4. — No. 5. — No. 7 ; 3-voice, unison, after 10 measures. — No. 10. — No. 11. — No. 12. — No. 13; 6-voice, in the following unique disposition: 4-voice Canon in upper parts, unison, after 9 measures; and, *as accompaniment,* 2-voice Canon in lower parts (8ve, after one measure).

Many other examples of the Round, both classic and popular, may be found in various collections of vocal music for instructive or social purposes.

189. Closely allied to the Round, but inclining toward the structure of the Progressive Canon, is a form of very pronounced **Lyric** character, in which (as a rule) there is no return to the beginning, and consequently no such rotation of parts as in the Round. The leading sentence is often of considerable length — 8, 12, or even 16 measures, in very definite Period, or Double-period, form; the number of voices is usually 3 (sometimes 4); and the form generally extends no farther than through the announcement of the *leading sentence* by the *last Follower.* A simple harmonic accompaniment is added (par. 201*d*).

Probably the most masterly example of this form is the famous mixed quartet in **Beethoven's** " Fidelio " (No. 3, in the First Act). The leading sentence is a regular Period of 8 measures; this, and the succeeding canonic counterpoints, are imitated in the usual manner by the Followers (in the unison by the other female part, and lower 8ve by the two male voices), until the last Follower has finished the original leading Period, whereupon a free homophonic coda of 12 measures is appended. The rhythm of the accompaniment is gradually accelerated from quarters and 8th-notes to 16th-triplets.

Rossini, " Semiramide," Act I, No. 3, Quartet, second division, *Di tanti Regi ;* 3-voice, auxiliary 4th voice during last announcement; independent Coda. A beautiful example.

Rossini, " Moses in Egypt," Act III, *Finale,* Quartet, *Je tremble et soupire ;* 4-voice ; slightly irregular near end. Also Act II, No. 8, Quintet, *O toi dont la clémence;* 5-voice ; *transposed* announcements of leading Period ; irregular ; independent Coda. Of similar design is the Quartet, *Urbs Syon inclyta,* from " Hora novissima " (**H. W. Parker),** No. 11, already cited among the vocal Fugues.

Mozart, No. 61 of the above volume, is an example of this kind, as far as lyric style is concerned ; but the imitation is extended to the characteristic rotation of the Round (cadence indicated by ⌒), and there is no accompaniment. It is 3-voice, unison, after 11 measures (extended Period).

A. Write two or more examples of the Round for 3 voices, in unison, unaccompanied; "endless," but with provision for a cadence.

B. One or two Rounds for 4 voices, in unison and 8ve, with Coda.

C. One or more Lyric canons for 3 voices (unison and 8ve), accompanied, with Coda, according to par. 189.

CHAPTER XVIII.

The Progressive Canon.

190. In the Progressive Canon the same principle of strict continuous imitation prevails; but any other interval (or species) of imitation may be used quite as well as the octave; and the time-interval is generally much shorter, — i.e., the *risposta* follows the *proposta*, or Leader, earlier than in the Round; and, finally, there is less distinctness or regularity of form, and no such characteristic recurrence of the leading sentence, — excepting the distinctive return to the beginning necessary when the 3-Part Song-form is chosen, or when Part I is to be repeated.

The Two–Voice Canon, Unaccompanied.

191. In the 8ve. Either part may be chosen as Leader. A simple melodic motive is devised, very similar in contents and character to the Motive of an Invention or a *short* Fugue-subject, but without cadence. Its length depends upon the time-interval between Leader and Follower. This is most commonly *one measure*, sometimes two measures, or one-half measure in any compound rhythm; more rarely one beat, or any other uneven fraction of a measure, for it is desirable that the prosodic effect of Leader and Follower (disposition of accents) should agree.

This leading motive is then imitated in the other voice, either an 8ve higher or lower, while the Leader proceeds with a contrapuntal associate devised in *strict conformity to the rules in par. 35a, which review.* The Follower imitates this Counterpoint, while the Leader again proceeds with a new one, — and so on, to the end of the Canon. If, for instance, the time-interval is one measure, the contents of every (or any) measure in the Leader will be literally reproduced in each following measure in the Follower; — though a duet, the contents of *one voice alone* will represent the entire melodic material of the composition. For illustration:

2nd Counterpoint : —

192. There are two characteristic difficulties persistently present in the constructive process of an unaccompanied Canon in the 8ve, namely :

a. The difficulty of avoiding **monotony.**

The 1st counterpoint is, presumably, a peculiarly fitting associate of the leading Motive. When it reappears in the Follower (3rd measure of the above example) it is necessary to devise an equally good, *but new,* associate, as 2nd counterpoint, whereby the natural temptation to *fall back upon the leading M.* must be resisted. In other words, constant care must be taken to use *new* contrapuntal intervals in successive measures ; also intervals occasionally foreign to the key, in order to effect necessary modulations. But no liberties are to be taken with the Follower; *in the 8ve-canon the imitation is* **absolutely** strict. It is also necessary to avoid monotony of *rhythm* and monotony of *register.* All of these considerations are skilfully observed in the following :

Follower (in lower double-8ve, after one measure.)

*1) The last beat of this measure was harmonized, in the Leader (preceding measure), with *b*, *d*, and *d♯*; here a totally new result is obtained by using *f♮*. This, and the persistent evasion of the distinctive Mediant *c* (in this whole measure of the Leader), prepares for the unique modulation (or change of mode) into *a* minor, at Note *2). — *3) The diversity of *register* during these 5 measures is noteworthy; from the high *e* of the Leader to this low *e* a range of 4 octaves is covered. — *4) Diversity of *rhythm* is here effected and sustained by the heavy syncopated formation of the Leader.

b. The difficulty of obtaining **intelligible form.**

The student will soon discover how galling the constraint of persistent strict imitation is; every desirable melodic aim is hampered, apparently to a fatalistic degree; and this is especially palpable *at the cadences*, or at any other point in the structural design where it is necessary to conduct the Leader in a certain definite direction. The dogged pursuit of the Follower is in itself a circumstance that militates against clear cadential effects, because the Leader can perform no act alone.

At the same time, it is absolutely necessary (particularly at the beginning, and from time to time in later sections) to preserve, at least *approximately*, the effect of regular Phrase- and Period-formation; to provide for a firm cadential separation at the end of the First Part; and, in case a *repetition of Part I* is required, or when the 3-Part form is used, to lead the voices back to the beginning.

The best device for such recognizable (if not strictly regular) syntactic formations is *a judicious use of Rests* in the Leader. The rests should not be so brief as to appear breathless, or so long as to sever the continuity of the sentence (excepting at strong cadences, where a whole-measure rest may be used); nor should the rests be so frequent as to defeat their own purpose.

In a word, it is mainly necessary *to impart to the* **Leader** *a good and intelligible melodic and syntactic form* — as far, and as continuously, as is possible under the canonic constraint. The Follower may then be left to take care of itself, as far as the "form" is concerned. For this reason, also, it is wise to introduce from time to time some *striking melodic or rhythmic figure in the Leader ;* not only because these contribute to the intelligibility of the form, but because they emphasize the relation of the Follower to the Leader, i.e., render the canonic imitation, as such, more recognizable. But see par. 202.

The "formation" is very distinct in the following:

*1) These rests mark the end, or semi-cadence, of the first 2-measure phrase-member.

*2) Here the second phrase begins, with the first melodic member (i.e., parallel construction, regular Period-form).

*3) Perfect cadence, marking the end of the First Part (meas. 26).

*4) This striking rhythmic figure is not only an important feature in the melodic delineation of the Leader, but also defines the canonic imitation clearly when it reappears (next measure) in the Follower.

c. The time-interval is a significant factor in the Canon, as it affects both the difficulty of structure and the recognizability of the imitation. The *shorter* the time-interval, the greater and more insistent is the canonic constraint. The imitatory effect can scarcely be brought out clearly when the time-interval is very brief, nor, on the contrary, can the connection between Leader and Follower be easily traced when more than two ordinary measures intervene. Long time-intervals may, however, conduce to regularity of design; for instance, a 4-measure interval is likely to resolve the Canon into a perfectly regular Phrase-group form.

The following is a unique example of short time-interval:

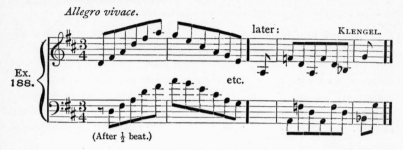

Allegro vivace.

later: KLENGEL.

Ex.
188.

etc.

(After ½ beat.)

d. The canonic imitation may extend to the very end, — in which case the Leader may pause, or may be a free counterpoint, during the final time-interval. Or it may be discontinued one, or several, measures before the final perfect cadence; the final measures will then assume the character of a free codetta or coda.

e. The Canon in **Unison** is very rare without accompaniment.

Analyze the following examples very minutely:

Clementi, "Gradus ad Parnassum," Schirmer ed. (Vogrich), No. 62 (orig. ed. No. 63); 8ve, after one beat; near the end the Leader is conducted back to the beginning and *repeated;* therefore it is, to that extent, "endless," but the last measure provides the perfect cadence. — No. 64 (orig. 26); 8ve, after one long measure; cited in Ex. 187. — No. 65 (orig. 67); double-8ve, after 1 measure; 2-Part form, Part I repeated ("endless"); cited in Ex. 186. — No. 67 (orig. 75); 8ve, after 1 measure; Part I "endless"; cited in Ex. 185.

Klengel, 48 Canons and Fugues, Vol. II, Canon 5; 8ve, after ½ beat; cited in Ex. 188. — Vol. II, Canon 11; 8ve, after 4 measures (see par. 192c); last 16 measures free. — Vol. II, Canon 23; 8ve, after 1 measure; the first 10 measures are monotonous (see par. 192a).

Bach, "Art of Fugue," Canon II; 8ve, after 4 measures.

Beethoven, C-minor Pfte. Variations, Var. 22; 8ve, after one beat (*very slight* modification).

Mozart, No. 43 (Breitkopf & Härtel, Serie 7); vocal Canon in Unison, after 2 beats; "endless," returning to beginning after 11 measures; no cadence.

Many other examples will be cited, later, among the Accompanied Canons.

193. In the 2nd. The Follower imitates the Leader, at the chosen time-interval, either in the 2nd above or the 7th below. The latter distinction is wholly unnecessary (though customary), for, as explained in Ex. 67, Note *2) — which see, — the imitation of any letter in the 2nd will be the *next higher letter*, whether placed above or below the leading part.

Each canonic Interval has its peculiarities, and it is left largely to the student to discover and learn to master them.

a. Probably the most characteristic difficulty of any other than the 8ve-canon, is that of preserving the natural harmonic relations of the tonality; it is the direct opposite of that shown in par. 192*a*, for these varieties of the Canon are apt to be too restless, and to contain *too much* variety. The constant uniform shifting of the parts tends to an unvaried *sequential* structure which must be prevented from destroying the unity of key, and must be mitigated by the best possible *collective* formal arrangement. See par. 192*b*.

b. Good modulatory results are impossible without free use of the changes in interval-*quality*, defined in par. 28*a*, — which review, in connection with the Notes to Ex. 69. Therefore, it is entirely legitimate to substitute the *major* 2nd for the *minor* 2nd, or vice versa, at any point; or even the *augmented* 2nd for either. But the *letter* must not be changed; i.e., the interval-quantity must be respected.

c. All the formal conditions correspond to those of the 8ve-canon. For illustration:

Ex. 189.

In the 2nd, below.

GOETSCHIUS.

etc.

*1) This rest defines the syntactic arrangement of the phrase in two 2-measure members.

*2) Here a definite semi-cadence is made on the Dominant of the leading key.

*3) It is often necessary, and *always permissible*, to cross the parts, as here.

*4) The first 2nd is minor, the next major.

See **Bach,** Air with 30 Variations for clavichord, Var. 27, Part I.

Other examples will be given among the Accompanied Canons.

194. In the 7th. This is the counterpart of the Canon in the 2nd, and exhibits precisely the same peculiarities, merely reversed. For example:

195. **In the 3rd.** This interval is somewhat easier to manage than the 2nd, though the same difficulties exist, and similar remedies are necessary (par. 193 *a* and *b*).

The same applies to its counterpart, the Canon **in the 6th.** For illustration:

GOETSCHIUS.

Cad.

etc.

*1) At the end of Part I (meas. 27) the Leader is conducted back to the beginning, and the Part is then repeated, with 1st and 2nd ending. — *2) From "48 Canons and Fugues," Vol. II, Canon 18. Analyze carefully. — See also **Bach**, "Art of Fugue," Canon III ; in 10th, — with Artificial Double-cpt. in 10th.

196. **In the 5th,** and its counterpart, **in the 4th.** For illustration :

In the 5th.

Ex.
192.

KLENGEL. *1)

N.B.

etc.

*1) "48 Canons and Fugues," Vol. I, Canon 19. Analyze to the end. See also Vol. II, Canon 3 (in 5th, after 2 measures).

Bach, "Art of Fugue," Canon IV; in the 5th, with Double-cpt. in the 12th.

For an example of the Canon in the 4th, see **Klengel,** Vol. II, Canon 6; after 4 measures.

EXERCISE 54.

A. Two examples (major and minor, different time and tempo) of the Unaccompanied 2-voice Canon in the 8ve. Review par. 192 *a, b, c, d.*

B. Examples of the Unaccompanied 2-voice Canon in the 5th, 4th, 3d, 6th, 2nd, and 7th. Either write one *brief* example of each; or a continuous example in sectional form, with a different interval in each section. Some experiments must, however, be made in 2- or 3-Part Song-form, *with repetition of Part I.*

OTHER SPECIES.

197. **The Canon in Contrary motion.** Here the choice of "corresponding tones" is of great importance. Review par. 29*a* thoroughly.

As there demonstrated, the best results are obtained either by answer-
ing *Tonic by Mediant,* or *Tonic by Dominant.*

All other conditions correspond to those of the above species.   See,
particularly, pars. 192*b* and 193*a*.

For illustration :

*1) *1) The Tonic *e* in the Leader is answered by *g*♯, the Mediant, in the Follower, throughout ; and vice versa — the Mediant by the Tonic (*g*♯ everywhere by *e*).

*2) "Gradus ad Parnassum," Schirmer ed. No. 66 (orig. No. 73). Analyze
to the end.   It is " endless," but with an added cadence.

See also, same work, No. 63 (orig. No. 10) ; exactly the same ; Tonic=Mediant,
after 1 measure, " endless," but with cadence.

Klengel, Vol. II, Canon 20 ; Tonic=Dominant, after 2 measures.

Brahms, Händel-Variations, op. 24, Var. 6 ; Part I, parallel 8ve-Canon, after
1 beat ; Part II, Contrary motion ; Part III, again parallel.

198. Canon in Augmentation.   The two parts generally begin together or nearly so, usually in the 8ve ; and the Augmentation constantly widens the distance between Leader and Follower, so that it is
of course impossible to imitate the *entire* Leader.   Usually, therefore,
the second half of the leading voice is a free counterpoint to the portion of the Follower still due ; but many devices, such as exchanging
the parts, or substituting Diminution after a while, may be resorted to.
For example :

8ve, in Augmentation.

Bach, Art of Fugue," Canon I; Augmentation *and Contrary motion.*

199. In Diminution. Here the distance between the parts is constantly decreased, so that the Follower overtakes the Leader after the first time-interval has been exactly doubled. Thereafter the calculation is reversed, and the imitation becomes " Augmentation." For example :

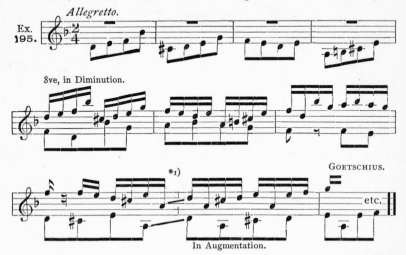

*1) The parallel octaves at the confluence of the parts are of course inevitable. From here on, the upper part is, *practically*, the Leader.

EXERCISE 55.

A. Two examples (major and minor) of the 2-voice Canon in Contrary motion.

B. One example, each, of the Canon in Augmentation and Canon in Diminution (the latter beginning with time-interval of 4, 6, or 8 measures).

———

CHAPTER XIX.

The Two–voice Canon, Accompanied. Instrumental.

200. This is by far the most practicable and valuable form of the Canon, because the added part (*parte libera*), or parts, disguise the constraint of the canonic imitation, and may contribute very significantly to the beauty and effectiveness of the whole. Any of the above canonic species may be thus treated, but the most common is that *in the 8ve,* parallel, — more rarely contrary.

201. The auxiliary (accompanying) part may be placed above, below, or between the canonic voices, at option; but much depends upon the degree of importance it assumes.

a. It may be distinctly *subordinate* (unessential), serving no other purpose than that of emphasizing the rhythm; or of supplementing the harmony where needed. For example:

*1) Vol. II, Canon 16; 8ve, after one beat. Analyze to end.

Schumann, Studies for Pedal-piano, op. 56, No. 1; 8ve, after $\frac{1}{2}$ measure; auxiliary Bass.

b. Or the auxiliary part may be *coördinate* with the canonic parts. In this case it may be a carefully conducted running voice (comp. par. 73*b*); or it may borrow its melodic and rhythmic figures from the Canon itself. For example:

*1) Vol. I, Canon 18.   Analyze.

*2) In Contrary motion, Tonic = Tonic (comp. par. 197).

*3) Vol. II, Canon 12.   Analyze to end, and see also —

Klengel, Vol. I, Canon 8 ; Contrary motion (Dominant = Tonic), after one measure ; auxiliary upper part, beginning in 3rd measure. — Vol. I, Canon 11 ; unison, after 2 beats ; auxiliary Bass. — Vol. I, Canon 16 ; Contrary motion (Tonic = Tonic), after one measure ; auxiliary Soprano, beginning in 2nd measure. — Vol. I, Canon 17 ; in the 2nd, after one measure ; auxiliary Soprano, beginning in 8th measure. — Vol. II, Canon I ; 8ve, after one measure ; inner part a running auxiliary. — Vol. II, Fugue 6, middle Division ; unison, after one measure, during Part I ; running auxiliary Bass ; in Part II the canonic voices appear in fairly exact contrary direction ; Part III as before. — Vol. II, Canon 10 ; Double-8ve, after 2 measures ; inner part auxiliary.—Vol. II, Canon 13 ; 8ve, after 2 measures ; auxiliary Bass, beginning 2 measures *before* canonic parts. — Vol. II, Canon 15 ; 5th, after ½ measure ; auxiliary Bass. — Vol. II, Canon 21 ; 5th, after one measure ; auxiliary Bass.

Bach, Air with 30 Variations, Var. 3 (unison, after one measure, auxiliary Bass). Var. 6 (in 2nd, after one measure, auxiliary Bass ; beautiful example).   Var. 9 (in 6th, after one measure, auxiliary Bass).   Var. 12 (Contrary motion, Tonic =Dominant, after one measure, Bass partly coördinate).   Var. 15 (ditto ; Bass coördinate). Var. 18 (in 6th, after ½ measure, auxiliary Bass ; fine example).   Var. 21 (in 7th, after ½ measure, auxiliary Bass).   Var. 24 (in 8ve, after 2 measures, auxiliary Bass).

Klengel, Vol. I, Canon 22, is in Augmentation, later Diminution (in 8ve), with auxiliary Bass ; the canonic parts begin on first beat ; the Augmentation, in inner part, extends to meas. 13½ ; Imitation in *uniform* rhythm follows (6-measure time-interval) to meas. 25½ ; then Diminution to end of meas. 28 ; then again Augmentation to meas. 35 ; then uniform Imitation (after 3 measures) ; in meas. 40 the time-interval is shortened to 2 measures ; the Coda, last 3 measures, is in Diminution.

Sometimes *two* such coördinate parts accompany the 2-voice Canon. This is rare, however, excepting in the free harmonic manner shown in *d* below.

See **Klengel,** Vol. II, Canon 8 ; in 8ve, after one measure, two inner auxiliary parts. — **Chadwick,** Canonic Studies for Organ, op. 12, Canon 2 ; in 8ve, after 2 measures ; two upper parts auxiliary.

c. Or the auxiliary part may be so conducted as to appear, as far as external effect is concerned, to constitute the *essential element,* which the canonic parts merely serve to sustain.   Here the danger of incoherent or unintelligible *form* is greatly reduced.   For example :

Ex.
198.

*1) Vol. I, Canon 7 ; analyze to end, and see also —

Vol. I, Canon 10; in 5th, after ½ measure ; auxiliary upper part. — Vol. II, Canon 7 ; in 2nd, *after two beats in 3-4 time ;* auxiliary Bass, beginning two measures before canonic parts.

d. Finally, the accompaniment may assume a distinctly *harmonic* character, imparting a more or less preponderantly homophonic effect to the whole.

It may be limited, as before, wholly (or largely) to one single auxiliary part, which exhibits the underlying harmony in broken-chord form (i.e., as *harmonic figuration,* in flowing rhythm). One of the canonic parts is almost certain to be given to the Soprano, the other to the inner voice, more rarely Bass. Thus:

*1) Pfte. Variations, op. 9, Var. 14 ; Canon in the 2nd, after 2 measures. See also Var. 15 ; in 3rd, after one measure ; auxiliary inner part. In both of these examples occasional, very slight, licences occur. — See further, **Klengel, Vol. II,**

Canon 19; unison, after ½ measure; auxiliary Bass. — Vol. I, Canon 3; in the 4th, after 2 long measures; auxiliary Bass. — Vol. I, Canon 5; in the 7th, after one brief measure; auxiliary Bass, partly coördinate.

Or, the auxiliary homophonic accompaniment may consist in concrete *harmonic bulk*, with little (or no) regard to the number or continuity of parts (i.e., variable volume).   Here, again, one of the canonic parts is assigned to the Soprano, almost without exception; the other may be placed in any lower part, but (unless in Bass) is frequently so confounded with the harmonic accompaniment as to be unrecognizable as a "canon."   See par. 202.   For example:

Ex. 200.

SCHUMANN. *1)

etc.

2. *Andante.*   BRAHMS. *3)

2)

*1) Pedal-piano Studies, op. 56, No. 2; Canon in unison, after one measure. Analyze; and see same work, No. 3; in 4th, after ½ measure; Prelude and Postlude added. — No. 5, in 8ve, after one measure; auxiliary accompaniment in inner parts and Bass; exquisite example.

*2) The Leader is in the Soprano; the Follower (8ve) in lower voice, in this broken form, throughout; an auxiliary Bass is added later.

*3) Pfte. Variations, op. 9, Var. 8; analyze carefully.
See also Ex. 201.

202. In order to appreciate the significance of the Canon-form, it should be contemplated in the abstract, aside from its uninviting mathematical aspect. As has been observed, each successive time-interval (one measure, or whatever section it may be) of the Leader is a counterpoint to the preceding section; that is, each such member is a *product* of the preceding one, through the strictest and most obvious process of logical derivation, or cumulation. The fact that the leading voice may thus accompany itself, may fit into itself, member by member, indicates a degree of cohesion and consistency of evolution which vindicates the rank of the Canon among those art-forms whose merit is founded upon close logic. This being the case, it is evident that the essential properties of the form are all present in the Leader *alone*, whether actually accompanied by the Follower or not; and though it might be injudicious ever to advocate the complete omission of the Follower,* it is interesting to question to what extent the presence of the Follower should be emphasized,—in other words, to what degree the canonic imitation should be made clearly recognizable. It is generally acknowledged that the merit of a Canon increases as the evidences of canonic labor decrease; that the more freely and naturally the leading voice runs, the more perfect the Canon; the less it betrays of its contrapuntal origin, the dry mathematical fact that one part is obstinately dogging the other, the better. Hence, the doctrine may be defensible, that a Canon need not be *recognizable* as such; but with one limitation, namely, not *incessantly* recognizable. The beauty and attractiveness of the act of Imitation, the calling of voice to voice, is so real, and so greatly appreciated by even the untutored musical listener, that it should not be banished from an art-form which, at its best, does not exhibit an excess of external beauty and grace. The proper balance between unimpassioned logic of structure on the one hand and romantic charm on the other, is most nearly achieved in the 8ve-Canon, with harmonic accompaniment, in which provision is made for *clear formal arrangement*, and for *fairly frequent evidences of the canonic imitation*. Review par. 192*b*.

203. When the last of the above varieties (par. 201*d*) is chosen, it is possible to mould the Canon in any of the Conventional styles of musical composition, as, for instance, the March, Minuet, Romanza, Étude, etc., etc. This is very desirable, as it lends definiteness of character and purpose to the Canon, and invites a certain legitimate freedom of treatment without violating any distinctive canonic condition (par. 186). For example:

1. MINUET.   GOETSCHIUS.

Ex.
201.

etc.

* This actually takes place in **Jadassohn**, Vocal Canon, op. 38, No. 1, during Div. I.

2. ROMANZA.
Adagio.
GOETSCHIUS.

etc.

Additional miscellaneous illustrations :

Schumann, *Jugend-Album,* op. 68, No. 27 (in the 8ve) ; 3-Part Song-form ; canonic voices exchanged in Part II. — *Jugend-Sonata,* op. 118, No. 2, second movement (8ve) ; 3-Part form, with all repetitions. — *Albumblätter,* op. 124, No. 20 (8ve). *Symph. Études,* op. 13, Étude 4 (8ve).

Guilmant, Org. Comp., op. 40, No. 3 (8ve).

Grieg, Lyric Pieces, op. 38, No. 8 (8ve).

Jadassohn, Pfte. Preludes and Fugues, op. 56 ; Prelude 2 (8ve). — Prel. 3 (8ve). — Prel. 6 and 8 (ditto).

Moszkowski, op. 15, No. 4.

Leschetizky, op. 36, No. 2 (Gigue) ; almost wholly unaccompanied.

Raff, *Frühlingsboten,* op. 55, No. 10.

César Franck, Violin Sonata, *A* major, *Finale ;* Sonata-allegro form, the Principal Theme each time an 8ve-Canon, in different modes of treatment.

G. W. Chadwick, Canonic Studies for Organ, op. 12 ; Nos. 1, 3, 4, 5, 6, 7, 8 ; different intervals ; all accompanied.

EXERCISE 56.

A. An example of the 2-voice Canon, with subordinate auxiliary part (par. 201*a*). Any interval may be used.

B. A 2-voice Canon with coördinate auxiliary part (par. 201*b*). Any interval, or Contrary motion.

C. A 2-voice Canon with essential auxiliary part (par. 201*c*).

D. A number of Canons with harmonic accompaniment (par. 201*d*). For each, some conventional Style may be chosen (par. 203).

THE TWO–VOICE CANON, ACCOMPANIED : VOCAL.

204. Among the conventional styles, frequently chosen for the outer vestment of the Canon, none is more effective than the vocal duet, with instrumental accompaniment.

The interval most commonly employed is the *unison* (when the voices are of similar register), or the *octave* (when parallel voices are used). But any interval is possible, and even Contrary motion is sometimes encountered. The time-interval is apt to be brief, as in the instrumental Canons.

The text is generally the same in both voices. The accompaniment is almost necessarily devoted, also, to an independent Prelude, occasional Interludes, and a Postlude; and, in general, it may assume considerable importance and independence of character. Sometimes the canonic Imitation extends to the end, but it is more common to add a free ending (par. 192*d*). For illustrations see —

Jadassohn, 9 Vocal Canons, op. 36. — 6 Vocal Canons, op. 38.

Henschel, 3 Vocal Canons, op. 4.

Mrs. H. H. A. Beach, Sea-Song for 2 Sopranos; in Part II the time-interval is enlarged; in Part III the voices are exchanged.

Haydn, 3rd (" Imperial ") Mass, *Credo in unum Deum ;* Leader in Soprano and Tenor in 8ve-duplication, Follower (after one measure *in the 4th*) in Alto and Bass; although the complex thus embraces four voices, it is evidently only a 2-voice Canon

Brahms, Motet, op. 29, No. II, 3rd movement (in 2nd, accomp.).

EXERCISE 57.

A number of examples of the 2-voice Canon as vocal duet, with instrumental accompaniment.

CHAPTER XX.

The Canon for More Than Two Parts.

205. The 3-voice Canon. This consists of a Leader and *two Followers* (similar to the 3-voice Round). In order to decrease the very great difficulties of this contrapuntal form, it is necessary, or at least customary, that *the same melodic interval and time-interval* should prevail between the first and second Follower, as preceded, between Leader and first Follower; in other words, that the contrapuntal relations between successive voices shall exactly correspond, thus ensuring at least this degree of continuous agreement. For instance, if the first Follower is in the 8ve, after one measure, the second Follower will also be in the 8ve, after one additional measure (or two measures from the beginning); or, if the first Follower is in the 5th, the second Follower will be in the next 5th, or *in the 2nd from the Leader;* if in the 4th, the second Follower will be in the 7th, and so on.   Thus:

Ex. 202.

In any other than the 8ve-8ve species, the same modifications of interval *quality* (not affecting the letters) are necessary, for the sake of smooth harmonic and modulatory succession, as were noted in par. 193*b*.

The difficulty of obtaining intelligible form is greatly enhanced; but much may be accomplished by wise and generous use of *Rests*.   Review par. 192*b*, thoroughly.

The 3-voice Canon is rarely accompanied, though the addition of one or even more auxiliary parts is possible.

For general illustration :

Ex. 203.

*1) The 2nd Follower is not again in the "2nd from the Leader," but in the 2nd from the preceding Follower, or *3rd from the Leader ;* the Canon is therefore "in the 2nd and 3rd," after one measure, respectively. The contrapuntal relations between the inner and upper parts in measure 3 therefore correspond exactly to those between the lower and inner parts in measure 2 ; and so on continuously, from measure to measure, throughout.

*2) Vol. I, Canon 14. Analyze minutely.

*3) Vol. II, Canon 9 ; in 8ve and 8ve, *after one beat ;* an extraordinary example.

*4) Vol. I, Canon 20; in 3rd and 5th; like the preceding, this has also a very brief time-interval (one beat), and is even more unique, in some respects ; analyze carefully ; the auxiliary Bass is coördinate.

*5) See Ex. 189, Note *3).

See further, **Klengel,** Vol. I, Canon 2 ; in 3rd and 5th, after one measure, unaccompanied. — Vol. I, Canon 4 ; in 7th and 6th, after one measure, unaccompanied. — Vol. I, Canon 9 ; 8ve–8ve. — Vol. I, Canon 12 ; in 6th and 4th, after six measures; very definite form, in consequence of long time-interval. — Vol. I, Canon 13 ; in 5th and 2nd, after one measure. — Vol. I, Canon 23 ; 8ve–8ve. — Vol. I, Canon 24 ; 8ve–8ve. —Vol. II, Canon 2 ; in 4th and 7th, after one beat ; at first unaccompanied ; later a running Bass is added, and still later an auxiliary upper part (5-voice texture) ; Prelude and Postlude. — Vol. II, Canon 14 ; 8ve–8ve, after 2½ measures. — Vol. II, Canon 17 ; in 5th and 2nd, after 2 beats; at first unaccompanied; in Part II an auxiliary Bass is added; later the canonic parts are shifted down (to 3 lower parts), and the upper part becomes a running auxiliary. — Vol. II, Canon 22 ; in 3rd and 5th, after 4 measures. — Vol. II, Canon 24; 8ve–8ve. — Vol. I, Canon 1 ; in 2nd and 3rd after ½ measure ; auxiliary running Bass. — Vol. I, Canon 6; 8ve–8ve, in *simultaneous Diminution and Augmentation ;* the 3 parts begin exactly together, the Leader in inner voice; 14 measures of the Leader are imitated in Augmentation (to meas. 28), and 28 measures are imitated in Diminution; the latter (upper part) becomes, therefore, "free" after meas. 14, and all the parts are free from meas. 28 to end.

Mozart (Breitkopf & Härtel, Serie 7), No. 42 ; unison. — No. 50; unison and 8ve. — No. 51 ; in 2nd and 3rd.   Both vocal.

G. W. Chadwick, Organ Canons, op. 12, No. 9 ; in 4th and 7th, after one measure ; auxiliary Bass. — No. 10 ; in 2nd and 3rd, ditto.

206. Contrary motion is employed as follows : The first Follower is the Contrary motion of the Leader, in any of the usual methods of correspondence (Tonic = Dominant being probably the best) ; the second Follower, being the Contrary motion of the first one, *returns to the original direction,* and the corresponding series of interval-relations is obtained by giving to the 2nd Follower, in every case, the exact tones of the Leader (i.e., 8ve-imitation of the latter).   Thus :

Ex. 204.

*1) The 2nd Follower imitates the Leader in parallel direction, in the double 8ve. The successive intervals described by Leader and 1st Follower (beginning with the 8ve, as indicated) are exactly reproduced between 1st and 2nd Followers, but, naturally, in *inverted forms.* This will be the invariable result, no matter what the location of the 1st Follower is, if the 2nd Follower corresponds thus to the Leader.

207. The 4-voice Canon. The principles of par. 205 apply here also, simply extended to include the 4th voice. For example (8ve–8ve–8ve, after one measure):

Ex. 205.

See also **Klengel,** Vol. I, Canon 15; in the 6th, 4th, and 2nd (comp. Ex. 202), after one measure respectively; unaccompanied.

Mozart (Breitkopf & Härtel, Serie 7), No. 54; vocal; all unison, after 4 measures.

Clementi, "Gradus ad Parnassum," Schirmer ed. No. 68 (orig. ed. 33), is a 4-voice Canon, *in unequal melodic intervals;* the succession is 4th, 5th, and 8th; hence, the *second pair* of parts (2nd and 3rd Followers) correspond in their relations to the first pair, but the interval-relations between the first and second Followers are so shifted as to involve Artificial double-cpt. Analyze minutely.

Brahms, Round-canons, op. 113, No. 6; *in contrary motion ;* indep. cadence.

EXERCISE 58.

A. An example of the 3-voice Canon in 8ve–8ve; unaccompanied; for pianoforte, organ, or *string-trio.*

B. Two or more examples in other intervals of Imitation, according to Ex. 202, with or without auxiliary part, at option.

C. A 3-voice Canon in Contrary motion.

D. One or more 4-voice Canons, for string-quartet.

CHAPTER XXI.

The Double–Canon, Etc.

208. Like the Double-fugue, the Double-canon has *two* Leaders, or a " Double-leader," imitated by two Followers. The number of canonic parts is therefore four ; to these an auxiliary part may be added, but it is rarely done.

The two Leaders may begin together, but it is more common to introduce the subordinate Leader (so-called) a beat or more, possibly a measure or more, later than its fellow. The rules of par. 165 apply, to a certain extent, and may be reviewed.

The interval of Imitation is optional, the 8ve being here again possibly the most convenient. The time-interval is apt to be a little longer than in the single Canon, but must be adhered to by *both* Followers ; i.e., the second pair of parts must agree with the first pair in time-relation. Any two of the four parts may be chosen for the two Leaders. For example :

2nd Follower (in 5th).

1st Follower (in 5th).

GOETSCHIUS.

etc.

This is a Double-canon in the 5th, after 3 measures. See further, **Klengel,** Vol. I, Canon 21 ; in the 5th, after one measure; unaccompanied; 2 Leaders begin simultaneously in Tenor and Soprano, 2 Followers in Bass and Alto. — Vol. II, Canon 4 ; in 5th, after 2 long measures ; 2 Leaders begin together in Bass and Alto ; they are contrasted through the novel device of making one *lyric* and the other its (apparently inferior) figural *accompaniment.*

Mozart (Serie 7), No. 41 ; Double-canon as *Round* (vocal, unacc.) ; in 4th, after one measure; no cadence ; 2 Leaders in Alto and Tenor, one measure apart, — hence the 1st Follower begins simultaneously with 2nd Leader.

Brahms, Sacred quartet, op. 30 ; in 7th, after one measure ; with accompaniment, including Prelude and Interludes. — Round-canons, op. 113 ; No. 8, unison, after 4 measures ; No. 9, in 4th, after one-half measure.

Clementi, "Gradus ad Parnassum," Schirmer ed. No. 70*b* (orig. No. 84*b*) ; in 8ve, after one beat ; unaccompanied.

209. The Triple-canon is far less frequent than the preceding. It consists in 3 Leaders, imitated by 3 Followers, and therefore involves six canonic parts.

See **Brahms,** op. 118, No. 4, Div. II (meas. 51–91) ; Leaders (simultaneous) on upper staff, Followers on lower, after one beat; unaccompanied.

The Quadruple-canon is still more rare ; it involves eight canonic parts, and is practicable only in Double-chorus or orchestral writing.

An extraordinary example of the Quadruple-canon is found in **Mozart** (Serie 7), **No. 49 ;** it is written for 12 parts (as triple-chorus), and consists in a full quartet of

Leaders, imitated in the unison, after $1\frac{1}{2}$ measures, by a quartet of Followers, and $1\frac{1}{2}$ measures later by still another quartet; it is designed as a Round, with cadence indicated.

EXERCISE 59.

A. One or two examples of the Double-canon; all conditions optional.

B. An example as " Song-form with Trio," for pianoforte, 4 hands; the principal Song a Double-canon, with auxiliary (subordinate) Bass; the Trio a brief Triple-canon, in the 8ve, unaccompanied.

CHAPTER XXII.

CANON AS CHORALE–ELABORATION.

210. Chorale as Canon. In this species the chorale-melody itself appears in two voices *as Canon,* while the other parts provide a contrapuntal accompaniment.

The interval of canonic imitation, and the time-interval, are optional. But the relations adopted at the beginning should be, as a rule, maintained uniformly throughout the chorale; therefore it is usually necessary to experiment repeatedly with the whole, before valid relations can be determined; and it is not considered unpermissible, in case the advantage is manifest, to adopt new relations for a new Section (or even for some single line) of the chorale. It is greatly preferable, however, to overcome the necessity for such changes of canonic relation by judicious (slight) rhythmic modification, or strictly unessential melodic embellishment, of the chorale-melody, in the manner shown in Ex. 125. For example (Table, Exercise 26, Chorale 29):

First version; canon in the 5th, after one measure.

*1) Observe the slight modifications of the original chorale-melody.

*2) The ⌢ simply indicates, as usual, the end of a Line, and is not respected.

*3) In the completed elaboration of this first version the canonic parts are Soprano and Pedal-bass,—the latter two 8ves lower than here written. The inner parts are thematic, as in the "Invention with chorale" (par. 99), preceding the Leader by two measures.

*4) Canonic parts are Soprano and Tenor; Pedal independent; Alto pursues constantly a Figure of its own; comp. pars. 93, 96.

211. The parts which accompany the canonic voices are in a sense their "auxiliaries," but should be strictly contrapuntal, and *thematic* (based upon some Motive or Motives), as described in par. 92, which review. See also pars. 99 and 93.

The number and choice of these accompanying parts, and the location of the canonic voices, are wholly optional. Either the small or large species of chorale-figuration may be employed.

For general illustration ·

*1) **Bach,** Org. Comp., Vol. V, No. 3. — See further, **Bach,** Vol. V, No. 8 ; in 8ve, outer parts ; 2 auxiliary thematic parts. — Vol. V, No. 19 ; 4-voice ; Canon in 8ve, Soprano and Tenor ; Bass independent ; running Alto. — Vol. V, No. 29 ; 4-voice ; Soprano and Alto, in 5th, after 2 beats ; running Tenor, independ. Pedal. — Vol. V, No. 37, 5-voice ; Soprano and Alto, in 5th. — Vol. V, No. 44 ; 4-voice ; Bass and Alto, in 5th, after 2 beats. — Vol. V, No. 35 ; 4-voice ; Double-canon (in 8ve) for 24 measures ; then single Canon, with longer time-interval, for 7 measures ; then free Coda (6 measures). In this example the triplet notation differs from modern usage (i.e., ♪♪♪ = ♩). — Vol. VI, No. 19 ; 5-voice ; Canon in two Tenors, after 2 long measures ; Pedal independent, Soprano and Alto thematic. — Vol. VII, No. 52 ; 5-voice ; Soprano and Tenor, 8ve ; Pedal independent, other two parts imitatory ; the canonic imitations *alternate* at each Line ; time-interval changed once.

A superb masterpiece is found in **Bach,** Vol. V, page 100 ; *Canon in Contrary motion ;* Sec. I (to meas. 14) in upper parts, Tonic = Mediant, Pedal auxiliary ; Sec. II (to meas. 27) the contrary motion of Sec. I, Mediant = Tonic, Pedal new ; Sec. III (to meas. 39), Canon in lower parts, Dominant = Mediant, two upper parts auxiliary ; Sec. IV (to meas. 52) contrary motion of Sec. III ; Sec. V is a Coda, containing Diminutions of first Line, and a remarkable stretto of all 4 Lines together.

212. Canon with Chorale, i.e., *canonic accompaniment* to the single chorale-melody.

All conditions are optional. Additional auxiliary parts are sometimes employed. For example :

See **Bach,** Org. Comp., Vol. V, page 92 ; Canon in 8ve, after ¼ measure, in outer parts ; *c. f.* in Pedal as Tenor ; Large species (with Prelude, Interludes, and Postlude). — Vol. V, page 94 ; Canon in 4th, after ½ measure ; other conditions similar to preceding. — Vol. V, page 96 ; Canon in 7th, Pedal-bass and Alto ; *c. f.* in Soprano ; additional *lyric* auxiliary part in 2nd Soprano. — Vol. V, page 98 ; *Canon in Augmentation,* Soprano and Bass, in 8ve ; the Leader ends in meas. 21, the Follower in meas. 42 (end of the composition) ; *c. f.* in Pedal as Tenor ; an auxil. Tenor is added.

EXERCISE 60.

A. Two or more examples of the Chorale as Canon (pars. 210, 211), for Organ.

B. Two or more examples of the Canon with Chorale (par. 212).

" CANONIC " COMPOSITIONS.

213. When the canonic imitation falls short of the characteristic requirements of the legitimate Canon (par. 180), either in being interrupted (periodic instead of *continuous*), or in containing more or less frequent licences (instead of being *strict*), the product forfeits the title of " Canon," and is called simply " canonic " composition.

To this class belong also the fairly numerous examples of homophonic (or even polyphonic) forms with canonic sections, or passages.

See **Beethoven,** Pfte. Var., op. 120, Var. 6 (1st section of Parts I and II) ; Var. 19 (the same) ; Var. 20 (similar). — Pfte. Var., op. 35, Var. 7 (Parts I and III ; Part II harmonic). — Pfte. Sonata, op. 101, 2nd movement, portions of the " Trio." — Symphony No. IV, first movement, meas. 103–119 of *Allegro.* — Violin Sonata, op. 30, No. 2, " Trio " of *Scherzo.* — Pfte. Sonata, op. **7,** 3rd movement, Part II. — Op. 31, No. 1, *Finale,* meas. 86–97.

Schubert, Trio, op. 100, *Scherzo.*

Schumann, op. 56, No. 4 ; Parts I and III ; in 4th, at first after 3 measures, then after one ; Part II free, but imitatory. — No. 6 ; Sec. I, 8ve-canon, harmonic accompaniment ; Sec. II, a 4-voice Fughetta ; Sec. III again canonic.

Chopin, Mazurka 34 (op. 56, No. 2) ; Part V, meas. 32–17 from end.

Brahms, Var., op. 9, Var. 10 ; contains several brief canonic passages, and duplications in simultaneous regular and contrary motion (belongs to the once popular species called " Quodlibet," a contrapuntal medley ; see the *Finale* of **Bach's** " Air " with 30 Variations).

Brahms, Motet, op. 74, No. 1, 2nd movement. — Op. 118, No. 4, Divs. I and III.

Jadassohn, op. 56, Prelude No. 5 ; Song-form with Trio ; Principal Song homophonic, Trio an 8ve-canon.

Bach, " B-minor Mass," No. 14, *Et in unum Dominum.* — Org. Comp., Vol. V, No. 15. — Vol. VI, No. 24.

THE END.